LORENZO IN TAOS

LORENZO IN TAOS
D. H. Lawrence and Mabel Dodge Luhan

Facsimile of 1932 Edition
by
Mabel Dodge Luhan

New Foreword
by
Arthur J. Bachrach

SOUTHWEST HERITAGE SERIES

SUNSTONE PRESS

SANTA FE

Sunstone books may be purchased for educational, business, or sales promotional use.
For information please write: Special Markets Department, Sunstone Press,
P.O. Box 2321, Santa Fe, New Mexico 87504-2321.

Library of Congress Cataloging-in-Publication Data

Luhan, Mabel Dodge, 1879-1962.
  Lorenzo in Taos : D.H. Lawrence and Mabel Dodge Luhan / by Mabel Dodge Luhan ;
new foreword by Arthur J. Bachrach.
    p. cm. -- (Southwest heritage series)
  Facsimile of 1932 edition.
  ISBN 978-0-86534-594-2 (softcover : alk. paper)
  1. Lawrence, D. H. (David Herbert), 1885-1930--Travel--New Mexico--Taos. 2. Lawrence,
D. H. (David Herbert), 1885-1930--Friends and associates. 3. Authors, English--20th century--
Biography. 4. Taos (N.M.)--Biography. 5. Luhan, Mabel Dodge, 1879-1962. I. Title.

PR6023.A93Z66 2008
823'.912--dc22
[B]
                              2007027392

Published in

WWW.SUNSTONEPRESS.COM
SUNSTONE PRESS / POST OFFICE BOX 2321 / SANTA FE, NM 87504-2321 /USA
(505) 988-4418 / ORDERS ONLY (800) 243-5644 / FAX (505) 988-1025

The Southwest Heritage Series is dedicated to Jody Ellis and Marcia Muth Miller, the founders of Sunstone Press, whose original purpose and vision continues to inspire and motivate our publications.

CONTENTS

I

THE SOUTHWEST HERITAGE SERIES /ix

II

FOREWORD TO THIS EDITION / xi

III

THE WOMAN WHO MARRIED AN INDIAN / xiii
from
The Stronghold
by
Phillips Kloss
Sunstone Press 1987

IV

PORTRAIT OF MABEL DODGE LUHAN / xvi
by
Harold Butcher
from
The Santa Fean
October 1940

V

FACSIMILE OF 1932 EDITION / xxi

I

THE SOUTHWEST HERITAGE SERIES

The history of the United States is written in hundreds of regional histories and literary works. Those letters, essays, memoirs, biographies and even collections of fiction are often first-hand accounts by people who wanted to memorialize an event, a person or simply record for posterity the concerns and issues of the times. Many of these accounts have been lost, destroyed or overlooked. Some are in private or public collections but deemed to be in too fragile condition to permit handling by contemporary readers and researchers.

However, now with the application of twenty-first century technology, nineteenth and twentieth century material can be reprinted and made accessible to the general public. These early writings are the DNA of our history and culture and are essential to understanding the present in terms of the past.

The Southwest Heritage Series is a form of literary preservation. Heritage by definition implies legacy and these early works are our legacy from those who have gone before us. To properly present and preserve that legacy, no changes in style or contents have been made. The material reprinted stands on its own as it first appeared. The point of view is that of the author and the era in which he or she lived. We would not expect photographs of people from the past to be re-imaged with modern clothes, hair styles and backgrounds. We should not, therefore, expect their ideas and personal philosophies to reflect our modern concepts.

Remember, reading their words and sharing their thoughts is a passport back into understanding how the past was shaped and how it influenced today's world.

Our hope is that new access to these older books will provide readers with a challenging and exciting experience.

II

FOREWORD TO THIS EDITION
by
Arthur J. Bachrach, Ph.D.

In September, 1922, the internationally known British writer D. H. Lawrence arrived, with his wife, Frieda, at the railroad station in Lamy, New Mexico. They had traveled from Australia to San Francisco, then to Lamy, to come to Taos at the invitation of Mabel Dodge Sterne, the patroness of arts and culture in Taos. Mabel Dodge met the Lawrences at Lamy, driven by her chauffeur, and later husband, Taos Pueblo Indian Tony Luhan. Stopping the night in Santa Fe, they arrived in Taos the following morning, September 11, Lawrence's thirty-seventh birthday.

It was the beginning of an intense, sometimes strained, relationship. Mabel, daughter of a well-to-do Buffalo, New York family, had a long history of cultivating arts and letters, surrounding herself with famous artists and writers in her salons in Florence, Italy and in New York City. She continued her support of literature and the arts in Taos and it was her hope that Lawrence would write the definitive novel of the Taos Pueblo. Lawrence did not write the novel Mabel had hoped for, but he did write a number of essays and articles on Indian life and culture.

The relationship between the Lawrences, living close to Mabel's big house and Mabel became difficult and was further complicated by the arrival, in March, 1924, of Dorothy Brett, a British artist and friend of the Lawrences, who accompanied them on their return from London to Taos. The interaction of the three women, all devoted to Lawrence, was intense and at times stormy.

Mabel offered the Lawrences a ranch of 160 acres in San Cristobal, some seventeen miles north of Taos. Lawrence refused, presumably unwilling to be any more beholden to Mabel, but Frieda accepted the offer and the deed was in her name. The Kiowa Ranch, as Lawrence named it, became a focus of one of the most productive periods of writing in Lawrence's life.

Lawrence encouraged Mabel to write about her own exciting life and, while back in Italy in 1925, continued corresponding with Mabel and edited manuscripts she sent to him. Her book, *Lorenzo in Taos*, is written loosely in the form of letters to and from D. H. Lawrence, Frieda Lawrence and Robinson Jeffers, the celebrated poet who had been a guest of Mabel's in Taos, with references to Dorothy Brett and Spud Johnson among others. The book is a highly personal and most informative account of an intense relationship with a great writer. It is an important work and its reprinting is welcomed by scholars and those of us who have come increasingly to respect Mabel's contributions in the world of arts and letters through her support of many individuals and her own creative spirit.

Aldous Huxley once claimed that D. H. Lawrence was blessed with an extrasensory perception, an awareness of what Wordsworth called "unknown modes of being." Huxley said, "He was always intensely aware of the mystery of the world, and the mystery was always for him a numen, divine. Lawrence could never forget, as most of us almost continuously forget, the dark presence of the otherness that lies beyond the boundaries of man's conscious mind. This special sensibility was accompanied by a prodigious power of rendering the immediately experienced otherness in terms of literary art."

Mabel Dodge Luhan must have felt the same way about Lawrence when she enticed him to Taos.

III

THE WOMAN WHO MARRIED AN INDIAN
from
The Stronghold
by
Phillips Kloss
Sunstone Press 1987

She was a conspicuity seeker, celebrity hunter, she drew
    artists and writers around her to draw attention to
    herself, built guest houses for them, dispensed largesse
    like a queen.
Born an only child of posh parents she grew up thinking
    she could buy anything she wanted. She collected four
    husbands, the last a Taos Indian not so riddable as the
    first three.
'Twas said she payed his Indian wife a stipend to release him,
    or rather to lease him, and she adopted his Spanish
    name Lujan, changing the j to h to read Luhan.
She wrote checks under the name Mable Luhan, wrote books
    under the name Mabel Luhan, distributed favors under
    the name Mabel Luhan, and was jocosely dubbed
    Queen Mabel.
She built an adobe palace wth a glass gazebo on top for her
    Indian consort, toted him with her to New York, his
    Indian blanket and braided hair adding to her
    conspicuity.
A strong likeable character nevertheless, Tony Luhan,
    capable, courteous, a British accent he had picked up
    from the English gentleman Arthur Manby and the
    Honorable Dorothy Brett, one of Mabel's coterie in the
    D.H. Lawrence days.
She had inveigled Lawrence to come to Taos, gave him a
    ranch at the foot of the Lobo mountains in exchange
    for one of his manuscripts, tried to detach him from
    his German wife Frieda.

Frieda saw through her, hung on to him till he died of T.B. in France, then brought his ashes back for burial at the ranch. Apparently he loved the ranch, proclaimed the view across the Rio Grande to the uplift of the Continental Divide the most beautiful landscape in the world.

It was his will to have his ashes buried there. Frieda brought them back in an unsealed urn. Mabel stole some of the ashes for a necrophiliac keepsake.

Frieda retrieved them, threatening a lawsuit, mixed them with concrete, buried the slab on the ranch, built a shrine over it, and hundreds of women who had wallowed vicariously in Lawrence's novels made pilgrimmages to the shrine to worship a sex-god.

Sterile sex-god. All his novels were repetitive extensions of his autobiographical *Sons and Lovers,* all his women were the same woman perpetually frustrated, all his men the same himself perpetually frustrated.

He never knew the meaning of the word love, except love of the land. Mabel wasn't frustrated, but her real love was love of the Taos country, Tony an indigenous part of it.

Lawrence's demise impelled her to look for another sex-writer to vanitize her domain. The Carmel poet Robinson Jeffers was available, his incestuous story *Tamar* qualified him a lurid trophy to hang on her literary wall.

She invited him and his wife Una to be her guests in the big house, the palace. They liked Taos, liked Tony, who chauffeured them around the country in Mabel's Chrysler Imperial.

Jeffers identified himself with the rock head of Taos Mountain looking down on the activities of Indians and White man. He wrote that only he and the Mountain understood civilization was an ephemeral disease.

Mabel was tempted to put a dent in such a lofty granite attitude, invited them again the next summer along with a former flame of his.

The flame reignited. Una, older than Jeffers, felt she was being cast aside, so during one of Mabel's evening parties she went to her room and shot herself with a pistol.

Tony heard the shot, told Jeffers. Jeffers rushed to their
    room, saw Una bleeding on the bed but not dead,
    swept her up in his arms and figuratively carried
    her back to Carmel.
They lived happily ever after till Una died of cancer and
    Jeffers took up with Judith Anderson, the actress who
    made a great success of his melodramatic version of
    Euripides' *Medea*.
Mabel arranged worser melordramers, instigated
    divorces among the Taos artists, Victor Higgins,
    John Young-Hunter, Nicolai Fechin, her own
    divorces a precedent, quite a mischief-maker.
On her better side she was very generous, helped artists,
    Indians, poverty-stricken families financially, helped the
    Indians with their land claims, John Collier appointed
    commissioner, and she was beset by moochers.
She built a house for Willa Cather, who rejected it, so
    Mabel donated it to a society of Polish Sisters for a
    hospital, and she tried to bring appreciative people to
    her beloved Taos.
Though she clashed with Georgia O'Keeffe she was a
    perfect hostess to responsive celebrities such as Max
    Eastman, A.A. Brill, Greta Garbo and Leopold
    Stokowski, the Vanderbilts, dozens of movers and
    shakers.
She might have been the right wife for Lawrence at that. He
    was the only one who loved the country as she did,
    every sagebrush, every rabbitbush, the incomparable
    views.
When Tony died and she suffered a slight dementia she
    hired a chauffeur to drive her around and around
    the Taos Valley communing with her favorite
    places.
She is buried in the historic Kit Carson Cemetery, an
    inconspicuous headstone marking her grave, often
    knocked down by local maurauders, reset by her
    friends.
Lawrence's ashes remain enshrined at the ranch she gave
    him, a cenotaph monument erected for him at
    Westminster Abbey.

IV

PORTRAIT OF MABEL DODGE LUHAN
by
Harold Butcher
from
The Santa Fean
October 1940

I first met Mabel Dodge Luhan, she of the "Intimate Memories" and dissector of D. H. Lawrence, at a tea given by Artist John Young-Hunter and his wife in their studio apartment near Central Park, New York. The room was so full of people, and Mabel was seated so quietly on a couch, that I came away with absolutely no impression of the most-discussed woman in the Southwest.

But when she invited me to lunch at Taos I had a closeup, and subsequent meetings have helped me to fill in the impression I caught then. I arrived at definite conclusions about her enigmatic personality.

For a woman who never bothers about smartness in dress or the style of the moment it is amazing how charming Mabel Luhan can be. She has been described as evil—interfering with soul stuff, bringing chaos into men's and women's lives—but even critics admit, while deploring, her charm. She can turn it on for the occasion. Beware the siren!

Gossips have been busy with her name; they have called her cruel, hard, cold, selfish. D. H. Lawrence quarreled violently with her— and then forgave and forgot. There's something about Mabel.

Which leads to an important point overlooked by the critics. Most of what we know of Mabel Luhan is what she has told us. There has been little in her external life that has not been duplicated again and again by women who are never criticized. To have had four husbands is almost conventional these days, and even if it is unconventional to have a full-blooded Indian, Tony Luhan—the fourth—as a husband, she is living conventionally with him, disclaiming any intention of seeking another divorce.

If Mrs. Luhan had bared her inner life in the confessional she would have received absolution, and that would have been the end of it. Because she chose the confessional of print she is that terrible Mabel. If she had elected to "hit the sawdust trail" at a Salvation Army meeting she would have been welcomed with open arms as a lost sister who had found her way to the fold. (What an intriguing picture!) She didn't choose that method, and so, instead of a few hundred people crowded into a stuffy mission hall knowing all about her past, the whole world knows—at least, all the world that cares to read her books.

In the writing of those books she attempted to achieve objectivity. There is, she told me, a conventional life, an external life, the front we present to our friends. But there is a real life within, hidden even from ourselves because we have not the courage to disturb it. This inner life she has uncovered, thereby achieving detachment. She can stand apart from herself, see herself as she is, face to face. She does not necessarily like herself, but she knows what she is like; and in that knowledge is freedom.

The external Mabel Dodge Luhan is a friendly, comfortable woman who was sixty-one last February. A woman with dark hair through which a red or pink ribbon is tied at the back, a woman with hazel eyes—not blue, brown nor green, but a combination of these colors. A woman wearing very little makeup, in clothes that never impress you one way or the other. You would pass her by if she were not pointed out as the famous—or infamous!—Mabel Dodge Luhan.

So much for externals, which are not very important.

How about her inner life? How could she bear to be so intimate in her "Intimate Memories?"

"They were not written originally for publication," she told me. The memoirs were written and shown to her friends, including the "victims," and the intention was to keep them locked away from the gaze of the curious. But that intention was destroyed by the success of her "Lorenzo in Taos," written quickly under publisher's pressure when Lawrence died, a time when the public was eager for anything that might throw light upon his life and thought. The writer who makes a hit cannot stay put. He may write for the million or for sophisticates and near-sophisticates as Mrs. Luhan does; but the public, large or small, once interested and intrigued, wants more.

The "more" that Mabel had was that which she had written to "know herself," to win detachment, to achieve that control over her life that comes with perfect knowledge and objectivity.

But all that Mabel had set down could not be published.

It went through a voluntary censorship so that it might become the personal news that was fit to print. But do not jump to the conclusion that she has deleted sins too sinister to be shared with a reader. To do that would be to miss her whole purpose. She believes herself to be as normal as any other woman save that she has actually written what other women hide. How many people who honestly bared their inner lives could hope to write a book that would go to the public unexpurgated? Precious few. There are conventions as to what may be printed with impunity, and although these conventions have dwindled with the passing years they still exist and have to be observed. D. H. Lawrence, in his novels, broke down many of the conventions, but only after constant conflict with the powers that be. And even he was only partially successful.

The inner life of the average human being is not pleasant to contemplate, and even the most honest—in which Mrs. Luhan is certainly included—can hope to reach only an approximation of the truth, the whole truth and nothing but the truth. The late Arnold Bennett, whose Journal never pretended to the intimacy of the Luhan memoirs, illustrated how difficult a feat it is to set down the truth about oneself on paper. He said one could go alone into a room, lock the door, sit by a fire into which the written words could be thrown at the first hint of disturbance; even then, despite all these precautions, only by a supreme effort could one be induced to write the whole truth. The inner life sets up such a resistance that only people of genuine courage can bear to tear aside the veil and·write of that which wishes to remain secret. Mabel Dodge Luhan has dared, and the very violence of her critics only goes to show that they are mad because they themselves wouldn't have the courage to do the same.

Mrs. Luhan could bear to write of her inner life because she is a woman of courage. She wanted to see her life, and to see it whole. Wholeness came with truthful writing.

An editor asked her to write an article describing what she had missed in life, the theory being that she was frustrated, always seeking something she could not find. When she was not laughing at this suggestion she felt annoyed. "I have missed nothing in life except time," she exclaimed. "When anything happens, whether pleasure or pain, it happens so quickly that one cannot feel all there is to be felt. It is only by reliving that experience that it is possible to feel all it contained. Time passed too quickly for all the feeling to be felt when the experience occurred." She is only just beginning to savour all that life has offered, and she does not expect to have time to catch up entirely. "Some day we shall learn how to hasten the process," she said.

Is Mabel Dodge Luhan a philosopher, a leader through the intricate ways of life? The answer is No. It is a great mistake to read into her books any more than the revelations of one woman's life. It is justifiable to hold, as she does, that these revelations show what goes on in the lives of ordinary human beings, that her experiences are not essentially different from those of other women whose human life she shares. The "accidents," as the theologians say, are different; the essentials are the same. It is an "accident" that she has had four husbands; a woman with one husband can have the same emotions, partake of the same human life of which Mabel Luhan is also a part. Therefore, if the faithful portrayal of her own life makes her a philosopher by explaining other lives which similar human beings live, then she is a philosopher. But she isn't. There may be a Mabel Dodge Luhan cult in Taos and among all who share the Taos atmosphere, but the whole thing is foolish. And I believe Mabel would be among the first to admit it.

She doesn't even believe in imposing her will on others any more. Women smile sceptically when I tell them that. She "willed" Lawrence to come to Taos; that is to say she did more than send him a few letters describing the attractions of the place and the opportunity it would afford him to do good work. She "willed" him to come in some esoteric and perhaps Indian sense of the word that resulted in his coming. He came because she willed it? At any rate, he came. Today she would not exercise her will in that fashion. "Lawrence showed me that was wrong, and so has Tony," she said.

Will Mabel be able to keep her hands from the soul stuff of other human beings? Perhaps not. She is fascinated by human beings. Crowds of writers, artists, musicians, philosophers, men and women of the world have enjoyed her lavish hospitality, and they will continue to come. Is she going to survey them all with the detachment she applies to her own life? It is not likely, not while life flows strong within her, not while the world grips her as it has done throughout her life. She wants people to be real, and to be real they must live their own lives. If she imposes her will on others it will involve them in struggles to make their own wills prevail. She believes in the independence, the individuality of every human being, and she wants people around her only when they are truly alive. Will she be able to keep "hands off" so that they may always live to the utmost?

Why not? She has had the courage of her beliefs so far. Why not in this also?

Harold Butcher, the author of this article and an English-born newspaperman, wrote for *The New York Times* and other American papers and acted as American correspondent for a string of British papers. He traveled all over the United States, of which he was a citizen, as well as over most of the rest of the world. A year spent in Santa Fe in 1938 and 1939 left him enchanted with the American Southwest. He was a contributing columnist for *The Santa Fean* in the 1940s.

V

FACSIMILE OF 1932 EDITION

Lorenzo in Taos

Photo Edward Weston.

MABEL DODGE LUHAN

LORENZO
IN
TAOS

ALFRED · A · KNOPF

NEW YORK   MCMXXXII

TO
TONY AND ALL INDIANS

Preface

DEAR JEFFERS—

This book tries to show you how we felt and acted some years ago.

When Frieda read it, she wrote me: "But Lorenzo was not like that any more. Taos changed him. . . ."

I told her that I could only tell in these pages how we all were then, that I had lived through the time we passed together here and recorded it, and so this recollection is only of the painful days that brought about changes in us all and not of the change itself. It tells of the process of change, of the permutations of the spirit worked upon by spirit. It does not end happily with all of us united once more, chastened and disciplined, for life is not concerned with results, but only with Being and Becoming.

MABEL DODGE LUHAN.

Taos, June 1931

Illustrations

Frontispiece

Tony Lujan, 1930   *page* 32

Mabel Dodge Luhan   97

Gate to the Big House   158

Robinson Jeffers, 1929   286

Part One

Part One

You know, Jeffers, after I met you, I felt that you and Lawrence ought to know each other, that you would have liked and understood each other; and I asked you to give me the two books of poems to send to him, and to write something in one of them especially for him. You chose so well when you wrote:

> This coast crying out for tragedy. . . .
> . . . I said in my heart,
> "Better invent than suffer: imagine victims
> Lest your own flesh be chosen the agonist. . . ."

Then, before they ever reached him, just in those two weeks, he was dead—and now you will never meet.

But I am going to try and tell you about Lawrence. I will tell you what I went through in my friendship (if that's what it was) with him, of the mass of contradictions and shocks one had to accept from him. And how, no matter what happened, once one really knew him, really saw the essential thing in him, nothing that he said or did mattered; everything finally seemed to one to be a deplorable but inevitable activity that he was compelled to carry on.

Of course one didn't really get the man in his books, although he spent twenty years trying to put himself and Frieda into them. I know when I read him in Taos, especially *Sea and Sardinia* and *Tortoises* and *Birds, Beasts and Flowers*, I thought: "Here is the only one who can really *see* this Taos country and the Indians, and who can describe it so that it is as much alive between the covers of a book as it is in reality." For Taos had something wonderful in it, like the dawn of the world. Lawrence always called it pristine, when he came. I had been right about one thing in him: He *could* see and feel and wonder.

It was after reading *Sea and Sardinia* that I wrote to him to come to Taos. That is one of the most actual of travel books, I think, for in it, in that queer way of his, he gives the feel and touch and smell of places so that their reality and their essence are open to one, and one can step right into them. Perhaps it is because, when he is writing, the experience is more actual to him than when it occurred. He is in the place again, reliving in retrospect more vividly than he was able to do at the time it happened. Lawrence couldn't live, with pleasure, in the real moment. He lived afterwards. . . . But I must go back and tell you about how he came to Taos.

I wrote him a long letter. I told him all I could about Taos and the Indians—and about Tony and me. I told him how much I wanted him to come and know that country before it became exploited and spoiled, before good roads would let in the crowds. I tried to tell him every single thing I could think of that I felt would draw him—simple things as well as strange ones. I remember I described it as a lofty, pastoral land far from railroads, full of time and ease, where the high, clear air seemed full of an almost heard but not quite heard music, and where the plainest tasks took on a beauty and significance they had not in other places.

This was true, but not true for me, for I had no tasks. I used to sit most of the time, sort of listening, before Lawrence came. After he came, he got me to really doing things, washing floors and making bread and wearing aprons for a while. But it's too soon to tell you about that. Anyway, I told him how in that place a woman would come to the door and stand smiling towards the Sacred Mountain, after she put her cake into the oven. For it was like that. The mountain and the fields were not separate from one's life. One did not go *out* to things, one was part of them. The mountain, if anything, came to one, came into the house; one ate it with the cake. At least it seemed that way to me. Yet afterwards, when he'd been there awhile, he was the one that upbraided me for being too cluttered up by things, and he wrote a poem that began:

Let us unhouse the women. . . .

I sent my long letter off to him. It was so long that it was rolled like papyrus. And I sent an Indian necklace to Frieda that I thought carried some Indian magic in it, to draw them to Taos. In the letter I put a few leaves of *desachey*, the perfume the Indians say makes the heart light, along with a little *osha*, the root that is a strong medicine—neither of which are in the botany books, but both of which are potent.

After a few weeks, he answered me from Italy:

> *Fontana Vecchia*
> *Taormina, Sicily*
> *5th November, 1921*

DEAR MABEL DODGE STERNE

I had your letter this afternoon and read it going down Corso: and smelt the Indian scent, and nibbled the medicine: the last being like licorice root, the scent being a wistful dried herb.

Truly, the q-b and I would like to come to Taos—there are no little bees. I think it is quite feasible. I think I have enough dollars in America to get us there. Are you practical enough to tell me how much it would cost, per month, for the q-b and myself to keep house in Taos? We are *very* practical, do all our own work, even the washing, cooking, floor-cleaning and everything here in Taormina: because I loathe servants creeping around. They poison the atmosphere. So I prefer to wash my own shirt, etc. And I *like* doing things.—Secondly, is there a colony of rather dreadful sub-arty people?—But even if there is, it couldn't be worse than Florence.—Thirdly, are your Indians dying out, and is it rather sad?—Fourthly, what do the sound, *prosperous* Americans do in your region?—Fifthly, how does one get there? What is the nearest port? I might get a cargo boat to bring us, from Palermo.

I believe I've heard of Taos, and even seen pictures of it, photographs—at Leo Stein's house in Settignano. Have I? And are you a relative of the Maurice Sterne, artist, who was at Anticoli this summer? I've only heard of him.

I believe what you say—one must somehow bring together the two ends of humanity, our own thin end, and the last dark strand from the previous, pre-white era. I verily believe that. Is Taos the place?

I have already written the second book to Psychoanalysis and the Unconscious, and posted the MS. to Seltzer,—called, provisionally, *Fantasia of the Unconscious*. I am satisfied with it for what it is. But it is the third book, which I have still to write, and which I can't write yet, not till I have crossed another border, it is this that will really matter. To me, I mean. I feel hopeless about the public. Not that I care about them. I want to live my life, and say my say, and the public can die its own death in its own way, just as it likes.

I think we may leave here in January or February. I think we will come to Taos. Write me what advice or instructions you think necessary, by return. I should have your letter by the new year.

I want to leave Europe. I want to take the next step. Shall it be Taos?—I like the *word*. It's a bit like Taormina.

D. H. LAWRENCE.

We could sail from any Italian port, or even from Malta. Do you know anything about ships from New Orleans or Galveston or anywhere near? I should really like to miss New York, for the first shot. If you should find it worth while to

cable I'll pay when I arrive—or send cheque.—I would prefer
to sail in January—don't know why.—Are there any trees? Is
there any water?—stream, river, lake?—How far are you from
El Paso or from Santa Fe. I don't see Taos on the map.

D. H. L.

If possible I would not go to New York: perhaps Galveston,
Texas, or Los Angeles. Please say.

D. H. L.

Please don't tell anybody that we think of coming to Taos.
Shall we bring any household things?—sheets, towels, etc.?
How warm must the clothing be? How cold, and how hot is
Taos?

The man who does most things for me is Robert Mountsier, 417 West 118 Street, New York. He might write you.

A few days later, Frieda's first letter came:

Fontana Vecchia
Taormina

DEAR MABEL DODGE

We are so keen on coming!—both of us. The mountain
lakes and the piazzas and Indians and I am very grateful to you
for giving us the impetus to a *real* move and putting our noses
onto the spot where I'm sure we want to go.—This Fontana is
very lovely early in the morning when the sun rises straight
onto us out of the Ionian sea, but by midday it goes round the
hill, the sun, I mean, and all the glamour goes, all feels empty
and meaningless and you go to *dull* tea parties in the afternoon,
exquisite young Englishmen and, you know, the usual travellers
in Italy and you rave about the beauty of Etna and with joy I
rush home here to our silent Fontana.—But it *is* time for Lawrence to get out of this, this is no life for a man and a man who
wants something genuine.—Well, I'll pack my few rags with
such joy already and before long we shall meet; and pray to those

Mexican Gods that we shall be happy, all of us!

This is still the old year, but how good to look forward into the new—

Best wishes to you.

FRIEDA LAWRENCE

geb. VON RICHTHOFEN.

We were completing Tony's house that fall. It is a five-roomed house, of adobe of course, near us, but across the *acequia madre* and on Indian land. The Indian land, you know, is all along behind our place and curves round our orchard to the north, so we are wholly protected from other buildings ever being put there. Tony took up a large piece of it for himself, as any Indian may do if he cultivates or fences it, and we put up this smaller house there to lend or rent to friends.

It is so lovely there with the water of the *acequia* running right behind it and cottonwood trees making a shadow over it, and the alfalfa fields directly in front of the low adobe wall we built around it, to keep the horses out. It is a long, low house with thick walls, and a portal between the two wings that project at either end. The portal roof is supported by twisted columns, the first ones ever put up in that valley. They were chiseled out of the trunks of pine trees by Manuel, who has done all the fine handwork on our houses. We painted them sky-blue. We use a tremendous amount of paint out there, and most of it is blue; it looks beautiful with the different shades of pale adobe color.

I hurried to finish this house for the Lawrences. I foresaw how he would love the isolation of it out there in the fields facing the low hills off in front of it, and with nothing between it and the Pueblo mountain to the north but Indian fields. The sun flooded the house, though the portal was shady. Inside, it was so fresh and clean with paint and whitewash. The ceilings were supported on heavy cottonwood and pine beams, glistening where the bark had been stripped off.

Most of the furniture was carpentered right there in the house and then painted, and each room had an adobe fireplace, whitewashed. It looked, when it was ready, as though it had been made with hands, as did all the houses in that country. Uneven surfaces, irregular lines, true as hand and eye could make them, but not mechanically squared, not *contracted*! I hurried to complete the last details of the little house. It must be as perfect as I could make it.

Another encouraging letter came from Lawrence in a short time:

> *Fontana Vecchia,*
> *Taormina, Sicilia*
> *21 Novem. 1921*

DEAR MABEL DODGE STERNE

This is a line to say I am persisting in my intention to come to Taos in January. I haven't yet heard anything about a ship: have a very great desire to find a cargo-boat that will land me in Los Angeles or San Francisco. I have a very great desire to land on the Pacific coast. I hope to be in Taos in February.

Look at Leo Stein bursting into a new Jewish psalmody!

I asked Robert Mountsier to chase ships for me at that end; am doing my best at this end.

Till we meet, then.

> D. H. LAWRENCE.

I cannot recall now, but I suppose I must have told him that Leo Stein had stayed with us in Taos, since he enclosed this disagreeable, malicious letter from him:

> *Settignano—Firenze,*
> *Nov. 9, 1921*

MY DEAR LAWRENCE

> Rich and red
> Bury the dead,
> And a soul prepare
> For the rich and the rare;

Rise from the grave
On a bellying wave;
Ganglionic back,
Hew snicker-snack;
Fly free O my heart
Light-quivering dart;
There, sheer, you behold her
Cling, amplectinous shoulder.

I have but lately read your book on consciousness, and re-call how once you would have sent to the New Republic the things that you were about to write on that subject. I am afraid that they would never have gotten by. The N.R.'s are a rather conservative lot and would have been inclined to judge rather harshly your flight on the wings of scientific imagination. I doubt whether they have gotten much beyond Tyndall in that direction.

Your work is of course in several respects in a familiar tra-dition. The title recalls Schopenhauer, and might well have been, The Fourfold Root of Sufficient Being. On the other hand it continues the work of the Natur-Philosophen. It makes me think of Oken and of science like the following: "Die Mathematik ist auf das Nichts begründet, und entspringt mithin aus dem Nichts." "Der Sehnerv ist ein organisirter Lichtstrahl, das Hirn eine organisirte Sonne, das Auge eine organisirte farbensonne, Regenbogen."

I am a little discouraged, however, by your materialism. Here we are started off from the belly. Disguise it as you will, the belly is made for food, and food is made for the belly. The back is, as everyone knows, made for resistance, for do we not in resistance get our backs up? Then we pass to a more lyrical note to "The Angel Israfel, whose heart-string is a lute," and so by ultimate progression, to the embracing arms which, of course, come from behind, else would we be left out from our own embraces if we embraced only from in front. That would make an embrace a sorry isolation, and so once more is the world justified in the wisdom of its poets.

The hour of war spiritualism is running to its end, and I should not be surprised if the moment were come for the founding, in the sunny glens of Southern California, of the new Laurentian Brotherhood of the Fourfold Root of Sufficient Being. It might carry as its Oriflamme the Blazing Beard of which the Sun in the High Heavens is the sufficing symbol, and the brethren might intone, in their triumphal progress, something like the following:

> In Plexus and Ganglion
> We rise, we rise,
> Freud and Einstein we leave
> To conceptual sties,
> In the Prophet's wisdom
> Alone we are wise
> As sensationally upward
> The spirit flies
> And warms to its home
> In the star-tented skies.

Of course I do not insist on the intrinsic importance of this chant. It is, perhaps, a little too much in the romantic temper and might not float easily in the amniotic juice of a modern womb. Pray accept the goodwill which prompts it rather than the evil deed which is the outcome,

and believe me ever yours,

LEO STEIN.

Kindest regards to your wife.

Leo had been with Maurice and me the first year we lived in Taos, when we rented Manby's house. He used to go for long climbs in the mountains behind the pueblo, carrying two bananas and a few whole-wheat crackers. He had a great appreciation for nature, and he always said that the landscape behind the Sacred Mountain up near Blue Lake was finer than the best Chinese painting—which is about the most that an art-critic could say!

I cannot tell you, Jeffers, how much I was counting on this visit from Lawrence. In his *Psychoanalysis and the Unconscious* there had been allusions here and there that seemed to point to capacities in him that would enable him to understand the invisible but powerful spirit that hovered over the Taos Valley. One could not say whether it emanated from the Indians or whether they as well as the rest of us dwelt under its wings. I knew the Indians believed they took care of the earth and the water; that they gave power to the sun; and they were proud of the crystal-clear streams from the mountains—Star Water they called Lucero Creek. And Tony used to say, laughing:

"The white people like Taos and call it '*climate.*' Do they know what *climate* is? Do they know why the sun is better in Taos and why they feel happy in it?"

But I did not know, really, whether they were responsible for the spirit of the place or whether there was over and above them all a consciousness that permeated all that place, that possessed it and called it Home. Anyway, I believed that Lawrence was the only person living, so far as *I* knew, who could penetrate and define that magic, in which we moved, but which we were powerless to understand—the laughing, aloof, genius of Taos.

His next letter was promising. He was ready to "believe." I did not understand what he meant by his words about the Indians believing in him, though, but I learned later!

Taormina, 28 December, 1921

DEAR MABEL DODGE STERNE

Your letter and the little MSS came this morning.

Good, we are coming. I haven't found a cargo boat yet, but from Bordeaux to New Orleans a boat on 15th January. It is just possible we may get that. But I have to wait for letters and money arrangements. If we miss this boat, we shall sail a month later—by the next. This is the Transatlantique passenger service. So at any rate we should be in Taos in March. I want very much to come, and wish I could start tomorrow.

Thank you for all the information. It seems to me we shall live as cheaply there as here—almost. If the rooms of the little house are not too small, we'll have that. And I'll pay you the usual rent. I hope I needn't all my life be so scrubby poor as we have been: those damned books may sell better. But money never worries me. I've got apparently about 2000 dollars to come with: enough.

I too believe in Taos, without having seen it. I also believe in Indians. But they must do *half* the believing: in me as well as in the sun. Vediamo.

I must learn Spanish. I don't know any.

allora, fra poco.

D. H. LAWRENCE.

A month after his first Taormina letter, he gave me the first glimpse of what I later called his Cult of the Unconscious:

Villa Fontana Vecchia
Taormina, Sicilia
4 December 1921

DEAR MRS. STERNE

I had your cable this morning. We are persisting in the Taos intention. I have written many letters: all I find so far is that I can get a steamer to New Orleans from England. That will do if nothing else. I wait still for answers from Genoa. I still hope to sail in January, or February at latest.

I must thank you for Bjerre's book, which I have read, and which I found interesting: pretty sound, it seemed to me. But I rather hate therapy altogether—doctors, healers, and all the rest. I believe that a real neurotic is a half devil, but a cured neurotic is a perfect devil. They assume perfect conscious and automatic control when they're cured: and it is just this conscious-automatic control that I find loathsome.

However—till we meet.

D. H. LAWRENCE.

I would prefer that the neurotics died.

Now in this letter I had my first shock from that man. He whom I was trying to draw to Taos because he seemed to me to have more consciousness than anyone alive was inimical to conscious activity! I was unable, then, to understand what he meant. Leo Stein had once defined genius as the capacity to leap without having to look—and I wondered if that was an explanation of an antagonism to it—to looking ahead, knowing, judging, "adapting," as the psychoanalysts called it. Could one really live, then, I wondered, by impulse, by letting "It" decide, as I had believed years ago until the Freudian analysts had deprived me of my faith in "hunches" and in intuitions?

But now, as I look back and try to find clear meanings in the old design of the last fifteen years, I can almost see, very dimly yet, that although everything went wrong with him, apparently, from first to last, right down to his death, somehow Lawrence was right and the analysts were not. Although he never "adapted" and never fitted into the environment, though he suffered and made anyone who came near him suffer; though he threw everyone over sooner or later, and not once, but as often as they rejoined his turbulent and intractable spirit; in spite of a most unsuccessful life from a sensible point of view; yet, beyond sense and expediency, beyond the average, practical, tight-lipped loyalties, and away beyond pleasure, Lawrence was right. Conscious activity is "of this world." Can we be satisfied to limit ourselves to it—even for happiness?

I see now, Jeffers, that Lawrence died because he was what is called a neurotic and because he scorned to learn the mundane mastery that may insure a long, smooth life if the living impulse is emasculated and overcome.

And yet we must doubt, too! Something in us longs to live and to be happy in this slum of the universe! To seize *now* the partial ecstasy; to conform and to obey; to overcome and override the inhuman dæmon that cares nothing for systems, but only for life. But to *think* about Lawrence makes one split asunder on the rock of the world and lose one's carefully fabricated analytic faith and begin to doubt it all—the whole small bag of tricks. Lawrence was always right, though everything he did was wrong and he made a mess of living and of friendship and love. Lawrence was always wrong, always in the wrong because he never learned to "control" himself, but let life rule.

How will I make you see it, Jeffers?

In January, when the little house stood ready and waiting, even with fires laid and plants in the window, Frieda wrote:

Fontana Vecchia
26. I. 22

Dear Mabel Dodge

We were coming *straight* to you at Taos, but now we are not. Lawrence says he can't face America *yet*—he doesn't feel strong enough! So we are first going to the East to Ceylon. We have got friends there, two Americans, "Mayflowerers" and Buddhists. Strengthened with Buddha, noisy, rampageous America might be easier to tackle. Now we propose this: Come and see us in *Ceylon* and we go with *you* to Taos from the other side.—It might be very thrilling. We really start on the 26th of February from Naples. In my mind I have already lived in Taos and suddenly when it was all fixed, our going to Taos, Lawrence sprang Ceylon onto me. Will you come? I hope you will. I would be very disappointed. I know it will be Taos before long. But I am sure the East would cure one of this sick Europe; to face America one has got to be strong and stand on very solid legs inside and out. I feel America has *almost* been too much for you. I hope you won't think we are horrid not to come yet after all your kindness, but you come to us. I am thrilled at going out of Europe for the first time. You will get this when we start at Naples. Write to us at Ceylon address.

Yours with my warmest greetings, and I say auf Wiedersehen.

FRIEDA LAWRENCE.

I knew what it meant. They were scared. They wanted to see me, take a look, take even a bite and be able to spit it out if they didn't like it! Someone had "warned" them. I was used to that. People were always warning other people about me. No matter if it was justified and I knew it was, still it always hurt my feelings and stiffened my backbone. Certainly I wouldn't budge to go and see them in Ceylon! I'd had the idea of having *him* come to *Taos*, and I'd sit there and draw him until he came. I'd go down inside myself and call that man until he would have to come.

A few days and he wrote:

> *Fontana Vecchia*
> *Taormina, Sicily*
> *27 Jan. 1922*

DEAR MABEL DODGE STERNE

Is it vile of us to put off Taos for the moment. But I have a Balaam's Ass in my belly which won't budge, when I turn my face west. I can't help it. It just stubbornly swerves away in me. I *will* come. But a detour. I am writing to book berths on the Osterley from Naples, Feby. 26th for Colombo, Ceylon. The address will be,

% E. H. Brewster, "Ardnaree," Lake View Estate, *Kandy*, Ceylon. But the telegraphic address just: Brewster, Ardnaree, Kandy. I feel it is my destiny to go east before coming west. Only to stay a short time: perhaps a year. But to get quite calm and

sure and still and strong. I feel America is so *unreligious*: it's a
bad word: and that it is on the brink of a change, but the change
isn't quite ready yet, so I daren't come. And I feel you yourself
are *harried* out there. Come and join us in Ceylon—as soon as
you can—and then after, let us go together to Taos.

I had your letter of New Year's Day. I sent you *Tortoises*.
I will come to the Indians, yes. But only via the East. There is
something will not let me sail west for America.

You want to send Brill to hell and all the analytic ther-
apeutic lot. And I don't like Stein, a nasty, nosy, corrupt Jew.
Voilà! Time we got clear of all that stuff.

No, *never* adapt yourself. Kick Brill in the guts if he tries to
come it over you. Kick all America in the guts: they need it.
Foul enough, with their over-riding of life. But when the hand
has fallen on them a bit heavier, they will change. Only wait. But
meanwhile withdraw for a little peace: a breathing space.

No, spit on every neurotic, and wipe your feet on his face
if he tries to drag you down to him. . . . All that "arty" and
"literary" crew, I know them, they are smoking, steaming shits.
My blood turns to gall: I want to go and have it sweetened a
bit: away from them all, in the old, old east. Later we'll tackle
'em.

Come to Ceylon. Come at once—via San Francisco and
China—and we'll prepare ourselves for the later Onslaught on
to that Land of Promise of yours,

Benedicite

D. H. LAWRENCE.

And a post card as he sailed!

Naples, Sat.

We are sailing tomorrow for Ceylon—you have the ad-
dress. I wonder if you will feel like a dash to the east. I feel rather
bad about suddenly backing out of all I had decided, Taos and
America. And you were so kind. But it is my destiny.

D. H. LAWRENCE.

But it was no use. I had sent him some powerful letters and I had used a lot of willing on him; and after a while he wrote from India:

Ardnaree. Kandy. Ceylon
10 April 1922

DEAR MABEL DODGE STERNE

I have your two letters, but still no sign of book or necklace. Speriamo.

No, the East doesn't get me at all. Its boneless suavity, and the thick, choky feel of tropical forest, and the metallic sense of palms and the horrid noises of the birds and creatures, who hammer and clang and rattle and cackle and explode all the livelong day, and run little machines all the livelong night; and the scents that make me feel sick, the perpetual nauseous overtone of cocoanut and cocoanut fibre and oil, the sort of tropical sweetness which to me suggests an untertang of blood, hot blood, and thin sweat: the undertaste of blood and sweat in the nauseous tropical fruits; the nasty faces and yellow robes of the Buddhist monks, the little vulgar dens of the temples: all this makes up Ceylon to me, and all this I cannot bear. Je m'en vais. Me ne vo'. I am going away. Moving on.

I have cabled for money from New York, and anxiously await the return cable so that I can book berths on the Orsova, on the 24th of this month, for West Australia: about 10 days from Colombo to Fremanth. The address there will be % Mrs. Jenkins, Strawberry Hill, Perth., W. Australia. I don't know how long we shall stay there: but I shall take my steamer-ticket right to Sydney. I want to look at Australia, and try what it's like. If I don't care for it, then I can very easily come on. There are steamers every fortnight from Sydney to San Francisco; and San Francisco is not far from Taos. And I shall be fulfilling my real desire to approach America from the West, over the Pacific. I hope I shall arrive in Taos with ten cents left in my pocket—ten cents left to me in the world, even. Knees of the Gods.

I still of course mistrust Taos very much, chiefly on account of the artists. I feel I never want to see an artist again while I live. The Indians, yes: if one is sure that they are not jeering at one. I find all dark people have a fixed desire to jeer at us: these people here—they jeer behind your back. But heavens, I don't see much in them to admire, either. They seem to be built round a gap, a hollow pit. In the middle of their eyes, instead of a man, a sort of bottomless pit. That's Buddhism too. Buddhism seems to me a very conceited, selfish show, a vulgar temple of serenity built over an empty hole in space. No, no, these little darkie people don't impress me, upon actual contact. The place, Ceylon, is a real prison to me, oppressive, and I want to get out. Two weeks today, pray God.

I wish I could come to America without meeting the awful "cultured" Americans with their limited self-righteous ideals and their mechanical love-motion and their bullying, detestable negative creed of liberty and democracy. I don't believe either in liberty or democracy. I believe in actual, sacred, inspired authority: divine right of natural kings: I believe in the divine right of natural aristocracy, the right, the sacred duty to wield undisputed authority. Naturally I find myself in diametric opposition to every American—and everybody else, besides Americans—whom I come across. Nevertheless, there it stands.

Well, so far so good.

Yrs.

D. H. LAWRENCE.

You see he *had* to come. He wanted it clean. He wanted the dawn of the world, Jeffers, and it was there waiting for him all the time he made that silly detour to India and Australia! But you see how he followed his impulses? Maybe he did well to wait. But it strengthened something in me that he hated. When he came, the strong-evil-will-of-the-American-woman thing, the very same wilful female principle that he hated and feared, was strengthened by his postponement.

About this time Leo wrote:

Copy of a letter that I have written to Lawrence. I don't know how he feels after that letter on the unconscious but no matter. The enclosure spoken of is that part of your letter that referred to him. Norman Douglas, by the way, said that in a recent letter Lawrence had said that he had enough of Europe and was thinking of N. M.

MY DEAR LAWRENCE—

The enclosed will speak for itself. It is part of a letter that I got from Mabel Sterne a few days ago. New Mexico is really one of the tremendous things. No landscape that I have ever seen elsewhere is so beautiful. It is the only place that for me actually realized the vision of the great Chinese landscape painters, and the Pueblo Indians are in many ways wonderful. The corn dance of the San Domingo Indians is the *biggest* thing in the way of a ceremonial expression that I have ever seen, the eagle dance perhaps the most beautiful, and there are many others. From Taos and Santa Fe as centers, one can see all but infinite wonders, and Mabel Sterne is the all but perfect hostess. She'll take you everywhere and show you everything. She has immense energy, and capacity to make things happen without any irritating restlessness. She's a kind of reposeful hurricane. She is completely at home in N. M., and is the only educated, cultivated woman that I know of who has broken through the barrier between red and white and keeps it open in both directions. If you are after something different, and Douglas tells me that you are, you'll find it there. Incidentally, Mabel is not a lion hunter. She's been used to lions all her life and is quite some little lioness herself. But she is a delightful and appreciative companion, and at Taos you can have society or solitude in such measure and forms as you prefer. I spent six months out there in 1917, and would have become the owner of a house if the ex-wife of the owner whose signature was necessary to transfer the property, had not gone utterly and irrevocably astray. It's good medicine, that country.

There you are and I hope that you like it.

Affectionately,

LEO.

Bien des amitiés et souhaits de Nina.

Another post card came as Lawrence left Kandy in April, which said:

Kandy. 3 April

I had your note, but neither book nor necklace so far. However, they will come. Ceylon is an *experience*—but heavens, not a permanence. I think we shall go right on, in about 3 weeks time and look at Australia—then from Sydney to San Francisco, if I've got any money. Write a line to me % Mrs. Jenkins, Strawberry Hill, Perth, West Australia. If we move on so quick, we'll soon see Taos.

D. H. L.

And in a little while he was in Perth:

4 April 1922

DEAR MABEL DODGE STERNE

Well, here we are—a raw hole it seems. Got here this morning. Shall have to wait a fortnight or so for a boat on to Sydney. Doubt if Australia will see much of me. At the rate I'm going, I ought to be in Taos easily by August. Will you still have a little house for me?

I never got the book and necklace you sent to Ceylon.

Yours,

D. H. LAWRENCE.

Sunday

Came out into the bush: wonderful sky and air and freshness. But don't think I shall stay long. Send me a line to Sydney, % Thomas Cook and Son. That is quite safe. D. H. L.

And then a letter came from Frieda:

P & O.S. N. Co. S.S. Malvoa
May 19th, 22.

DEAR MABEL DODGE

We are on the way to Sydney and the boat rolls. We had your letter in Perth, so we are coming nearer, you see. I *love* the idea of spending some of the winter with you and Tony. I am so full of hope that it might be happy for all of us. Only we won't tell anybody that we are coming, I am frightened of people's spite and vulgarity. I want to stay in Sydney till the middle of August, I am sick of boats, so we may be with you sometime in September. Ceylon was a wonderful experience and deeply satisfying but the past and the known. We will unite our efforts in a jolly life. Your book on "glands" reached Ceylon, Brewster read it. I suppose it will follow us. . . . I hope the necklace and other book. Ashsah Brewster was quite simple and nice, but a kind of New England "culture" was very irritating; if she had only been content to be her simple self instead of all her flights! Pictures of huge St. Francis's and unbirdy birds and white chiffon clouds of garments round her solid flesh. He was "Elder" Brewster, still only Elder Brewster turned to Buddha! *Poor* Australia, we stayed in the bush but the pathetic penscratchy attempts at civilising the poor country was oh so depressing and the people are so *over*-civilised in one centre of themselves!! I hope Sydney will be bearable for a few months, it will be very hot, won't it, in the summer in New Mexico. If we can only keep it dark for a little while that we are coming, let's have our meeting without the spiteful comments of New York on *all* of us. We must think about an address for letters. I *liked* the picture on your note paper!

Looking forward to be with you quite soon.

FRIEDA.

I am sure it was wise that we came round this way, you see we had neither of us been out of Europe!

It seemed as though she were rather harried herself. And how discontented they were everywhere! Would Taos suit them? What was the matter? From Sydney, Lawrence wrote a letter that seemed a trifle more settled:

% Thomas Cook & Son
Sydney, N.S.W.
3 June 1922

DEAR MABEL DODGE

Here we are in a little house on the edge of the Pacific, which ocean rolls loudly nearly into the house. We've come about 40 miles south of Sydney. Australia is not a bad country, qua country. But I am so weary of these utterly à terre democratic peoples. Probably America will be as bad.

I have started a novel and if I can go on with it, I shall stay till I've finished it—till about end of August. But if I can't work I shall come on to America. I'll send you a cable merely saying the boat. I suppose Sterne, Taos, New Mexico, will find you. The steamers are. . . . .

These sailings may be altered a bit, but not much. . . . It seems to me it is a good thing I came round the world to Taos. I shall be much more likely to stick it when I get there.

I hear the glands book arrived in Ceylon and was sent on, so I shall get it.

I do hope I shall get from your Indians something that this wearily external white world can't give, and which the east is just betraying all the time. Meanwhile have patience with our vagaries.

If I was really going to give up struggling with life, I'd come to Australia. It is a big empty country, with room to be alone.

I want this to catch the Tahiti, which sails June 8th and is due in Frisco on July 3d.

tanti saluti

D. H. LAWRENCE.

And soon it was followed by another:

> *"Wyewurk," Thirroul*
> *New South Wales*
> *9 June 1922.*

DEAR MABEL DODGE

I have as good as decided to stay here till August—because I think I can finish my Australian novel, or near enough, by then. We shall probably take the boat Tahiti, arriving in San Francisco Sept. 4th. I'll write again when I book berths. The Tahiti sails August 10th.

I want you please *not* to tell anybody we are coming. I want to be really apart from most people—same as here. Here I have not let anybody know I am come—I don't present any letters of introduction—there isn't a soul on this side of Australia knows I am here, or knows who I am. And that is how I prefer it. It's a queer novel I'm writing, but it interests me.—I have ordered Seltzer to send you a copy of *Aaron's Rod* and of *Fantasia of the Unconscious*, which follows Psychoanalysis and the Unconscious.

I build quite a lot on Taos—and the pueblo. I shall be so glad if I can write an American novel from that centre. It's what I want to do. And I have learned a lot coming here.

We shall have blewed all our money on steamships, so shall want to be very obscure and economical till a little more grows up. Of course I shall have enough to get along with.

I wonder if we shall find the winter very cold! But I look forward to it very much. I wonder if we shall go to that farther off pueblo you wrote about.

I feel now it actually won't be long before we are in New Mexico.

D. H. LAWRENCE.

My Indian necklace to Frieda seemed to be rather far behind their tracks! He kept saying they hadn't it.

20 June, 1922

I had your letter of May 12th today—and two days ago the *Glands* book. But no sign of the necklace. I suggest you write to the Postmaster, Kandy, and ask where it is, and ask to have it returned. I will write to him also. Am stuck in my novel. Wish we could get away from here in July, but fear I shall have to wait till August for money. I am sending you a copy of Aaron's Rod by this post. I asked Seltzer to send you a copy of Fantasia. Hope you got it.

D. H. LAWRENCE.

And Frieda's letter:

"Wyewurk" (*the name of this bungalow. It's an "Australian" joke, we believe, on Why Work!*)
Thirroul, New South Wales

DEAR MABEL DODGE

We are sitting here perched on the Pacific, lovely for that and the air and space, but the tin cans and newspapers flung over the ugly little town behind are not to be thought of. And quite a nice statue of an "Anzac" stands at the corner, just like a forgotten milk can, no grass around it or *anything*, only filthy paper flying and a tin cinema show near. I can not bear it—except this place alone on the cliff of the sea with a nice big beautiful room and big terraces all round. We are reading the Gland book in turns. I find it interesting, but it always is funny when a man sees salvation in "glands" they know in "part." L. has written a novel, gone it full tilt to page 305, but has come to a stop and kicks. I am glad to sit still for a little before we start the 24 days to San Francisco, but it will be I hope the jolliest part of the journey—and we are *both* looking forward to Taos. Keep us dark at *first* anyhow, but *terribly* dark. We don't know a soul here, rather fun. Nobody has "discovered" L. The necklace must wait till I come to you. I shall be so cross if it is lost—but I am sorry that you had so much bother with it, the post can be so irritating. I looked inside the gland book for the necklace and had a genuine ten minutes of disappointment, till I remembered that it wasn't with the gland book—with relief. August the 10th we start. By the way, *don't* give us too little a place to live in, we are much too quarrelsome and it's quite fatal. We can afford it nowadays, I mean we aren't as poor as we used to be—but we mustn't be too much on top of each other or we get on each other's nerves. I cannot really imagine Taos, in spite of pictures. So I shall see it in the "flesh" soon. . . .

Every good wish

FRIEDA LAWRENCE.

With the following postscript from Lawrence at the end:

June 21. We'll get this off by the Niagara via Vancouver. I posted you Aaron's Rod yesterday. Asked Seltzer to send you *Fantasia of the Unconscious*—which should be out. I wrote to Ceylon with very careful instructions to have the necklace returned to you. It *may* turn up here meanwhile: also the notes.

Unless something untoward happens, unless the Consul refuses a visa or my money doesn't come from Mountsier or anything tiresome like that, we should be in Frisco on the morning of Sept. 4th. Why don't you come for a trip and meet us? I'll cable you the boat just before we sail. I expect we shall have to go first class on these small boats. Damn steamer fares.—Of course I must pay rent for whatever house you let me have. No, not too small, if it can be avoided—the house. We both like to keep sufficiently clear of one another.

D. H. L.

The address: "Wyewurk," Thirroul, New South Wales, is good till August. And *New South Wales* is one word.

This was followed by two more from him:

"Wyewurk," Thirroul, N.S.W.
9 July 1922

DEAR MABEL DODGE

Just a word to catch the Sonoma, sailing on Wednesday.

I had your cablegram: "Expecting you." I am only waiting for Mountsier's cable with my money to engage berths on The *Tahiti*. I was in Sydney, and the consul will give the visas all right. I'll cable you the word Tahiti the day before we sail, if nothing goes wrong: and nothing will go wrong. That will mean we are in San Francisco on September 4th. It would be great fun if you came to meet us, but of course not unless it would amuse you to. Seltzer *might* come.

I have nearly done my novel: such a novel. I hope you have Aaron's Rod, and Fantasia.

I wish we could settle down at—or near—Taos, and have a little place of our own, and a horse to ride. I do wish it might be like that.

I had a note from the Customs—some sort of parcel from the U. S. A. It may be the necklace. There is one more boat sails —to Vancouver—after the Tahiti, so I can send you one more note.

Till then.

Yrs.

D. H. LAWRENCE.

"Wyewurk," Thirroul
New South Wales
18 July 1922

DEAR MABEL DODGE

The notes of Taos and the photographs—very interesting— but not the necklace. F. laments this. But I wrote urgently about it to Kandy.

I still haven't got the money from Mountsier, so can't finally engage berths. But they are holding Cabin No. 4 for me on the *Tahiti*. I see the advertisement of her sailing has suddenly

changed the date from the 10th to the 16 August. If she sails on
the 16th then I don't suppose she arrives in San Francisco till
September 10th instead of 4th. I very much want to catch the
Tahiti—have done my novel and have nothing further to do
here.—I wish the money would come. I'll cable you the date of
arrival when we are leaving.

à bientot.

D. H. LAWRENCE.

This will catch the Makura via Vancouver: and that is the last
boat before the Tahiti—the last mail. We shall stay a couple of
days or so in San Francisco anyway: just to look at it.

And the last one, finally, from San Francisco, some time in
September:

Palace Hotel, San Francisco
Monday

DEAR MABEL DODGE

I had your letter and telegram on board—sounds perfectly
lovely—very many thanks. The General Post Office is shut today
so I can't get the other letter till tomorrow. And I can't telegraph
you our day for arrival in Lamy because once more, like an ass,
I spent all my money and arrive here with less than $20, so must
wait till Mountsier wires me some. I have telegraphed to him
already. There is money in the bank.

I think we shall leave Thursday—perhaps even Wednesday.
I thought of stopping off at Yosemite Valley but feel— Oh damn
scenery. So intend to come straight to Lamy.

Shall telegraph you immediately I am fixed up—tomorrow,
I fondly hope. And we ought to be with you by Saturday. It
sounds all so delightful.

Tante belle cose di noi due

D. H. LAWRENCE.

So you have been able to follow them and how they moved
all through a year—a year's journey to Taos—and our strange
poignant time together.

Difference

Difference

Why does the white man hate you so, Indian, Indian?
I know.

You stand together and smile.
You trade, you joke, you touch hands,
But something deep down in you stands apart
All the while.

I have heard Indians say of their good friends
Among the whites: "White man smells bad—
I do not like his smell."

This keeps him always really aloof from his friend.
They may play together, eat together, live under the same roof;
But the inner alchemy of the Indian separates them,
And will until the end.

White man, you know, 'way deep down in you,
The Indian is the better man.
Deeply you are ruined—spoiled—inferior—lost, lost!

Now you hate him for his difference from your kind—
For his joy in life, his immediacy, his well-being.
You call him lazy, dishonest, stupid—
But these are only attributes of your mind!

Indian alchemy is not lazy, stupid, dishonest—
It is swift, true, and infinitely knowing.
It is *your* inner chemistry that has lost its "natural"
And grown lazy, stupid, and dishonest.

31

You think everything is as it should be
Because your brain thinks things that are
Noble-seeming and superior.
Foolish white man, your brain is traitor to your living;
It has taught you far-fetched false ways of being.

It has brought you to rank, curious eatings and drinkings,
And many foul mechanical substitutes for action.
It has led you into poisonous wisdoms—
You scarcely know when the sun is shining.

The sun, moon, and earth, the rains and rivers,
Still nurture Indians,
And these are no poisons.
While you, white man, have run fast and loose
Into bad ways and mirage-horizons.

This is why the Indian hates your smell.
And this is why, in sick envy, lost to life, you hate him.
But neither of you knows all this.
And that is just as well.

Photo Edward Weston.

TONY LUJAN, 1930

Part Two

Part Two

Through the months while Lawrence and Frieda hesitated about coming to Taos, I willed him to come. Before I went to sleep at night, I drew myself all in to the core of my being where there is a live, plangent force lying passive—waiting for direction. Becoming entirely that, moving with it, speaking with it, I leaped through space, joining myself to the central core of Lawrence, where he was in India, in Australia. Not really speaking to him, but *being* my wish, I became that action that brought him across the sea.

"Come, Lawrence! Come to Taos!" became, in me, Lawrence in Taos. This is not prayer, but command. Only those who have exercised it know its danger. And, as before, when I had tried to bring about my wishes, I had Tony with his powerful influence to help me. I told him we must bring Lawrence to Taos because I knew he could do a great deal to help the pueblo. Tony had helped to bring Collier there and he had seen Collier take up the work in behalf of the Indians, and when I told him that if Lawrence came he would bring power for the Indians by his writing, he, too, used his magic to call him. But with some reluctance—just some reluctance to believe that writing about the Indians would help them. His instinct somewhat opposed it. The Indians believe that utterance is loss and that the closed and unrevealed holds power. But I overruled him and he gave way—and together we called Lawrence; and in the darkness and stillness of the night *became* Lawrence in Taos.

In those days it was a long, difficult trip down to Santa Fe over a narrow, dirt road full of ruts and rocks. We always had to rest at least an hour at noon to recover from the bumps and jolts of the car. So when Tony drove me down to Lamy, twenty miles beyond Santa Fe, to the station, we started in the morning and took all day to meet the early evening train.

We stood waiting in the sweet air, all scented as it was from the charcoal kilns burning piñon-wood. That was always the first impression of New Mexico when one got off the train at Lamy station—the thin, keen air full of a smell of incense.

Lawrence and Frieda came hurrying along the platform, she tall and full-fleshed in a suit of pale pongee, an eager look on her pink face, with green, unfocused eyes, and her half-open mouth with the lower jaw pulled a little sideways. Frieda always had a mouth rather like a gunman.

Lawrence ran with short, quick steps at her side. What did he look like to me that first time I saw him? I hardly know. I had an impression of his slim fragility beside Frieda's solidity, of a red beard that was somehow too old for him, and of a nervous incompetence. He was agitated, fussy, distraught, and giggling with nervous grimaces. Tony and I felt curiously inexpressive and stolid confronting them. Frieda was over-expansive, vociferous, with a kind of forced, false bonhomie, assumed (it felt so to me, at least) to cover her inability to strike just the real right note. As usual when there is a flurry like that, I died inside and became speechless. Tony is never any help at such a moment, and he just stood there. Somehow I herded them into the lunch room of the station, for we had to eat our supper there because it would be too late when we reached Santa Fe.

We got seated in a row at the counter, the atmosphere splitting and crackling all about us from the singular crash of our meeting. There was a vibratory disturbance around our neighborhood like an upheaval in nature. I did not imagine this: it was so. The Lawrences seemed to be intensely conscious of Tony and somehow embarrassed by him. I made out, in the twinkling of an eye, that Frieda immediately saw Tony and me sexually, visualizing our relationship. I experienced her swift, female measurement of him, and how the shock of acceptance made her blink. In that first moment I saw how her encounters passed through her to Lawrence—how he was keyed to her so that he felt things through her and was obliged to receive life through her, vicariously; but that he was irked by her vision; that he was impatient at being held back in the sex scale. He did not want to apprehend us so and it made him very nervous, but she was his medium, he must see through her and she had to see life from the sex center. She endorsed or repudiated experience from that angle. She was the mother of orgasm and of the vast, lively mystery of the flesh. But no more. Frieda was complete, but limited. Lawrence, tied to her, was incomplete and limited. Like a lively lamb tied to a solid stake, he frisked and pulled in an agony, not Promethean so much as Panic.

Can it be possible that it was in that very first instant when we all came together that I sensed Lawrence's plight and that the womb in me roused to reach out to take him? I think so, for I remember thinking: "He is through with that—he needs another kind of force to propel him . . . the spirit. . . ." The womb behind the womb—the significant, extended, and transformed power that succeeds primary sex, that he was ready, long since, to receive from woman. I longed to help him with that— to be used—to be put to his purpose.

Lawrence scurried to the far seat away from us on the other side of Frieda and she and I sat next each other, with Tony beside me. The meal was an agony—a halt—an unresolved chord, for me, at least, and for Lawrence, I knew. Tony ate his supper with a calm aloofness, unperturbed in the midst of alarm. Frieda continued her noisy, running ejaculations and breathless bursts of emotional laughter. Lawrence hid behind her big body. I scarcely saw him, but we all knew he was there, all right!

As we made our way out into the dark road where the motor waited, he exclaimed:

"Oh! Look how low the stars hang in the southern sky!" It was the first simple, untroubled notice he had taken of anything since they had left the train.

When we reached the automobile, I directed him to the seat beside Tony and took Frieda into the back seat with me, though I wanted it the other way round. But I thought it was easier for Lawrence that way, and that Tony would soothe him down.

As we moved off into the still night, Frieda exclaimed loudly, motioning to Tony's wide back:

"He's wonderful! Do you feel him like a rock to lean on?"

"No—o," I answered, hesitantly, unable to confirm her. Her words passed over to Lawrence with a thump. I saw his shoulders twitch. He did not want Frieda to think Tony was a rock to lean on; he could scarcely avoid understanding her unconscious comparison, or feeling again the old, old lack in himself. We ran smoothly on for a little while, and then, quite suddenly, the car simply stopped in the road.

"Well," said Tony.

He got out and looked under the hood, though I well knew that, no matter what he saw, he would not understand it. He had never learned much about the motor. Only by having the car checked quite often by garage people, we rarely had any difficulty any more, though when he first learned to drive, things were always going wrong. It was extremely unusual for anything to happen as late as 1922, for Tony had been motoring about the country for four years by that time.

We sat there for ages under the stars while Tony tried different ways to make it go again. We didn't talk much. It was peaceful, but it was growing late and I had not engaged rooms anywhere in Santa Fe. The only hotel possible to stay in then had burned down and I had intended to go to a boarding-house I knew about, for the night. As we sat there, quietly, our emotions subsided, our nerves quieted. Suddenly Frieda cut in:

"Get out and see if you can't help him, Lorenzo! Just sitting there! Do get out!"

And Lawrence answered angrily:

"You know I don't know anything about automobiles, Frieda! I *hate* them! Nasty, unintelligent, unreliable things!"

"Oh, you and your hates!" she returned, contemptuously.

A moment of silence broken by a vague picking sound out in the front where Tony pried round inside the machinery. And then Lawrence leaned over from the front seat and said:

"I am a failure. I am a failure as a man in the world of men. . . ."

Tony got into the car and tried it and it moved again.

"I guess there is some snake around here," he said, as we drove on.

I was flustered when we reached Santa Fe. The city was sleeping. We drove to the Riches' house, where I'd hoped to find rooms, but after rousing the house we were told it was full. Lawrence had unloaded their huge bags onto the sidewalk while they waited for me to go in. Frieda had made him do that. When I came out, I found him stamping his foot in a rage and trying to yell quietly in the night at her:

"I won't do it, Frieda! You stop that. . . ."

I interrupted him:

"We can't get in there. But I'll tell you what: Witter Bynner knows you're coming. He's always up. He has room. I know he'd love to have you—and we can go to some other friends here."

They were dubious and upset. But there was nothing else to do and we drove over to Bynner's house. Of course he and Spud Johnson were still up. I was so tired by now, I have forgotten how it seemed; anyway, we left the Lawrences to Bynner and we went and slept somewhere else.

"Do you like him, Tony?" I asked, before we closed our eyes.

"I don't know yet," said Tony, but he made a face.

It was a comfortable, jolly scene at Bynner's in the morning.

They were finishing breakfast in his gay kitchen, and everyone seemed to be in good spirits.

Frieda and I stood looking at a Chinese painting in the living-room after they all left the table, and she motioned with her head in her lusty, hearty way:

"Un ménage, hein? The young thin one seems rather nice."

We made off as soon as we could, for it was a long, tiring drive we had ahead of us. In the car, Lawrence exploded, peevishly:

"These men that leave the world—the struggle and heat of the world—to come and live in pleasant out-of-the-way places—I have little use for them."

"Just what he does himself," I thought. "But he has little use for himself, either. He is a frail cargo that he hauls through life with perpetual distaste."

I find, Jeffers, that I have given you no real, concrete portrait of Lawrence and Frieda. But I have here among their letters a description that a girl wrote of them and sent to a friend and me some time during the year we were all waiting for them to come. This was a girl who had known them in England—the only woman with whom—Frieda told me later—Lawrence was ever "unfaithful" to her!

"But it was unsuccessful," she added, with a kind of bitter triumph!

I think I will add this description of them, so you will be able to *see* how he looked:

"Lawrence is tall, but so slightly built and so stooped that he gives the impression of a small man. His head seems too heavy for his very slim body and hangs forward. The whole expression of his figure is of extreme fragility. His movements are quick and sure. He has a very heavy crop of ash-colored hair that is cut round in a bang and falls in sort of Greek-like locks. In contrast to his hair, is a very soft, silky beard of bright red. He has very large, wide-apart grey eyes, a long, slender face with a chin that

is out of proportion long, a defect that is concealed by the afore-
said beard. His under lip protrudes from the dainty decoration
of the beard in a violent red that makes his beard look pink. In
the midst of all this, is a very podgy, almost vulgar, certainly un-
distinguished nose. There! Can you see him?

"On the whole, it seems foolish to talk about Lawrence to anyone who has read his books, for he is all there, more than any
other author I ever knew. *Sons and Lovers* is a fairly authentic
picture of his own life. I think the events are absolutely true.
His mother's death almost killed Lawrence. He had such a
frightful mother-complex, and still has, I fancy, that the book
had to be written. His wife told me that when he wrote the
death of his mother, she had a perfectly terrible time with him
for many weeks.

"But what you want to know particularly, I suppose, is what
he is as a human being. He is one of the most fascinating men I
ever met. The first time I ever saw him, he talked for a whole
afternoon, almost steadily. He will do this at once and without
the slightest self-consciousness if he feels a sympathy in his
listener. He talks as brilliantly as he writes, and as frankly. Have
you read *Women in Love*? because that *is* Lawrence—his word.
It is his final philosophy. It pours out of him like an inspired
message, and no matter how much you may differ when you are
away from him, or how little able you are to follow his own particular mysticism, he makes you believe it when he is with you.

"But at the slightest touch of adverse criticism or hostility,
Lawrence becomes violent. His vituperation is magnificent. I
have never heard its equal. He spares none. He has quarreled
with everyone. He says he has no friends that he has not quarreled with. And yet all these same friends, I noticed, are very
likely to come back for the same treatment again and again.
Lawrence is a Puritan, really, and his intellectual reaction against
it is so violent that he hurls himself against it with all of himself,
destroying himself as he does it. In the marvelously sweet side of

his nature, he is inarticulate. And yet he is the gentlest, kindest person in all human relations that anyone could be on this earth. The peasants around where he lived in Cornwall adored him, blindly. They looked upon him as the new Messiah come to lead the world out of the dark into a light that they couldn't understand, but which they had infinite faith in, simply because he was he.

"Lawrence lives the life of a workman. He says that no matter how much money he has, he always will live just the same. I think this is true. When I visited them in Cornwall, he and his wife lived in a little stone cottage of three rooms. It was spotlessly clean, mostly done by Lawrence. All their cooking was done on an open fire in the living-room. I have even known Lawrence to do the washing, though they usually sent it out. Money means nothing to Lawrence. He is very frugal, with all the thriftiness of his working-class background, but he would share whatever he had with another without a thought. The little spotless sunny house in Cornwall had the most beautiful simplicity that I have ever seen.

"His wife is a big, rosy German, who, as the daughter of a Prussian officer, never knew anything but luxury in her girlhood. She is highly impractical now, and the little she knows of housework, Lawrence taught her. She is an expansive child-nature, very sunny and rich, living only in her emotions. The story of their love life is all to be found in the poems, *Look, We Have Come Through*. She is really all light and sun while Lawrence is dark; there seems to be always a weight on him. He is rarely really gay—he is truly the sombre Anglo-Saxon, which he hates with a bitter hatred.

"After all, Lawrence is best known in his books, for he writes all the things he cannot say. And yet he says such a lot! But the inner tumult wears him out. He is very fragile, physically. He says that he is always well when he is happy. It is said that he has something the matter with his lungs, yet not since he was a child has a doctor ever found any actual lung trouble. When he was a little boy, I believe, his lungs were affected, but he seems to have outgrown it.

"People are always making pilgrimages to him. He hates it, but is infinitely sweet to them. His awareness of other people is unbelievable. When you are with him, you feel that there is not a corner of your mind or spirit or whatever you have that Lawrence doesn't see and be tolerant of. And he bares himself perfectly frankly. When a mood or an impulse is in him, there is no such thing as repression. It all comes out in a mighty gust.

"He cannot live in big cities. The excitement kills him. He is too aware all the time. The war was a horrible thing to him, came darned near killing him, through the intensity of his emotion about it."

We passed alongside the Rio Grande River in the clear morning sunlight. In the warm valleys between Santa Fe and Taos the apples were ripening and the air was sweet from the juicy apricots. Corn, wheat, and alfalfa filled the fields, and the Mexicans and Indians were singing.

The September day was sunny and still about us all the way home, but when we made our final long climb up the mountain to reach the table-land of Taos Valley and pulled round the curve at the top, we saw the Sacred Mountain over behind Taos looming half-darkened by cloud shadows that hastened over it in great eagle shapes. Wide wings of eagles spread, sinister, over the huddling mountain while its peaks, forming a wide bow, held the last red rays of the sun.

Lawrence caught his breath. Everyone is surprised at that first view of Taos Valley—it is so beautiful. The mountains, eighteen miles away, curve half round it in a crescent, and the desert lies within its dark encircling grasp. Taos is an oasis, emerald-green beyond the sage-brush, drinking water from the high mountain lakes and streams.

We had just that one long look at Taos in sunlight and shadow, Jeffers, those few moments of sharp light with the eagle clouds in shadow flight across the face of it, when a long, slow flash of lightning zigzagged out of the sky above the mountain and disappeared into it like a snake. And then came, all of a sudden, a terrific explosion of thunder that seemed to fill the whole valley far and near—out of the stillness, out of the windless sky—with a crash so sharp and wild that we could only cower for an instant and cover our ears with our hands.

Tony stopped the car at once, and as he hurried to get out and put up the side-curtains, he threw me a swift, strange look. He was just in time to get us covered, for the rain broke over us in stark sheets, straight down in undivided steel sheets, nipping cold and shutting out all the world around us. It turned almost immediately to hail, battering upon the top of the car like cannon-balls, cracking open on the ground like splitting shells; hail like large stones piled up around the car until the earth was covered with them, and the air was suddenly like a winter night. Crash after crash of thunder, and the lightning zigging now on all sides as though a parent snake had peopled all the world in one immediate creation and filled the universe with serpentine light. East and west and north in turn flashed up out of the rain-darkened land. We saw now Taos, now far Colorado, or the low foot-hills east of Ranchos. Only the south, from where we had come that day, lay open and free of the storm.

In the car, no one spoke till Tony said to Lawrence:

"The white people say that the thunder comes from clouds hitting each other, but the Indians know better," and Lawrence giggled in a high, childish, nervous way.

The storm did not last long, but when it was over, all the crops in Taos Valley lay on the ground, ruined. There were practically no harvests taken in and the Indians and Mexicans suffered all that year.

It was dark when we reached our hill, a mile out of Taos village. I was shaking and weary, as always after the long, tiring ride. I led the Lawrences into the house and wished I myself were free to leave them and go to bed. But again we had to eat. I had hoped for so long that Lawrence would like our house. It is a strange house, slow grown and with a kind of nobility in its proportions, and with all the past years of my life showing there in Italian and French furniture, pictures from many hands, books from New York, bronzes from Venice, Chinese paintings, and Indian things. And always a fire burning in the fireplaces— "To make life," as Tony says.

Supper was ready. I saw the candles burning on the table in the big, dim dining-room and I led the way down the five round steps from the living-room. I was in a blind retreat behind my face, as always when I get tired from one thing or another: when there is a weight to pull for too long and things don't flow of themselves. After a little while I don't care any more what happens if things don't go of their own accord. Then I am alone, separated, divested of all wishes, indifferent to the whole outside world, forgetful of my high plans and hopes.

I sat them down at the round table, scarcely aware of anything. Blind, departed, nobody home. When I rang the bell to call Albidia, Lawrence giggled as he looked round into the surrounding dimness, from the island of our lighted space, and he said:

"It's like one of those nasty little temples in India!"

I didn't care what he said. I longed to get through—through with the day and away from them to my own room and to sleep —sleep—sleep!

Now this had all been a very inauspicious beginning, hadn't it, Jeffers? And yet when I saw Lawrence the next morning, none of that mattered. He was as sunny and good as a rested child, and his wide-apart eyes were blue like gentians.

I was rested, too, and we took a good look at each other,

neither of us seeming to be doing so. I'm not going to waste any time saying how or why, Jeffers; you must just take it as a fact when I tell you briefly that, from the first, Lawrence and I knew each other through and through as though we were of one blood. In fact, he told me many times afterwards, both in irritation and in sympathy, that I seemed like his sister. We never knew each other any more than we did at the beginning, for it was complete and immediate in the first hours. I wonder if this is not generally true. We do not know people by experience; experience through the passing of time merely ratifies the first full realization we have received entire. With some people it is a thin surface one penetrates, and bottom is soon reached; pleasant, shallow folk to know and like and find always the same. But of course there is a deep knowing when there is depth to sound. Like a diver and with instantaneous perception one plunges through the universe contained in some people, finding all time and all space, with what the past has won and everything that has bloomed and withered on this earth. Generally, however, sooner or later one touches bottom in them. When I was a girl, I had a friend named Violet. She was only twenty, but she was wise. I lost her, for she died; and since her there have been only two people I never reached the end of: Tony and Lawrence.

"You have gone a long way, but I have gone a longer," Lawrence said to me soon.

I had a friend from Buffalo days staying with me: Bessie Wilkinson. One of those prematurely white-haired widows who skim rapidly about the world like swallows, dipping here and there, enjoying themselves, taking life lightly. Lawrence seemed to like her. There was no danger. She did not make Frieda glower, either. Anything that was likely to make Frieda glower, Lawrence avoided. When he was at outs with her, he was thrown off his balance, for she was the root of his existence. He drew life from her so that when anything shook or disturbed that even flow, he was like a cut flower, drying up.

Bessie and I helped them to settle into Tony's house. They liked it very much, and it looked as though we should all have a happy time together.

They were to take their suppers at our house, and when we finished eating that night, Lawrence started telling us about the people on the boat. He was perfectly horrified at the way movie people go on. There had been a great many Hollywood people among the passengers, coming back, evidently, from making an island picture, and apparently Lawrence had observed them to the last!

Their unrestraint and their wild, care-free love-making amazed and at the same time infuriated him. He became acquainted with some of them. They were like a new species of creature he had never seen before. He watched and registered every move—not like a scientist, with coolness and interest—not like a poet—more like a dog in the manger, really, come to think of it, for he was so angry, so incensed when he told us about them. And evidently he had not got away without an antagonistic scene on board—for in the end he had a scene with some of them, and they, angered too—"jeered at him," as Frieda says in the following note.

Lawrence made us *see* that ship; the long, slow passage through the blue sea, the reckless, sensational crowd on board, and his own watching, angry, righteous, puritanical presence among them.

Tony was leaving to go to the Apache fiesta the next day and I begged him to take Lawrence along. Lawrence and Bessie Freeman. I wanted awfully to go, too, but there was not room for Frieda, so I knew I had to stay home with her. Tony didn't want to take Lawrence, but I made him!

He is so good-natured, Jeffers, and I am always *making* him do things that are nice for other people, but that leave him indifferent. You see, I wanted Lawrence to get into the Indian thing *soon*. I counted so much on that. On his understanding, his deep, deep understanding of the mystery and the other-worldness, as he would call it, of Indian life. My need to bring Lawrence and the Indians together was like an impulse of the evolutionary will, apart from me, using me for its own purposes. I could no more help trying to bring this about than I could help staying with Tony. I got tired, bored, indifferent, as with a difficult task; I wished I'd never started it; at such times all I cared for was to rest; but inevitably the same strong compulsion would return after a few hours of quiet.

So Bessie and Tony and Lawrence were to leave for the Apache Reservation, where they would have a dry camp on the side of a hill, opposite the Apache camp, where hundreds of tepees would be set up.

I forget who else was there staying with me at that time, but there were evidently others, for Frieda, in answer to a note from me, speaks of our all going over to her house:

DEAR MABEL

I am glad you feel like that. It's true, what you say. I have suffered tortures sometimes when Lawrence talked to people, when they drew him out just to "see his goods" and then jeered at him. I was happy last night. And for all that you will detest Lawrence sometimes and sometimes he talks bosh—but that is so human in him that he isn't "suberbo." It's a joy to me that Tony wants to go with him—but tell Tony that he is frail, he can't stand so very much! Won't you all come here again after your evening meal? I am cleaning and washing.

Love

F.

Yes, I will say if there is anything. I only wish with all my heart we had known you long ago!

She and I had a long talk that day. She was good company when Lawrence was not there, as is the case with nearly all wives. She talked with heartiness and vigor—always with a real, deep, human warmth, albeit sometimes with such obtuseness, such lack of comprehension. So long as one talked of people and their possibilities from the point of view of sex, she was grand. She had a real understanding of that. But one had to be careful all the time—to hide what one knew—to stay back with her. Any reference to the spirit, or even to consciousness, was antagonistic to her. The groping, suffering, tragic soul of man was so much filthiness to that healthy creature. Offensive. I learned early to keep away from her any sight or sound of unhappiness that was not immediately caused by some mishap of the bed— for really she admitted no other. You see, Jeffers, she was hedged in by her happy flesh, for she had not broken her shell when I knew her. Yet Frieda was very alive to all the simple sights and sounds of the earth. To flowers and birds; to the horses and cows and sheep. She responded to things vigorously with boisterous explosiveness, and with passionate oh's and ah's!

When we first drove them out to the pueblo and they saw it planted there at the foot of the mountain, solid, eternal, and as though its roots were fastened deep in the earth of which it was built, Lawrence was silent and seemingly unaware; but Frieda expressed herself all over the place:

"Oh! It is *wonderful*! How ancient and how perfect! Oh, to think it will probably be spoiled! Oh, Mabel, why don't you *buy* it and keep it like this forever!"

"Oh, Frieda! Don't be vulgar," Lawrence broke in on her delight. "Of course Mabel can't *buy* it. And if it has to go, it will go."

I felt, though, that he was getting it through her, experiencing it, seeing it, and that she was, in a sense, giving it to him. Quite soon afterwards, I think, Frieda and I were alone and again out in the pueblo together, for I remember the cottonwood branches over our heads when these words come back to me. I believe it was while Lawrence was away at the Apache fiesta. I said to her:

"Frieda, it seems to me that Lawrence lives through you. That you have to feel a thing before he can feel it. That you are, somehow, the source of his feeling about things."

"You don't know how right you are," she answered. "He has to get it all from me. Unless I am there, he feels nothing. Nothing. And he gets his books from me," she continued, boastfully. "Nobody knows that. Why, I have done pages of his books for him. In *Sons and Lovers* I actually wrote pages into it. Oh, it was terrible when he was writing that one! I thought it would kill him. That mother . . ."

It was no time at all before Frieda's grievance—her great grievance—appeared on the surface.

"Everyone thinks Lawrence is so wonderful. Well, I am something in myself, too. The Kot thinks I'm not good enough for him!"

"*Who?*" I broke in.

"Kotiliansky. My enemy. He thinks I should just be willing to scrub the floor for Lorenzo. And he would like to separate us. Well, I'd like to see *him* live with Lawrence a month—a week! He might be surprised."

It was right away in these first few days that Frieda and I had together that she told me so much. Afterwards there was nothing between us. This probably added to her old sore feeling of not being appreciated as much as Lawrence was. We started being friends. She was excellent company. She had the gift of immediate intimacy that I had myself, which, compared to ordinary intercourse, is like a live baby beside a talking doll. And there was a quick, spontaneous flow between us. But as soon as Lawrence returned to the scene, he stopped it. He was, in all possible ways, jealous, just as she was. He was annoyed that Frieda and I had become friends, and not only jealous of me, but jealous of her as well. The flow immediately ceased between Frieda and me and started between Lawrence and me. He somehow switched it.

It is terribly difficult for me to explain these things to you, Jeffers, these tides and currents that comprise the relationships between people—the fluid come and go that constitute so different a reality from the solid, staring, fixed appearance of faces.

Sometimes I see all of us human creatures, Jeffers, as so many gases, stimulating, beneficent, or poisonous, occasionally bursting into flame, or transformed from one degree to another by meeting a new element. Anyway, the least that we are appears, actually, in the flesh, and the truth lies behind bone and muscle.

I saw that Lawrence and Frieda tried to hold each other in a fixed, unaltered, invariable combination. Each of them immediately checked every permutation that the undomesticated, wandering instinct in the other sought to indulge. Anything that deflected the flow between them, deprived one or the other of his lawful, oh, so lawful! prey, though neither one nor the other was satisfied with what he or she had.

Frieda told me about the two times Lawrence had evaded her. One time was with the American girl in Cornwall when she was absent for a visit to her mother, I think. She had returned to the little house and found a feeling in the air that she had not left there. She forced Lawrence to tell her about it and then showed the girl the door. It had, or at least so he told her, been a miserable failure, anyway. The other one had been a young farmer, also in Cornwall.

"Was there really a *thing* between them?" I asked.

"I think so. I was dreadfully unhappy," she answered.

"It is a woman's place to hold a man *centered*," Lawrence said one day when he and Frieda were momentarily in harmony. "And it is a man's place to keep the woman centered," he added.

Well, when he came back after that few days with Tony and Bessie Wilkinson and found Frieda and I had flowed together in sympathy, he was in a rage. But it must be admitted once and for all that Frieda and I were friends and could have been good friends and had fun together if he had never returned.

That very evening he asked me if I would work on a book with him. He said he wanted to write an American novel that would express the life, the spirit, of America and he wanted to write it around me—my life from the time I left New York to come out to New Mexico; my life, from civilization to the bright, strange world of Taos; my renunciation of the sick old world of art and artists, for the pristine valley and the upland Indian lakes. I was thrilled at the thought of this. To work with him, to give him myself—Tony—Taos—every part of the untold and undefined experience that lay in me like a shining, indigestible jewel that I was unable either to assimilate or to spew out! I had been holding on to it for so long, solitary and aware, but helplessly inexpressive!

Of course it was for this I had called him from across the world—to give him the truth about America: the false, new, external America in the east, and the true, primordial, undiscovered America that was preserved, living, in the Indian bloodstream. I assented with an inward eagerness, but with the usual inexpressive outwardness. I saw him, though, reading my joy, and he gave me a small, happy, sympathetic nod.

I have among my papers a part of an article he wrote when he came back from the Apache Reservation. I don't know where the end of the manuscript is or if he ever published it. It does not seem to me to be very good. Was it because Frieda was not along with him on that occasion?

"Supposing one fell on to the moon, and found them talking English; it would be something the same as falling out of the open world plump down here in the middle of America. 'Here' means New Mexico, the South West, wild and woolly and artistic and Indian and sage-brush desert.

"It is all rather like comic opera played with solemn intensity. All the wildness and woollyness and westerity and motor-cars and art and sage and savage are so mixed up, so incongruous,

that it is a farce, and everybody knows it. But they refuse to play
it as farce. The wild and woolly section insists on being heavily
dramatic, bold and bad on purpose; the art insists on being real
American and artistic; motor-cars insist on being thrilled, moved
to the marrow; high-brows insist on being ecstatic, Mexicans insist on being Mexicans, squeezing the last black drop of macabre
joy out of life, and Indians wind themselves in white cotton
sheets like Hamlet's father's ghost, with a lurking smile.

"And here am I, a lone lorn Englishman, tumbled out of the
known world of the British Empire on to this stage: for it per-
sists in seeming like a stage to me, and not like the proper world.

"Whatever makes a proper world, I don't know. But surely
two elements are necessary: a common purpose and a common
sympathy. I can't see any common purpose. The Indians and
Mexicans don't even seem very keen on dollars. That full moon
of a silver dollar doesn't strike me as overwhelmingly hypnotic
out here. As for a common sympathy or understanding, that's beyond imagining. West is wild and woolly and bad on purpose, commerce is a little self-conscious about its own pioneering
importance—Pioneers, Oh Pioneers!—high-brow is bent on getting to the bottom of everything and saving the lost soul down
there in the depths, Mexican is bent on being Mexican and not
yet Gringo, and the Indian is all the things that all the others
aren't. And so everybody smirks at everybody else, and says,
tacitly: 'Go on. You do your little stunt, and I'll do mine'—and
they're like the various troupes in a circus, all performing at
once, with nobody for Master of Ceremonies.

"It seems to me, in this country, everything is taken so damn
seriously that nothing remains serious. Nothing is so farcical as
insistent drama. Everybody is lurkingly conscious of this. Each
section or troupe is quite willing to admit that all the other sections are buggoon stunts. But it itself is the real thing, solemnly
bad in its badness, good in its goodness, wild in its wildness,
woolly in its woollyness, arty in its artiness, deep in its depths, in

a word, earnest.

"In such a masquerade of earnestness, a bewildered straggler out of the far-flung British Empire is myself! Don't let me for a moment pretend to *know* anything. I know less than nothing. I simply gasp like a bumpkin in a circus-ring, with the horse-lady leaping over my head, the Apache war-whooping in my ear, the Mexican staggering under crosses and thorns and bumping me as he goes by, the artist whirling colours across my dazzled vision, the high-brows solemnly declaiming at me from all the cross-roads. If, dear reader, you, being the audience who has paid to come in, feel that you must take up an attitude to me, let it be one of amused pity.

"One has to take sides. First, one must be either pro-Mexican or pro-Indian: then, either art or intellect: then, republican or democrat: and so on. But as for me, poor lost lamb, if I bleat at all in the circus-ring, it will be my own shorn lonely bleat of a lamb who's lost his mother.

"But I arrive at a moment of crisis. I suppose every man always does, here. The crisis is a thing called the Bursum Bill, and it affects the Pueblo Indians. I wouldn't know a thing about it, if I needn't. But Bursum Bursum Bursum!! the Bill! the Bill! the Bill! Twitchell, Twitchell, Twitchell!! O Mr. Secretary Fall, Fall, Fall! Oh Mr. Secretary Fall! you bad man, you good man, you Fall, you Rise, you Fall!!! The Joy Survey, Oh Joy. No Joy, Once Joy, now Woe! Woe! Whoa! Whoa Bursum! Whoa Bill! Whoa-a-a!

"Like a Lindsay Boom-Boom bellowing it goes on in my unwonted ears, till I *have* to take heed. And then I solemnly sit down in a chair and read the Bill, the Bill, the Printed Bursum Bill, Section one-two-three-four-five-six-seven, whereas and wherefore and heretobefore, right to the damned and distant end. Then I start the Insomuch-as of Mr. Francis Wilson's Brief concerning the Bill. Then I read Mr. C's passionate article against, and Mrs. H's hatchet-stroke summary against, and Mr.

M's sharp-knife jugglery *for* the bill. After which I feel I'm getting mixed up, and Bear ye one another's Bursum. Then lamb-like, ram-like, I feel I'll do a bit of butting too, on a stage where every known animal butts.

"But first I toddle to a corner and, like a dog when music is going on in the room, put my paws exasperatedly over my ears and my nose to the ground, and groan softly. So doing, I try to hypnotise myself back into my old natural world, outside the circus-tent, where horses don't buck and prance so much, and where not every lady is leaping through the hoop and crashing through the paper confines of the universe at every hand's turn.

"Try to extricate my lamb-like soul into its fleecy isolation, and then adjust myself. Adjust myself to that much-talked-of actor in the Wild West Show, the Red Indian.

"Don't imagine, indulgent reader, that I'm talking *at* you or down to you, or trying to put something over you. No no, imagine me lamb-like and bewildered, muttering softly to myself, between soft groans, trying to make head-or-tail of myself in my present situation. And then you'll get the spirit of these effusions.

"The first Indians I really saw were the Apaches in the Apache Reservation of this state. We drove in a motor-car, across desert and mesa, down canyons and up divides and along arroyos and so forth, two days, till at afternoon our two Indian men ran the car aside from the trail and sat under a pine-tree to comb their long black hair and roll it into the two roll-plaits that hang in front of their shoulders, and put on all their silver and turquoise jewellery and their best blankets: because we were nearly there. On the trail were horsemen passing, and wagons with Ute Indians and Navajos.

" 'Da donde viene, Usted?' . . .

"We came at dusk from the high shallows and saw on a low crest the points of Indian tents, the tepees, and smoke, and silhouettes of tethered horses and blanketed figures moving. In the shadow a rider was following a flock of white goats that flowed like water. The car ran to the top of the crest, and there was a hollow basin with a lake in the distance, pale in the dying light. And this shallow upland basin dotted with Indian tents, and the fires flickering in front, and crouching blanketed figures, and horsemen crossing the dusk from tent to tent, horsemen in big steeple hats sitting glued on their ponies, and bells tinkling, and dogs yapping, and tilted wagons trailing in on the trail below, and a smell of wood-smoke and of cooking, and wagons coming in from far off, and tents pricking on the ridge of the round *vallum*, and horsemen dipping down and emerging again, and more red sparks of fires glittering, and crouching bundles of women's figures squatting at a fire before a little tent made of boughs, and little girls in full petticoats hovering, and wild, barefoot boys throwing bones at thin-tailed dogs, and tents away in the distance, in the growing dark, on the slopes, and the trail crossing the floor of the hollow, in the low dusk.

"There you had it all, as in the hollow of your hand. And to my heart, born in England and kindled with Fenimore Cooper, it wasn't the wild and woolly west, it was the nomad nations gathering still in the continent of hemlock trees and prairies. The Apaches came and talked to us, in their steeple black hats, and plaits wrapped with beaver fur, and their silver and beads and turquoise. Some talked strong American, and some talked only Spanish; and they had strange lines in their faces.

"The two kivas, the rings of cut aspen trees stuck in the ground like the walls of a big hut of living trees, were on the plain, at either end of the race-track. And as the sun went down, the drums began to beat, the drums with their strong-weak, strong-weak pulse that beat on the plasm of one's tissue. The car slid down to the south kiva. Two elderly men held the drum and danced the pat-pat, pat-pat quick beat on flat feet, like birds that move from the feet only, and sang with wide mouths, Hie! Hie! Hie! Hy-a! Hy-a! Hy-a! Hie! Hie! Hie! Ay-away-away—!!

Strange dark faces with wide, shouting mouths and rows of small, close-set teeth, and strange lines on the faces, part ecstasy, part mockery, part humorous, part devilish, and the strange, calling, summoning sound in a wild song-shout, to the thud-thud of the drum. Answer of the same from the other kiva, as of a challenge accepted. And from the gathering darkness around, men drifting slowly in, each carrying an aspen-twig, each joining to cluster close in two rows upon the drum, holding each his aspen twig inwards, their faces all together, mouths all open in the song-shout, and all of them all the time going on the two feet, pát-pat, pát-pat, pát-pat, to the thud-thud of the drum and the strange, plangent yell of the chant, edging inch by inch, pát-pat, pát-pat, pát-pat, sideways in a cluster along the track, towards the distant cluster of the challengers from the other kiva, who were sing-shouting and edging onwards, sideways in the dusk, their faces all together, their leaves all inwards, towards the drum, and their feet going pát-pat, pát-pat, on the dust, with their buttocks stuck out a little, faces all inwards shouting open-mouthed to the drum, and half laughing, half mocking, half devilment, half fun. *Hie! Hie! Hie!—Hie—away—awaya!* The strange yell, song, shout rising so lonely in the dusk, as if pine-trees could suddenly, shaggily sing. Almost a pre-animal sound, full of triumph in life, and devilment against other life, and mockery, and humorousness, and the pát-pat, pát-pat of the rhythm. Sometimes more youths coming up, and as they draw near, laughing, they give the war-whoop, like a turkey giving a startled squeal and then gobble-gobbling with laughter—*Ugh!*—the shriek half laughter, then the gobble-gobble-gobble like a great demoniac chuckle. The chuckle in the war whoop.

"Listening, an acute sadness, and a nostalgia, unbearable, yearning for something, and a sickness of the soul came over me. The gobble-gobble chuckle in the whoop surprised me in my very tissues. Then I got used to it, and could hear in it the humour, the playfulness, and then, beyond that, the mockery and the diabolical, pre-human, pine-tree fun of cutting dusky throats and letting the blood spurt out unconfined. Gobble-agobble-agobble, the unconfined, loose blood, gobble-agobble-agobble, the dead, mutilated lump, gobble-agobble, agobble, the fun, the greatest man-fun.

"So I felt. I may have been all wrong, and other folks may feel much. . . ."

The article breaks off here; and then I have two other paragraphs descriptive of the happenings of the following day:

"We waited three hours for the race to begin, and it was over in half an hour. Then the two groups of racers clustered on their drums again at opposite ends of the track, the drumming began, the ritual song, and slowly the two groups advanced to meet in the centre of the course. They should dance the bird tread all the way, but only the elder ones do so. The others just shuffle. Like the white boy, who stares with a kind of half-ashamed, half-defiant outcast look from side to side.

"The groups meet in the centre, and circle round each other, continuing the singing, while there is a great whooping of the elders. The crowd presses close, and gorgeous Apache women on big horses fling little round loaves of bread, and apples, and small peaches, at random into the cluster of dancers, who catch and pick up from the ground such things as they want. The daubed racers are dully singing, the two drums thud; only the white boy glowers silent. Then the two sides have passed one another, and proceed to their respective goals. There is one tall, lanky young Indian with a square of red cloth hanging at his rear. One of the elders lifts this hind flap and switches the small, loin-clothed posterior of the lanky one as he passes. . . ."

Lawrence hurried over to our house in the morning ready to begin our work together. As I never dressed early in the morning, but took a sun-bath on the long, flat, dirt roof outside my bedroom, I called to him to come up there. I didn't think to dress for him. I had on moccasins, even if my legs were bare; and I had a voluminous, soft, white cashmere thing like a burnous. He hurried through my bedroom, averting his eyes from the unmade bed as though it were a repulsive sight, though it was not so at all. My room was all white and blue, with whitewashed walls, sunny, bright, and fresh—and there was no dark or equivocal atmosphere in it, or in my blue blankets, or in the white chest of drawers or the little blue chairs. But Lawrence, just passing through it, turned it into a brothel. Yes, he did: that's how powerful he was. We went out into the sun on the long, flat roof. The house seemed to be sailing on a quiet green sea—the desert behind us bordered by the cedar-covered foot-hills, and the alfalfa fields in front, and Taos Mountain north-east of us, looking benevolent that day.

That mountain really seems to have a conscious life of its own. The Indians, passing upon it all through the centuries, have filled it with greater life, and the Pueblo canyon is full of magic —from the perpetual passage of Indians back and forth upon their mysterious errands. The mountain changes its moods: sometimes it is dark and unfriendly, and sometimes it radiates joy. But it is always alive, always alive.

We squatted down in the hot earth of the roof, and the sun shone on Lawrence's red beard, making it look like the burning bush. He dropped his chin on his chest in a gloomy silence and I waited for him to say something. The birds were singing all around, and the pigeons, cosy on the roofs of their upraised cottages, were roucouling as they paced amorously up and down before each other. Everything was calm and quiet and lovely until Lawrence began to talk.

"I don't know how Frieda's going to feel about this," and he threw an angry look over towards their cottage that lay there, harmlessly enough, like a cat in the sun, with no sign of her about.

"Well, surely she will understand . . ."

"Understand! She can't *understand* anything! It's the German mind. Now, I have always had a sympathy for the Latin mind— for the quick, subtle, Latin spirit that . . . but the north German psyche is inimical to it. The blond conquerors! The soldier soul, strong because it does *not* understand—indelicate and robust!" He ran rapidly on and on. I was immediately on his side. He made a perfect cleavage between the blond, obtuse, and conquering German and ourselves. We were Latin together, subtle, perceptive, and infinitely nimble. And from that moment to this I have been Latin, and Frieda has been Goth.

And also in that spoken sympathy Lawrence drew me to him and would hold me, I believed, forever, for he knew that he and I were the same kind of people. As we were. As we always were.

In that hour, then, we became more intimate, psychically, than I had ever been with anyone else before. It was a complete, stark approximation of spiritual union, a seeing of each other in a luminous vision of reality. And how Lawrence could see!

I won't try to tell you what we said, Jeffers, because I can't remember. I could invent sentences that would give you an idea of our conversation; I could almost tell you what words passed, but not quite. I will not put into this story, Jeffers, a single thing that I have not actually, whole and real, in my memory. What remains there must be the essential truth for *me,* no matter how slight it may turn out to be. Don't you think so? Don't you think that all that was not ours finally escapes us? I do. I always mistrust, in written or recounted memories, those long, interesting conversations that we sometimes enjoy very much. Because talk, real talk between people, is as unexpected and surprising to them as it is uttered as any movement in nature. It flows through one like the wind. The fire shapes, the forms of clouds, or waves, or sand, are sudden and immediate, and as quickly gone. Does the sea remember every pattern in the sand? One *cannot remember* one's own real talk. One cannot remember the quick, evanescent, exact movements of one's own independent soul. The most one can do is to recall the general feeling or mood of a long conversation in after years.

That is why, Jeffers, in telling you about this thing between us all, I feel I am perhaps quite unconvincing. It is all about the invisible, intangible, real world; and with so very little to make it appear concrete. Curiously enough, I suppose that if I were to fake it a little, I could make it come more true for you, but that, Jeffers, would be art—and I want this to be a real scrap of life itself, for that is the only respectful way to attempt to give you anything of Lawrence.

But it was in that first long talk together that he repudiated Frieda so strongly, with an intention, apparently, to mark forever in my eyes his desperate and hopeless bondage to one who was the antithesis of himself and his predilections: the enemy of life—his life—the hateful, destroying female.

"You cannot imagine what it is to feel the hand of that woman on you if you are sick," he confided in a fierce, lowered voice. "The heavy, German hand of the flesh. . . . No one can know . . ."

A great desire to save him, who could not save himself, was surging in me. I *would* save him!

As we got up to go into the house, his eyes shining blue and seeming to be assuaged, he paused an instant and said:

"The burden of consciousness is too great for a woman to carry. She has enough to bear with her ever-recurring menstruation." But I was glad at last for being what I was, for knowing, sensing, feeling all I did, since now it was to have its real, right use at last.

Lawrence went downstairs and I stayed to throw on my dress and my stockings. He was in the big room when I came a few minutes later, and I walked over to his house with him. Being with him keyed one up so that everything was humming and one felt light and happy. We were happy together. We reinforced each other and made each other feel invulnerable: more solid and more sure. When his querulousness left him, he was such fun! He was without fear and without reproach and needed no longer to carp and criticize.

As we strolled over to Tony's gate and entered his alfalfa field, we saw Frieda, in the distance, hanging clothes on the line.

"She is mad!" chuckled Lawrence, giggling. As we got nearer, she saw us coming and stopped what she was doing. The big, bonny woman, she stood there in her pink cotton dress and faced us with her bare arms akimbo. Lawrence was laughing almost delightedly into his beard and bending down his face to hide. At a distance of two or three hundred yards one could read the mounting rage gathering in her, the astonishment and the self-assurance.

"I guess I'll go back," I murmured, and as he did not press me to go on, I turned and retreated before that figure of wrath. It was not my way to fight in the open—although I certainly would fight!

That long, complete talk on the roof was practically the only time I saw him alone. I had supposed, of course, that he would have his own way about his work at least, but no. I did not see anything more of them that day until evening, but when we met again, they had had it out. There was a tired serenity about both of them when they came over, like pale sunshine on a battlefield. Lawrence looked diminished. He said to me, aside, when he had a chance:

"Frieda thinks we ought to work over in our house."

"With her *there*?" I asked.

How could I talk to Lawrence and tell him my feelings and experiences with *Frieda* in the room? To tell him was one thing —that was like talking to oneself—but one couldn't tell her *any-*

thing. She wouldn't understand and she would make one terribly uncomfortable and self-conscious.

"Well, not in the room—all the time. She has her work to do."

Then and there I saw it was over and I should never have the opportunity to get at him and give him what I thought he needed or have, myself, the chance to unload my accumulation of power.

You know, Jeffers, how there comes a time when formulation becomes imperative for assimilation, which, with people, is understanding. And without understanding experience we can perish from it. I had reached the saturation point in impressions. I had taken in so many impressions both in my past life in America and Europe and in my new life in New Mexico without ever translating them into words and defining them, that I was full. A deep reservoir in which I could perhaps drown.

I had told Lawrence in our talk the day before, how at different periods in my life, clear-cut and visible, I had awakened at the different great centers: first in Buffalo, the lower sex center; in Italy the emotional, nervous, æsthetic center at the solar plexus; in New York the exciting, frontal brain center where ideas stimulate and whirl one about; and then how in Taos, Tony had gradually awakened my dormant heart, Tony and the mountains of Taos.

"The unfolding of Kundalini," Lawrence had said.

In all that time I had been taking life in, but never formulating it and never giving it back to the universe. I knew it must be given back, otherwise my ability to live any more would cease. But how could I give it back? Tony developed my latent feeling and made me learn to love for the first time in my life, but he had no need to talk to me or have me talk to him. We communicated silently. He knew me through the pores of his skin and by his intuition. Our love needed no words. But something else in me needed words. My total ego needed to pass off into words, else the accumulation of energy-carrying impressions, which made me like a Leyden jar charged to the brim, would destroy either me or my environment.

But you know, Jeffers, one can't hand oneself out to just anyone. I had never met anyone that could understand all I had to give. Part, yes, but no one the whole. I had been in a psychic jam once or twice and had been eased out by Dr. Jelliffe and again by Dr. Brill. But, heavens! With these analysts one has to be so careful, one has to weigh everything lest one give them more than they can swallow and they turn and rend one for it! Unless one fits oneself into their systems and formulas so they can pigeon-hole one into a type or a case, they grow puzzled or angry or sad. I knew Walter Lippmann was right when he told me I was "a sport" and unclassifiable, but psychoanalysts do not seem to admit exceptional people. One has, then, to be continually assuaging them and measuring down to them out of sheer kind-heartedness. When I think of the time I have spent assuaging analysts at twenty dollars an hour!

No, I thought, Lawrence could have done it. He is the only one deep enough to hold it and transform it and in return be fed and assuaged himself—a fair exchange. And this woman will not let it be. "She is inimical to the spirit," Lawrence had said. Life must never pass beyond her vision of it. She was the enemy of change.

"You *need* something new and different," I cried to him in our corner by the window. "You have done her. She has mothered your books long enough. You need a new mother!"

"She won't let any other woman into my books," he answered, hopelessly.

So that was that.

I rebelled. I said that if I couldn't do it my way, in my house, then I wouldn't do it at all.

"Very well," he acquiesced, without opposition.

But I did try it once in her house. I went over there in the morning and he and I sat in a cold room with the doors open, and Frieda stamped round, sweeping noisily, and singing with a loud defiance. I don't think that anything vital passed between Lawrence and me, for all the dead times are blank in my memory and are not lighted up at all.

The next day he was sick in bed and I was off to Santa Fe with Tony for something or other. Lawrence asked me to try to write out some things for him to work on while I was gone. Here is a note he sent over to me as I was leaving:

So you are *mise en scène*. Now I want:

1. The meeting with Maurice
2. John, M. and You in Santa Fe
3. How you felt as you drove to Taos
4. What you *wanted* here before you came
5. First days at Taos
6. First sight of Pueblo
7. First words with Tony
8. Steps in developing intimacy with Tony
9. Expulsion of M.
10. Fight with Tony's wife
11. Moving into your house

While away, if away long, *post* me the notes.
Sempre Pazienza

D. H. L.

You've got to remember also things you don't want to remember.

Please write me a note about how it was when you met Maurice at Lamy, just how it felt. You see this is the jumping off ground.

You told me you wrote—sometimes during Maurice's "reign," a sort of story you thought was good. I wish you could find that for me. I might incorporate it, perhaps. I might also, later, incorporate some poems of yours that you sent me—about Tony and being alone in a strange house at night before he came. I've got that.—Then, anyhow, would be your own indubitable voice heard sometimes.

I don't want you to read my stuff till the end—it will spoil your view.

I have done your "train" episode and brought you to Lamy at 3 in the morning.

Always with patience! And I had none of that! I remember trying to write things out for him in my bedroom at Santa Fe, but it was an agony for me. I was not a *writer*. I was accustomed to the personal equation. I needed the living hand held out before my eyes to take me. I was alone when I was alone: alone and in a static, latent state. I could not *start* the flow of myself. To make the little dynamos inside begin to hum and discharge sparks, I had to have the living hand of the creator transmit to me its compelling authority. The hand of God, I suppose!

Frieda's opposition to me released, of course, all my desire for domination. An invisible struggle went on between us for possession of Lorenzo. This accentuated the division in him—for he was already split. Loyal to neither of us, who represented corporeally the separated sides of his nature, he kept us both on tenterhooks by vacillating between us. When he was in a temporary harmony with Frieda, he would, in brilliant vituperative talk, sling mud at the whole inner cosmos, and at Taos, the Indians, the mystic life of the mountain, and the invisible, potent powers of the embodied spirit or at everything, in fact, not apparent, scheduled, and concrete. Then, sometimes, he would go back on the limited scale of obvious, materialistic living and, forgetting Frieda's presence or defying it, would talk just wonderfully, with far-reaching implications, of the power of consciousness, the growth of the soul, its dominion and its triumphs. Talk to me outright, his eyes shining like blue stars.

"I hate all that talk about *soul*," Frieda would rap out viciously, as she sat over her embroidery.

But sometimes he hated us both. I remember one day we were all down in the orchard picking apples and sorting them. It was a still, autumn day, all yellow and crimson. Frieda and I, in a lapse of antagonism, sat on the ground together, with the red apples piled all around us. We were warmed and scented by the sun and the rich earth—and the apples were living tokens of plenitude and peace and rich living; the rich, natural flow of the earth, like the sappy blood in our veins, made us feel gay, indomitable, and fruitful like orchards. We were united for a moment, Frieda and I, in a mutual assurance of self-sufficiency, made certain, as women are sometimes, of our completeness by the sheer force of our bountiful health.

Lawrence dropped out of a tree and caught sight of the two of us; and we were suddenly made one in his eyes. He drooped over us in a funny, wry despair.

"O *implacable* Aphrodite!" he moaned, and hastened again up into the thick branches and out of sight.

I do not want to give you the impression that there was a continual strain between us all, Jeffers, though everything tended to strain. No matter how flowingly the day began, someone would tighten up.

We were soon leading each other into new ways. Lawrence gave great dissertations upon activity; upon *doing* things. This *doing* business has been one of the principal problems of my whole life. Nothing to do! From childhood until now I've been suffering a great deal of the time from a blank feeling that seems best-expressed in those words, and I have passed countless hours just sitting and staring straight ahead. Now, I don't believe I *ever* saw Lawrence just sit. He was forever doing something. Rather fussily, too. He did a good deal of the housework at home; he always did the baking, and at least half of the cooking and dish-washing. When Frieda and he went off together, he taught her how to do all of these things. He taught her how to wash clothes, how to scrub them clean and rinse them in cold water with bluing in it and to hang them in the sun to make them come white; and one of the few things Frieda really liked to do about the house was this washing. She always made quite an affair of it, and it usually put her in a good temper.

Lawrence really had very little sense of leisure. After the housework was done, he usually crept into a hedge or some quiet corner and wrote something, sitting on the ground with his knees drawn up. Midday brought another meal to prepare and to tidy up—and in the afternoons he made up tasks if he had none, odd jobs of carpentering or cleaning, unless he was out somewhere with us.

The only time he appeared to relax at all was at tea-time. He didn't seem to mind chatting then—and he liked his tea. But in the evenings—and we always spent them together in our house or theirs—he either delivered a monologue—a long, passionate harangue or narrative about something that he addressed to himself, his eyes not seeing us, but bent upon his inner picture, usually ending in an argument with Frieda—or else he got us all doing charades or playing some game. He loved charades —and he was so gay and witty when he was playing! He could imitate anything or anybody. His ability to identify himself intuitively with things outside himself was wonderful. We had some boisterous evenings, with Ida and Dasburg and Spud and others, that left us hot and happy and full of ease.

He hated just sitting round and letting things come of themselves. I preferred letting life take its course, and, in talk or in anything else, I was so lazy that I had never attempted to direct it. Only in my relations with people did I ever try and steer things. Lawrence was just the opposite. He was purposeful in impersonal things and left it to the impulse of life in human things. That was where Frieda triumphed. Because he either could not or would not use his will to make things go the way he wanted: she, with less scrupulousness about it, had always had complete control of him. It was, in effect, as though he had no will of his own. I wonder if he had or hadn't! Perhaps he only made a virtue of his passivity and in reality had no choice in the matter.

But everyone needs a bite and a sup occasionally of something more than daily bread. Though Frieda tried to stand with a flaming sword between him and all others, he, subtle, exchanged with me more and more sympathy, but secretly, I think, almost, though not quite, unconsciously. Of course one can never know another person completely, though we came as close to it as is humanly possible, I believe. I can only say for myself for certain that *I* knew when there was passing between us the mysterious effluvium that crosses space and reaches its goal, and that I sought, by nearness to him, to shorten its passage and increase its intensity. When we washed the dishes in the porch outside his kitchen, and our fingers touched in the soap-suds and he exclaimed, with a blue and gold look through the clamor of the magnetic bells: "There is something more important than love!" and I, defiant of definition at the moment, and sure of myself and him—sure that no barriers were able to shut him away from me—questioned: "What?" and he answered, grim: "Fidelity!"—I wondered just how conscious he was then—how passive or how much in control of everything.

Sometimes I think that perhaps, far beyond my own conception of the facts, he knew what was what.

Perhaps this is the time to tell you, Jeffers, what I think *I* wanted, and not to beat about the bush and cover it up in a maze of words. I wanted to seduce his spirit so that I could make him carry out certain things. I did not want him for myself in the usual way of men with women. I did not want, particularly, to touch him. There was no natural, physical pleasure in contact with him. He was, somehow, too dry, not sensuous enough, and really not attractive to me physically. But I actually awakened in myself, artificially, I suppose, a wish, a willful wish to feel him, and I persuaded my flesh and my nerves that I wanted him. Never approximating any actual touch or union, body to body, with him, that would destroy my illusion of desire, I was able to imagine any amount of passion in myself.

I did this because I knew instinctively that the strongest, surest way to the soul is through the flesh. It was his soul I needed for my purpose, his soul, his will, his creative imagination, and his lighted vision. The only way to obtain the ascendancy over these essential tools was by way of the blood.

That is one of the things we know, Jeffers; realists like you know it. The idealists, as they call themselves—masking under a nice word their short-sightedness—they never know it. Of course some people stop short at the gate of blood. They are satisfied with that. But others, all those who get things done— they go on from there.

I was always trying to get things done: I didn't often even try to do anything myself. I seemed to want to use all my power upon delegates to carry out the work. This way—perhaps a compensation for that desolate and barren feeling of having nothing to do!—I achieved a sense of fruitfulness and activity vicariously.

Whenever you hear anyone criticized, Jeffers, for wanting power and using it on others, don't blame them. It is only because they haven't learned yet to use it upon themselves. So desperate is our need, on this planet of achievement, to return to the universe all we have taken out of it that when we haven't learned just how to do it ourselves, we try to make others do it for us if we can.

I wanted Lawrence to understand things for me. To take *my* experience, *my* material, *my* Taos, and to formulate it all into a magnificent creation. That was what I wanted him for.

When this crept gradually into his consciousness I don't know. I certainly tried to hide it. I almost succeeded in fooling myself into thinking I was in love with him and into hiding my real intention from myself. Sometimes he would need to come nearer to me. He was so sensitive that he could get one's emanation and one's vibration by coming near one; and he would pass behind me and stand a moment in the radius of that swinging, swirling circle of force of which each one of us is the core.

I have to be careful not to go too far in trying to define these shades of action, Jeffers; for, crystallized into speech, they become too ponderous and indelicate. Also rather ridiculous, to tell the truth! Assume for yourself, then, those obscure and groping chanced encounters and imagine for yourself what structure they gradually built up between us.

A chemical congeniality is eternal. That is axiomatic, I suppose. Once two atoms meet who are drawn to each other, they will never cease to feel that attraction. They are not meant to cease feeling it. Being of one substance and vibration, their tendency is to join so as to lessen the tension of separation. Nothing in nature cares for tension for its own sake—that is one of the reasons why the maxim "Art for art's sake" is foolish, for only the angels overcome gravitation willingly and without effort! Anyway, I think he didn't realize that I was using my will on him until he was well implicated.

Very soon, in those first September days, I discovered that Frieda would not let things slide. I mean between them. Their relationship was never allowed to become slack. When, as between all married people, they were going along smoothly, not noticing each other much, when the thing between them tended to slip into unconsciousness and *rest*, Frieda would burst a bombshell at him. She *never* let him forget her. What in the first days must have been the passionate and involuntary attention of love in the splendor of fresh and complete experience had become, when I knew them, the attack and the defense between enemies. To keep the fire burning between them, Frieda would sting him in a tender place—she could attract his attention away from anything or anyone in the world by one of her gibes. She could always get his attention and start him flaming. Friction between them had become necessary, to take the place of the natural heat, and she undertook to keep life burning between them.

At the end of an evening when he had not particularly noticed her, she would begin insulting him. He would almost dance with rage before her where she sat solid and composed, but with a glare in her green eyes, as she puffed her cigarette into his face or—leaving it drooping in the corner of her mouth, a sight he always detested—mouthed some vulgar criticism up at him, one eye closed against the smoke, her head cocked: a perfectly disgusting picture, when she did so!

"Take that dirty cigarette out of your mouth! And stop sticking out that fat belly of yours!" he yelled once, shaking his finger in her face.

"You'd better stop that talk or I'll tell about *your* things," she taunted. All of us there were appalled. This was the end. They had certainly come to the end of hate this time. Frieda gathered her sewing into a bag and nodded good-night to us. He, his head sunk, avoided our eyes. He was ashamed.

"Well!" someone exclaimed.

"But *look*," I whispered in amazement. They had gone round the corner of the house and were passing the long, low window in the moonlight. They were close—close together—arm in arm —in a silent world of their own.

The next day he told me that the bond of hate can be stronger than the bond of love. . . .

Lawrence, being a very active person himself, did his best to start me moving. He wouldn't have a servant in his own house, because, he said, they poisoned the air; but I believe it was also because it would have interfered with the noisy fights he and

Frieda were always having. It would have cramped their free and easy rowdiness. He railed at me for having servants to do all the work for us and said I had no contact with life if I let them come between me and my food and my floors and everything.

"You don't *know* your floor until you have scrubbed it on your hands and knees!" he announced. That was all very well, I must say, for the cottage life. But I had positively *miles* of floors in my house! Nevertheless I scrubbed out my living-room. Once!

Oh, yes! But I must tell you first that before he got me to scrubbing, he completely altered my way of dressing. Now, I have always been, if not fat, well, square. Though longing to be like a willow, I have always resembled a pine tree. Not the lofty kind, more the Christmas-tree variety. I tried to mask my solidity in so-called flowing lines, and all my clothes hung from the shoulders. I had recently had some new dresses made, of cotton crêpe with wide, embroidered sleeves and round, embroidered necks. I thought they were beautiful. The colors were exquisite, and nobody had any like them.

The first time I put on the rose-colored one worked in turquoise-blue and pale yellow, I was obliged to go over and see Lawrence directly after breakfast. I felt so nice in this dress. I walked proudly up to him where he was splitting kindling wood beside the porch, hopeful of appreciation. He looked up and immediately made a wry face and cocked his head sideways impatiently.

"Sancta Maria!" he groaned, and threw his eyes to the sky. "These jibbahs! These Mother Hubbards! We grew a little weary of them in India! What is the idea in veiling the 'human form divine'?" he asked, satirically.

"Well, I guess if you had *my* form, you'd veil it," I answered angrily. Frieda appeared, to enjoy the row. She had on a full, striped, cotton skirt, with a peasant bodice lacing up her plentiful bosom. She was smiling and her mouth curved up like the crescent moon when it will hold water. I was discouraged. This man reversed all my ideas! He saw my discomfiture and went on in a gentle voice:

"No, no. A woman is a woman. A waist-line is a waist-line. I have always thought the kind of clothes my mother wore were the most lovely pattern any woman could have: a long, full skirt and her little waist buttoned snugly down the front over her breast! I always make Frieda wear that kind of dress, though sometimes she longs to be *chic*!" He threw her a pleasant, sympathetic humorous look.

"No, nice full skirts, with maybe a ribbon around the waist —and white stockings—that's the correct dress for a *woman*!"

My heart sank, but I determined to be equal to this need of his to be entirely surrounded by all sorts and sizes of persons dressed like his mother. That very day I got yards and yards of gingham, calico, and dimity and very soon I sailed about dressed like *that*. Anyway *he* liked it. He said so.

Aprons came next. All women must wear aprons when they work. I got me several of different prints, some polka-dots, some stripes. Checked pink-and-white and blue-and-white gingham pleased him and melted him.

Now, I will admit it's a lovely feeling to step out into the early morning sunshine in fresh, starched petticoats and to feel the cool calico tight around one, holding one in at the top; while below there's a swing and a rustle from the hips down. It *is* congenial to the spirit and it feels natural.

Well, sleeves rolled to the elbow, I fetched a pail of hot water and a brush and brown soap—and I pushed the furniture all to one end of the big room and I started to scrub. My Indian girls stood round looking half-distressed and half-amused. I frowned and paid no attention to them, because I wanted this to be real. I didn't want to experiment, I wanted to be really *washing* the floor. They turned it into an unnatural caprice, so

I soon got them to return to the kitchen.

I didn't seem to be able to get into a rhythm of scrubbing. The soap kept sliding off and trying to evade me, and almost at once my knees ached. I kept at it, though, with the water running down my face and onto my eyelashes, until I did half the room—and that had taken me ages! Here my memory fades out. I wonder if I or Albidia finished that floor.

The next recollection is of bread-making out in our large, sunny kitchen after lunch one day. Frowning and serious, I thumped the dough while the girls, I knew, exchanged looks behind my back. I shoved it into the oven and heaved a sigh. When I left the kitchen, I smelled to myself of damp calico, flour, perspiration, and violet powder. I liked it.

Lawrence ran in at tea-time, and together we drank tea in front of the fire, with the sun shining into the chimney place. I had changed my calico dress for a white muslin one, and I had a red ribbon tied around my waist. I thought I would be praised, but he never noticed it! Albidia brought in tea and bread and butter. *My* bread! Alas! The least said about it the better! Lawrence giggled at my expression.

"Better luck next time," he said, kindly, and threw his piece into the fire. He was generally kind when he had one at a disadvantage. Then, really, he quite approved of one. No matter, his kindness was sweet.

As I look back, I discover that Tony was away most of the time. I think I did not notice it then, my thoughts were so much with Lawrence. Of course Tony had that threshing-machine and he was always away all day long in the fall, so probably that is why I miss him from these scenes when I go back to them.

But he and I taught Lawrence and Frieda to ride horseback; that much he was with us all. At least, the horses taught them to ride! We merely went along. The first time Lawrence got up on one over there at his house, the horse ran right off down the field, with him bobbing up and down, light as a feather, and humped over the animal's neck the way monkeys ride, in the circus. Tony sat square on his stallion and laughed heartily. By the time Lorenzo had pulled his horse round and run back to us, he was still laughing. Really amused, not malicious. But Lawrence, holding on to his nervous beast, threw half a quick look at Tony and cried furiously:

"That's all right, Tony. Others can laugh, too." I know that at such moments Lawrence took refuge in the thought of the pen, which only then became, for him, mightier than the sword. Ordinarily he kept his writing level, in his mind, with other living acts, like cooking and chopping wood. For him it was just another activity of life. It was not writing, and separate from life. It was the speech or song, for him, of his own voice, and the writing of it never seemed as important to him as the living behind the pen. That is why he was *never* literary —never a writer.

"I'm not laughing," replied Tony, his shoulders still shaking. "It's very nice." He meant he was not being mean—he was just feeling happy. Lawrence caught the idea, but he didn't like to make Tony feel happy because the horse cantered off with him. There was never a moment of sympathy between them after that.

We were soon going on long rides together—Frieda and Lorenzo and I. He was absolutely fearless and he never fell off, no matter what the horse did. Though he was unaccustomed to riding, he took to it naturally and easily, though he always looked uncomfortable on horseback, bent over forward and riding as though the saddle hurt him. He rode with a very free rein. Fast. He couldn't endure to have me go ahead of him across the fields, and I adored to lead him chasing after me if I could get a good start ahead of him. I had a good fast horse named Contentos, who liked me very much, and in those days I was far more free myself on a horse than I am now. I would

get a little ahead of the other two and then start agalloping,
and Lawrence would immediately start after; and when I
turned and looked back, I saw him bent forward, his face set
and stern, pounding along as though his fate depended upon
catching me. I suppose he simply couldn't stand the idea of a
woman in the lead. I remember walking one day across our
alfalfa field with him and Leon Gaspard, over the narrow
board walk that divided the tall green stuff. They went so
slowly, talking as they went, that I *couldn't* linger behind them,
and so I brushed by them and got in front where I could go
at my own pace. I don't know how to walk slowly! I didn't
think they noticed, but in a flash Lorenzo dashed by me, throwing a furious look as he went, and, beckoning Leon after him,
he got me to the rear again. He never let little things pass.
Everything was significant and symbolic and became to him
fateful in one way or another. Perhaps that is why he made
life so thrilling for one. I was used to hearing that I made the
house alive and made living exciting around me, but now someone made it intense for *me*. Lawrence raised the pitch. Life became radiant wherever he appeared.

I don't remember whether John (my son, Jeffers, twenty
years old) was staying up at the ranch then or not. I had given
him this ranch up on Lobo Mountain that I had bought from
old Mr. McClure some time back. Lawrence has described it in
St. Mawr. John and other boys used to go up there and hunt;
and he was up and down all the time between there and Taos.
He and Alice were engaged then to be married soon, and Alice
was staying there with us for a few days along with her mother,
Alice Corbin. I had some silver things to give them, and one
night when we were all together, I got them out, and my jewel-
box, too, and unceremoniously began, saying:

"Well, here they are: spoons, knives, forks. And—"

"But wait—wait!" Lawrence hastened over to where John
and Alice and I sat together on the couch. "Let us count them!

Lovely silver spoons! Twelve of them—" and he piled them all together. "And then the forks."

He was making a party out of it. I never had the patience to make a nice thing like that myself, but when he played a game, I liked to play it with him.

"Beautiful, heavy silver knives! Twelve of them."

The children were handling the odds and ends in the Chinese box. I gave Alice a few things and then I was through with that game. John was handling the silver things, contemplatively.

"Well, take them away," I began.

"Wait! Let him have his moment," Lawrence said, gently, in a low voice. "This is *his* moment." How kind he was! How entirely understanding! He made me feel unfeeling and un-responsive, as, indeed, I was! I never did know how to feel like a mother to my own son!

I wished he would have a talk with John before he married. *I* did not know what I ought to say to him. I wanted Lorenzo to say it for me—whatever it was that needed to be said.

"Will you, Lorenzo?"

"I'll see. If it comes naturally."

So one night they were in John's log cabin together with the doors closed for an hour; and when they joined us in the big room, John looked quite elated. When Lawrence and Frieda went home, I asked John what he'd said.

"He said a lot. He said for me to be always alone. Always separate. Never to let Alice know my thoughts. To be gentle with her when she was gentle, but if she opposed my will, to beat her. And he said, above all, to be alone. Always."

"Well!" I said.

One day Frieda and I were talking in her sitting-room. She was showing me a piece of lovely pale-blue velveteen she had found in her trunk.

"Look! Won't it make a lovely little jacket?" And she held it around her big bosom.

"Frieda, I feel so fat in these clothes!"

"Lawrence likes fat. He says my stomach is like a big loaf of bread."

"But your legs are long. You have long, thin arms, too. It's different with me. . . ."

Lawrence came in from the back porch.

"Look, Lorenzo! Won't this make me an ador-r-r-able little jacket?" She held the velvet about her. She certainly did look huge in pale-blue velvet. Lawrence was standing behind her. He could not resist throwing me a roguish look of malice, which I could not acknowledge, facing her as I was.

Yet he was loyal, too. I was already writing him long letters. I had so much to say to him and we had no chance to talk. My letters were intimate—I could not have given them to anyone but him, and though I forget now what I wrote, I remember how they felt. They were just for that one, single, separate person, Lorenzo. I know there was a good deal about mothering his books, because our book had lapsed. The interference of Frieda had killed that. I never even saw the chapter he did; I presume she tore it up. Though in the beginning, when she had us coming to her place to work, she told me that the first pages he had done on it were like nothing he had done before.

"There is a kind of vitality and eternal youth in it," she cried.

But, as I was saying, I had started to write him my thoughts, since I could no longer speak them. And as we went out the picket gate into the field one morning, Lawrence said:

"I showed Frieda your letter. Just to make everything square and open."

"Good Lord!" I was shocked to the ground.

He giggled. After that it was hard not to include her in my messages to him.

Lawrence was double in everything. No sooner had he gone close to John in that intimate talk than he hated him for it.

The next night, when he was talking or, rather, monologuing about American women and their evil, destructive wills, John, not interested, I suppose, jumped up and went bounding out of the room.

"Young jack-rabbits, all of them," Lorenzo muttered, throwing a dark look after him. "We shall see what we shall see!" And from that time there was no more rapport between *them*, either.

At the end of September the Fiesta of San Geronimo was celebrated in the pueblo. In those years it was entirely an Indian festival and had not been taken up by the "Lions Club" in Taos village for purposes of commerce and exploitation.

San Geronimo was the Indians' patron saint, handed to them by the Catholic priests several hundred years ago. A wooden image of him dwelt in the church at the pueblo, along with a statue of the Virgin. The Indians regarded these two as their guests, and the church as their house. The Virgin had a chestful of different costumes in which they clothed her, changing them from time to time. Succeeding fashions followed each other down the years, but I think the Victorian one was the most becoming to her pale, meek features. It consisted of a white crinoline with lace flounces, a black jet shoulder cape, and a small, close bonnet.

In the evening before the race, the Indians always built bonfires of pitch-wood, piled all over the pueblo in hollow squares of split kindlings. In front of the church there was a long avenue of them leading out from the entrance, down through the pueblo and around and back. There was one in front of every house, and some were on the roofs. The priest always came out from town to give them a mass, and when it was over, he drove rapidly away in his buggy, drawn by two black horses. Then the Indians lighted all the fires, and some of the young men stood on each side of the church doors ready with their guns to fire a salute, while the head men of the pueblo lifted the Virgin from the altar and brought her out for her walk. One of them carried her aloft in his arms while four others marched along holding four poles with a white sheet knotted to them to spread over her head.

The fires blazed and the young men fired their guns. A small handful of Mexicans walked with the Indians, piously singing a Catholic tune, but their voices were almost drowned in a sea of shouts and war-whoops and exultant cries. The whole pueblo followed her in her slow progress—men, women, and children. Once a year they took her thus for a walk around the pueblo, down the avenues of fire, and home again; for the irrelevant, pale Virgin had become, by the transforming power of the psyche, the Goddess of the Harvest. It was no mere coincidence that made them celebrate San Geronimo's Day when the wheat was garnered.

The flames of blazing pitch-wood soared high and the wind raced round them. The whole pueblo was given over to a fiery joy and the wonders of the earth.

"What is so powerful as fire?" Tony asked me where we stood together at the church wall. Indians never cease to feel the mystery of it—they never grow used to it so that it becomes for them a matter of course.

Early the next morning they carried the Virgin and San Geronimo to the leafy shrine of yellow cottonwood branches they had erected at the head of the race-track; and at sunrise they started that race that Lawrence has described so well: the race that is not run to win, but to give back power to the earth from whom they have drawn their food. Emerging from the kiva, each one blows a bit of eagle-down to the rising sun to give him eagle power and receive it back again.

The Indians *know* it is all a give and take, Jeffers. They never forget, until they go to school.

Lawrence and I sat together on the top of one of the high

structures made of trees and boughs that stand in front of the pueblo houses, carry firewood and hay, and shelter their wagons. The race went on and on. Brown bodies and black hair and the sun shining on them. It is always beyond any telling. Lawrence was really in it—he was able to go into it and participate with them and understand. It dissolved his painful isolation—breaking the barriers around him so that for a while he shared a communal effort and lost himself in the group. Vicariously he too raced and spent himself, offering the sum of his energies to the Great Mother.

It was in him easily to comprehend and readily to sympathize with such an immolation. Had we in our evolution (if one may call it that, Jeffers!), had we only some provision for that need to love and spend ourselves, some Idea to which we might give all and from which we might receive all, there would be no more "mother-complexes," Jeffers. I suppose the genius of the race is working out some solution that will take care of us, but while we wait, we die.

When they came to an end of the relayed padding and thumping up and down the track, they broke the pattern and fell into two great groups, singing for a few moments a triumphant harvest song; and then they separated and ran, all variously, down to the river to bathe. Lawrence was out of his spell and released. His eyes shone, Jeffers, he was so happy and free. Oh, why can't *we* learn how to live like the Indians, I wonder. Is it really "backward" to be happy?

Of course he was often gay. I don't want you to think that in those first years he was cross or morose all the time. He was all right so long as things went his way. That is, if nothing happened to slight him. He simply couldn't bear to have anyone question his power, his rightness, or even his appearance. I think his uncertainty about himself, a vague feeling of inferiority, made him touchy. I suppose a *sense* of inferiority comes from some inferiority actually present in one, or one would not have it.

Did Lawrence realize, I wonder, that in spite of all his charm, his sensitiveness, and his sympathetic intuition he had a vulgar nose?

He was deeply uncertain about his clothes, like many delicately balanced people, and watchful for looks. He *did* look funny in some kinds of clothes, too. They had to be just right or he looked common. Well, he had a little white homespun coat with no collar that he wore a good deal, and he was most of all lovable in that. Up at the ranch he always wore tan corduroys and a blue shirt that made his beard flaming and his eyes more blue.

He didn't care for men much. Very few, anyway, and never for what we call manly men. He had quite a grudging feeling about cowboys and that kind, and he once wrote an article, or said in a novel, that those strong, silent characters were all inhibited neurotics!

So, really, he was best off when alone, with no one about to poke the hidden wound. He could have got along indefinitely with just the few of us up there on our hill. I was building a protection around him, keeping people away from him as I thought he wished. As I knew he wished, really. But he was perverse. He always suspected one's motives or one's acts. When he found I asked no one to the house, and that no one came, he began to resent it—the very situation I had arranged for *him*!

People that lived down in the Plaza—that "arty" set he had written me he feared were there and that he would have to be bothered with—I myself knew only slightly. I rarely saw them. Once a year I gave a party and had them all. I never wanted them running up casually to the house, though I wanted to be on friendly terms with them.

Lawrence began to be uncomfortable, then, at the absence of this "arty" and "literary" element. He did not know that when I encountered them in the Plaza, they inquired eagerly for him and hinted they would like to meet him. Now, naturally, I had taken him at his word—and so I kept them off him. But since I didn't bother to tell him of it, there was an unresolved question in his mind. Were they ignoring him? He had to know!

Somehow, then, he began to meet them and invite them to his house. There was in particular one of these, a painter, who had suggested to me one morning in the Plaza that he would like to know Lawrence, and though I did nothing about it, I found him over at Lorenzo's one night.

I sat and silently watched that evening unfold. The visitor was determined to please Lawrence. To that end he violated every decency. He began, cathartically, to give his father away to Lawrence. In a whining, self-pitying voice he described how his father, in the war, had been forced by the economic conditions of the country to prostitute his genius. He had been driven to get a living by making delicate loaded dice. I saw Lawrence's eyes shine with vivid interest. This was humanly *very* interesting, he thought. The man went on talking. He had quite a gift with words, but no sense. Soon he was telling how a friend of his was bitten by a rattlesnake; how he took him home to his house and saved him with whisky and nursed him. The dénouement of this story was quaint. The guest sat forward on his chair, to make Lawrence the gift of this intimate revelation.

"And when I *bathed* him," he said, dropping his voice to the confidential note, "I suppose it was the *poison*, but his balls and his sex were black!"

There wasn't a move in the room as these words fell into our midst. Everyone was frozen. I looked into my lap. I don't know where the others looked.

"The action of the *poison*, I suppose," the voice went on, less certainly. Still no response, till his wife, shaking a little, broached, timidly:

"But Arthur . . . Surely so much whisky must be poisonous for a man." He turned his disappointed and irritated attention roughly to her, in a snub.

They left soon after. Lawrence had seemed unable to cope with him after the snake story; not able, either, to show indignation or to show interest. He just sat and seemed to muse, until they were out of the room, and then he exploded with fury at the man's *daring* to tell such a story to *him*. He was insulted as well as horrified and shocked, Lawrence was. He felt he had been smirched. His delicacy was outraged.

Do you see, Jeffers? He had so deep a veneration for sex and everything connected with it. Imagine how it hurt him when people tried to please him and win him with strange or bizarre episodes about it, as though they thought he stood for mere outspokenness, without regard for taste or feeling. As if he put the value in the mere exhibition of sex. Nothing was further from him. Will the world ever know how delicate, how reserved he was; and how religiously he stood in his attitude to the creative powers?

"How dared he, how *dared* he talk like that to me?" he cried. "Never in my house again—never!"

"I pity the wife," put in Frieda, a cigarette hanging out of the corner of her mouth. She made a droll picture. That cigarette made her face look tough and formidable, while her hands held a bundle of knitting-needles and yarn!

"Oh, the woman isn't so bad—if she'd take that Norwegian *egg* out of her mouth!" And he began to imitate her, vociferously.

"Well, I don't see why you had them." I was unable to resist this small dig.

"One must *know* people," Lawrence cried. "One can't shut oneself off from the world."

"But why *him*? *I* have never known him, hardly!"

"No," said Frieda, spitefully; "he told us: 'We do not call on Mrs. Sterne.' "

"Oh, shut up, Frieda. That canaille—that *canaille*!"

And I, I was so mad at that that I cried. I guess we were all quite worked up from the evening.

So it is when one lives in the country: one is more vulnerable and sensitive to people. One feels them more. Each one is an experience. How differently city people are organized, toughened as they rub up against others more and more!

Well, Lawrence was acutely aware of people, of their thoughts and feelings and the inner boiling caldron from where everything is distilled; so each person was a real event to him. He was able to draw an infinite amount of experience from a chance encounter. He took a look at people and sized them up. One day when we were all out motoring, I overheard him say to Frieda, in the back seat, about somebody:

"I suppose she was attractive. You know a man *always* unconsciously judges a woman by deciding whether he'd like to be in bed with her or not. *I* always do. Even your mother, Frieda. You know how fresh and appetizing she looks lying in her great bed!"

He judged everybody swiftly, by his essential quality. After drinking tea with anyone, he *knew* them. And he rarely had extended, long relationships with people—nor needed to, perhaps.

So you can see, Jeffers, that our daily companionship grew to have more and more significance for him. He and Frieda had spent all their married life in little country places with few acquaintances and hardly any friends. They did not know how to live easily and casually with people. I came to know from each of them in turn how they had quarreled, now here, now there. His novels show that. Either he would get jealous and break up the situation or she would grow jealous or, worse, envious. She hated worst of all to feel slighted, left high and dry by Lawrence when he'd soar away from her in a flight she could not follow. One can hardly blame her. He was sorry for her himself at such times, feeling just as he felt the day when we were riding in the desert and, looking back after a fierce, long gallop, we saw Frieda hanging ludicrously, head down, from her saddle. His face was full of compunction as he rode back to extricate her. After that he never rode away from her again; no matter how I tried to make him forget and follow me, I rode away alone.

In every way possible, then, Frieda held him back with her. He told me that what she wanted—the way she liked best to live—was to be off alone somewhere, with him writing his books in the next room while she did her housework in peace.

"Frieda's at her best that way," he said. But sometimes she drove him outside himself with exasperation when she had him to herself.

One morning at nine o'clock I was writing letters in the big room and he came in the door like a current of wind. I was taken aback at seeing him so early, for he hardly ever left his own place before dinner; and when I looked at his face, I couldn't believe my eyes. He was shining, radiant, perfectly transfigured with rage. His eyes had a weird light in them: a high, clear, pale light, so that they looked like two stars. His features were stern. There was really something godlike about him, Jeffers, and he seemed to be immeasurably tall and strong and to tower over me. The real Lawrence stood there at last, burst out from the equivocal chrysalis that showed him, falsely, a dominated and diminished creature.

"I can't stand it over there," were the words that fell from this figure of an archangel. "Frieda has got a woman there sewing! She has your sewing-machine going and there are yards and yards of stuff all over." His irritation was discharging itself into power. The sharp radiance poured over me from his starry eyes. His eyes were flashing messages his reason never knew, I think. He challenged me and claimed me, and, fear forgotten, it was as though all of him was saying to me: "Nothing else matters save this excitement, this flow, this ecstasy."

So we sat together and I became conscious, as often before, that his presence was alterative, that it set up, perhaps involuntarily, changes in whoever came in contact with it. I said:

"I am changing. You are changing me, Lorenzo."

"Perhaps. It is too soon to know. Only a real emotion can change anyone—and I don't know whether your will has given way yet."

"How *can* I give up my *will*?" I asked, uncomprehendingly.

"Unless you do, you will be destroyed," he answered.

"Never. I have a protection," I told him, lifting my head.

"Oh, you have gone far, but I have gone farther," he said then, as he had said in the first days in Taos, "and I know a destruction that passes over your protection. . . ."

Of course I suppose we were a great deal together, though hardly ever alone, for even if Frieda was not there, I think he had promised not to be alone with me. But the communication between us grew deeper all the time and we quickened each other increasingly so that merely being near, even with others there, gave Lawrence more insight and gave me more vitality.

We were living at high pitch, with occasional crashes back to earth when Frieda would recapture him by an irresistible jab and engage him in a fight. At such times he would be severed from me completely—the spell broken—the thread snapped between us—the sympathy no longer flowing back and forth. It was all to make over again! I never got used to his cold, unfriendly face, his repudiating, indifferent look. Never. Any more than I ever got used to the visible signs on Frieda of what took place between them. For when we went to the Hot Springs, I saw the big voluptuous woman standing naked in the dim stone room where we dressed and undressed, and there were often great black and blue bruises on her blond flesh. And sometimes I found her with eyes red and swollen from weeping.

One morning in particular, I remember, I found her in her kitchen, spent and old from too many tears. I asked her what was the matter and she, still undone with misery and discouragement, broke out again into sobs.

"I cannot stand it," she wept. "He tears me to pieces. Last night he was so loving and so tender with me, and this morning he hates me. He hit me—and said he would not be any woman's servant. Sometimes I believe he is mad. . . ."

I knew well that when he revolted away from her, he caromed over to me. That was always the way it went. He vacillated between us and hated each in turn. Every time we went off into the far-away places of consciousness and of the imagination, he did a tail-spin; and whenever, reunited to Frieda, he capitulated to her and sank into the flesh, he beat her up for it afterwards.

And so as the weeks went on, this life of ours grew more extreme and its ups and downs more intense. Seeing him fade away from her too often those days, into what probably seemed to her to be thin, unpalatable, and hostile air, she found her hatred of him grow uncontrollable, so that she could not contain it and had to vent it—even to me, for whom in her heart she felt no real congeniality any more, for I was bad, she thought, for Lawrence. Perhaps she thought of me as bad in myself, apart from any effect I had on him, for she had said to Alice Henderson soon after she first came to Taos:

"What a *person* Mabel is! You can't say she's *good*, of course. She's just *there*!"

"Well, if she doesn't think I'm good, it's likely she thinks I'm bad," I had replied with some assumed defiance. I didn't want anyone to think I was bad. I wasn't bad.

Whenever Frieda and I were left alone now, she began to defame him to me.

"He's done, Mabel. He's finished. He's like glass. Brittle. You don't know what it's like—living with him. Sometimes I think I'll leave him. I could make a real life for myself!"

How terrible this was. He of the warm living flow, whose tenderness was so instant and responsive, he had constantly to watch out that it did not betray him!

I wonder why I swung away from him to her in that moment. I think it was my fatal ability to see any point of view
that presented itself. Anyway I was suddenly on her side, seeing
him as a rare and specialized creation of nature, something separate and strange and alone except for her. Untempting. I did
not want him. Neither did anyone else. Frieda must keep him.
He was hers—good luck to her!

"Frieda, you must never leave him. You're the only woman
he can live with. Besides, you know, he's not physically attractive
to women. I don't think women want to touch him. . . ."

"Of course they don't," she assented, angrily. "He's dry. Well,
sometimes I think I'll just get out before it's too late. . . ."

Lawrence came in at the garden door—and my heart ached,
for I saw he could feel in the air our antipathy and our abandon;
and from that time on they worked together to get away from
Taos.

Did she repeat that very night what I had said to her about
him? I never knew. But from that day on they were gone, in
reality, even though they lingered on for a while in the flesh.
They broached departure the next day. They could get a little
cottage from the Hawks up on Del Monte Ranch.

"But why? Why?" I questioned in despair. I could not bear
to have him go now, when he had lightened life and made it
so thrilling.

"Oh! We are better off alone," said Frieda, ambiguously.

"There is destruction here," Lorenzo shot in. "There is a queer
menace in the air. Oh, there's a witch's brew on this hill! And
the Indians struggle against it—and I will fight it, too. Yes. I
value my own little bit of life, and I will fight for it."

I felt perfectly helpless against such an attack. We were
friends no more. There was nothing but antagonism between
us, scarcely veiled, and Frieda was triumphant and glad.

One day I made a last appeal to them. We were driving all
over the valley for a farewell look at the yellow cottonwood

trees. The sky was almost black-blue, and the yellow plumes were motionless against it. In Cordovas the white village was peaceful. Great round white clouds boiled up behind it, and the desert was a carpet of yellow between there and Taos. In Seco the alfalfa was piled on top of the corrals, and the earth was pale yellow. The trees were like beaten gold in the sunshine, and the mountains behind Seco were plum-color. Everything was quiet. It was impossible to be unhappy.

"Lawrence, I believe we shall remember this day and wish we could come back to it. We do not know when we are well off."

"It is a miraculous day," assented Frieda.

"Why don't you stay, Frieda?" I begged. "Don't go up to Del Monte. You keep moving and moving and it's always the same. You won't change anything by moving."

"Perhaps that is true, Frieda," Lawrence muttered. "We are always moving on—but we take ourselves along! Shall we try awhile longer?"

"No. I am packed. I have decided to go and we will go. But we'll come down all the time—really we will," she flashed, reassuringly.

But I wanted none of that. I did not care for what I knew would be broken, breathless visits full of errands and practical needs. No. I wanted the flow and the rhythm of daily living. Unless I could have what I wanted, I wouldn't have anything. *My* will be done!

We parted then without good feeling or friendliness. The sympathy was gone. Almost the last thing I remember Lawrence saying to me was:

"You in your fur cap! You are like a great cat—with your green eyes. Well, I snap my fingers at you—like that!"

They were gone. It was the end of the first part, Jeffers. Do you make anything out of it all, the contradictions and the moods, the lively joy and the subsequent swift darkness?

Can you discern how, though he was always mistaken, yet he was always right?

Sometimes I think I have attempted an impossible task in trying to have you know Lawrence, Jeffers!

The Ballad of a Bad Girl

The Ballad of a Bad Girl*

When I was a baby, Mother pushed me from my cradle,
But I didn't fall! Oh no, sir! Though it's odd, odd, odd.
I snatched up in the hall Father's silver-headed walking-stick,
And, a-straddle it, I hastened after God, God, God.

I flew, flew, flew on the silver-headed cane,
Little girls and women were gaping down below,
Higher, higher, higher, past the Higherarchy.
(Mother didn't know of it till Father told her so.
But she didn't care!)

I passed the seven cycles of the old, old men,
All the ancient mariners were gathered safe in rows,
Safely making magic to keep the world a-going,
And from them I found out things no other woman knows.

I passed the ducky angels all busy with their songs,
No way to tell the boys from the girls, girls, girls,
Together they were making the music of the spheres,
And they all wore dresses and they all wore curls.

In these airy regions it was fun, fun, fun!
Honey-cake and ether was a sweet, sweet fare,
And every day I higher went among the secret-masters.
(I'd left my doll below, but I didn't care.)

I was lost among the stars and I was glad I was lost,
For I was learning things I'd have never learned at school;
Higher mathematics is to put it very mildly!
(The last thing I'd learned on earth was called the Golden Rule.
But I forgot that up there.)

* Published in *Laughing Horse*, May 1924; illustrated with a drawing by Lawrence.

For æons and æons I spiraled through the heavens.
Father died raving, and Mother? Mother married again.
And sometimes, very queerly, in the middle of a secret,
'Way down below upon the earth I felt a little pain.

But that was not important. I kept going, going, going,
Pushing past all barriers and beyond locked gates,
I dodged three gray-haired ladies who all looked very knowing.
Somebody whispered: "Those are the Fates."

And then one day! . . . (Heavens, what a day for me!)
I pushed past a curtain to where God lay fast asleep.
I knew I'd finally found Him and forever, ever, ever.
And I knew He had the secret that it wasn't His to keep!

Very, very warily I stole to His shining side,
Ready to plunge my eager hand within His burning breast,
When out of His heart there up and jumped a very, very angry man,
With blue, blue eyes and a red, red crest.

"Quit that! Get out of here! Down, down, down you go!
Back, back to earth to where you belong.
This is no place for *women* here! Don't you know your business?
You took the wrong turning, and you're wrong, wrong, wrong!"

He pointed a freckled finger down, and I looked down there.
Down, down, down again? How *could* I go?
But all of a sudden I forgot my lovely secrets,
For it ached me, it ached me, the little pain I'd left below.

But that man! He didn't care a bit! He raised a foot and threatened,
"*You clear out of here!* Get t' hell, hell, hell!"
I looked amazed and waited, but he meant it, oh, he meant it!
While I looked he gave a kick and I fell, fell, fell!

Well, I fell, and I fell, and I fell, fell, fell,
Never any end to it at all, at all, at all.
On the way I learned a secret, the best one of any,
That a *woman* can be saved by a fall, fall, fall!

Photo John Evans.

MABEL DODGE LUHAN

Something made me sorry for what had taken place.
I took my father's silver cane and put it in the hall.
Then I lay down in the pansy-bed and whispered: "Mother! Mother
   me,
And teach me how to mother and that's all, all, all!"

Part Three

Part Three

I went away, down to Santa Fe, the day before they were to leave, to show them that I didn't care—but in reality because I couldn't bear to see them go.

Oh, we had such fun together! Lawrence made every least thing in life into something amusing and worth while. The dreadful sense of futility left one. I was never depressed when he was there. I might be angry or hurt or baffled by his incalculable, changing ways, but I never sank into the humdrum boredom I had known so often before, and I never *questioned* life or lost my trust in it. He connected me with the life of everyday things and put value into them for me. I had a tendency to lapse away, growing cold and indifferent to everything. But Lawrence restored one's faith and conviction. With him there, anything might be true, but with him gone, anything might be true, too! Horribly.

Of course I did not feel any really fatal loss, because the rock bottom of my life was Tony, and I threw myself on the thought of him. But in the daily hours Tony was away from the house a great deal, and though other people came and went, no one took the place of Lorenzo. I missed our everyday rides and walks. Hardly a morning had passed that a note had not come over from him about doing something together:

DEAR M

Frieda says she doesn't want to walk this afternoon. Would you like to ride a bit with me—? Would you feel safe.

Did an Eagle poem, and I'll type it on your Corona if I may.

D. H. L.

The "Eagle poem" he speaks of here came from a drive we
had one day far out in the desert that leads down to the Manby
Springs. As we silently turned a curve, we came upon an eagle
sitting on a low tree close to the road. Hoary, immeasurably old
and wise-looking, and so silent and alone. Lawrence was im-
mensely moved by the aspect of that bird, who never budged as
Tony drove very slowly by him. He knew we had no gun
with us and he had no fear. All the wild animals are gun-wise
nowadays—they all know by some instinct whether a person
has fire-arms along or not, and they act quite differently when
gunpowder is absent.

I remember going to Lorenzo's house that afternoon to see
the poem. He brought it and laid it on the table. Frieda was
silent, looking cross and contemptuous. When I read it, I recognized the depths and depths that it plunged into, and that he
had written it for me. I knew that, and he meant me to know it.
I read it and laid it down again on the table without any
comment. But I couldn't forget it. Three months later I wrote
to him at the ranch to ask him for a copy of it and he replied:

> *Del Monte Ranch, Valdez*
> *15 Jan., 1923*

DEAR MABEL

I looked for that first eagle poem, but am sorry I could not
find it. No doubt I burned it—which is just like me.

> Yrs,
> D. H. LAWRENCE.

I wonder if Frieda destroyed it and whether he knew or not,
if she did. Anyway, it was wonderful, but it is gone and even
I cannot remember it, only the feeling that it gave.

There are other notes here with the letters that recall all
those first days so plainly, and even the conflicts in them come
back to one without the bitterness. Here's a note to him:

DEAR LAWRENCES

Don't you think it's too windy and dusty to ride the horses?
Tony will take us out with the buggy about 3 o'clock if you like.

MABEL.

And his answer on the back of it:

Yes, we won't ride—neither do I want to go in the buggy
today—am gathering the last apples and will finish them later.

D. H. L.

Also another similar one:

Best walk.—Or else ride. Frieda won't ride, though I prefer
it. Perhaps best walk.

We'll mail a copy to Thayer this evening. I'll get it done
now. But it will take me about an hour.

D. H. L.

Frieda had had to mask her interest and affection for her
children from Lawrence. He couldn't stand having her even
speak of them. He had taken her away from them and she had
had to go through that separation by herself—with no help
from him.

When her Nottingham husband—that professor of English
—told her he had a very promising student, she had told him
to ask the young man to tea with her. Lawrence came into the
room, and when their eyes fell on each other, it was all over. In
twenty minutes she had taken him. She told me this herself.

Now, for Lawrence this was the inevitable—the fatal—attach-
ment. He was far less experienced than she was, for she had
the habit of having a little love-affair every summer when she
returned to Germany to see her mother. Casual, simple, spontaneous relationships contracted easily here, there, and everywhere. Easy come and easy go, Frieda was as flowing in her sex
life as any antique pagan.

Nottingham had no temptations to allure her, so she was circumspect at home. Her professor used to call her his "pure white lily"! Lawrence never stopped twitting her about that when he was angry with her, and quoting about the lilies festering. . . .

She had imagined that this red-bearded young man was just another gigolo—someone to add a spice to Nottingham. But no! For Lawrence the sword had fallen. This was forever. He said they would not live in a hole and corner way, they would tell her husband what had happened and then they would leave together. Leave him and his three children. What an upheaval! Lawrence took her—and all communication ceased between Nottingham and their own new world. Not only her husband forbade her to ever see or try to write to the children, but Lawrence forbade it, too. She was cut off on two sides.

She often told me, when we sat together in momentary sympathy, all she had gone through—of loneliness that was like a terrible hunger for the children. She missed their little clothes, she said. She had spent so many hours making little dresses and underclothes for the girls! Now her hands were empty.

You know, Jeffers, how Lawrence tells their story in the poems called *Look, We Have Come Through*, which is one of the realest and most anguished books ever written. But it is all Lawrence's anguish. He says very little—very little—about Frieda's side of it.

It took her and Lawrence years to fill the hungriness in her. By the time it was filled, he came round to agreeing to let her see the children again, for they were old enough to ask it. The girls asked it, but the oldest one, the boy, couldn't forgive her. He went completely English and blotted out of himself his German blood. When she tried to see him, during the war, he answered, saying that his mother was the enemy:

"Every time one of those bombing planes circles over London, I know it is my mother. . . ."

Poor Frieda suffered over her children more than Lawrence

ever knew. He would not know it. He must be everything to her: the child, the son, as well as the lover. He couldn't admit any rivals.

So Frieda was always worrying about them. She had heard nothing from them all the time they were in the East. One day—one dark and rather sinister morning—when the weather made one feel nervous and apprehensive, Frieda sent me this note:

DEAR MABEL

I want you please to send a cable about the children. I feel worried about Elsa. She is frail and overgrown and was *not* well when I last heard. Two of her father's brothers died of consumption. If she isn't well, we must find somebody who would bring her to America. We could find somebody surely. And then from New York either Mountsier or Seltzer or somebody could bring her. I feel so happy, otherwise, but this worries me.

F.

It had to be done clandestinely. And I had them send the answer to me. Fortunately it was reassuring.

When Tony and I came back from Santa Fe, the little house was closed and still, and these notes from Lorenzo and Frieda lay on the table in the big room:

Friday

DEAR MABEL

Just leaving. No word yet about horses: will send a note by Sabino.

I think you will find everything in the house, except a dish and a plate, smashed, and two blankets, the red stripe and the blue stripe, which we borrow to wrap up in. I'll see these come back safely. Then I feel a bit guilty about the big water-tin, accepting the loan of it.

Hope everything was nice in Santa Fe.

So very many thanks for lending us this new house.

Let us hear what is happening. We shall see you soon.

D. H. L.

30 November, 1922

DEAR TONY

Thank you so much for letting us live in your house. I hope you won't find it much the worse for wear.

Let me give you a few dollars for its christening.

Come over soon with Mabel to see us at Lobo.

Yrs,

D. H. LAWRENCE.

How cold they were! And how self-sufficient, apparently, Lorenzo felt—going off without me. Yet he had seemed to need me and want something from me all through those three months.

Del Monte Ranch
Saturday

DEAR MABEL

Got here after a struggle yesterday. Spent a hard morning getting wood.

We shan't want the horses—better not have them, anyhow, as Hawk lets his stay out all winter. But Tony's were in stable last night—and well fed and watered.

Frieda says among the washing is one of her pillow-slips. We'll have it some time, as we've only four.

Jerry Mirabal brought good wood—hope nobody steals it. And his wife is tanning five skunk skins for Frieda—hope she'll do them nicely.

Jolly up here. Come and see us.

D. H. L.

Say if you want me to send back your two blankets at once. I can give them to John.

D. H. L.

Del Monte Ranch
Valdez. Wednesday

DEAR MABEL

Did you get the little clock from Mama? I got one! Also Mrs. Ennis wrote from Ceylon that she sent tray and all those hobs! We will come and see you soon with Mountsier. I miss the nice Tony house in many ways, I shall always be grateful that you brought us here. I love this place. Europe *is* in a mess— O Lord! When are you going to New York?

Yours,

FRIEDA.

Thank you for sending on letters.
Seltzer went to Los Angeles. They may film "Women in Love" —queer, wouldn't it be; but it would mean dollars!

Very well. I would do without them. I shut him out of my heart and plunged deep into some work for the Indians that I had been neglecting. After persuading John Collier to come to Taos and spend a year there with his whole family, just on the chance that he would become interested in the problem of protecting the pueblo and perhaps saving the Taos Indians from going the way all the other tribes have gone; when the thing finally got hold of him and he became involved—as he did, per- haps forever—in the interminable struggle between the races, there was I with all my attention and interest turned away from the Indians on to Lawrence! I came back to it now.

That story is another one, Jeffers. I will not go into it here. I will just tell you that I put all my force into another kind of fight, another effort than the one I felt I had lost, and I effected a kind of division between myself and Lawrence by turning my sympathy away from him, back to the Indians, by an effort of my will.

He and Frieda were not alone. I knew that he couldn't face that. They had annexed two stray Danish artists who wandered into Taos—simple, unremarkable characters, whom they persuaded to go up to the mountains with them. I was quite mad at this, too. It seemed to me that Lorenzo perhaps sought to fill my place too easily. I would not go up and see them. In fact, I didn't want to see them up there. What I wanted, as I told you, Jeffers, was the daily, rhythmical interchange of power and life with him. I would *never* be satisfied "to go and see them," to drink tea with them, or to drop to the ordinary intercourse of other people. So I stayed away, but when Christmas drew near, he wrote:

> *Del Monte Ranch*
> *Valdez, New Mex.*
> *Sunday*

DEAR MABEL

Thank you for the honey, which came from you or via you, I don't know. Also Frieda's shoes from Santa Fe: fit.

I don't know now if you are home or not.

We are settled in—very nice—Danes in their cabin. Today we rode all four to the hot springs—Manby's—did me good to soak. I rode Elizabeth's horse—nice horse to ride.

Seltzer says he and his wife leave New York on the 22nd Dec. and come straight to Taos. His wife has a fortnight's leave: from what, I don't know. I said I would meet them in Taos: and see the Christmas dance at the pueblo. I want you to let me know at once if you wish us to come to you for a day or two, or not. Of course you may be full up—or you may be going away. Then I would just stay a night with the Seltzers in Taos and come on here. Tell me, so I can arrange.

Why don't you come over here and see us? Or if you don't want to come here—don't you?—then we'll meet you at John's Ranch and picnic there.

Life has been just a business of chopping wood, fixing doors, putting up shelves, eating and sleeping, since we are here. There is still much more to do, but it can wait.

No news from the outer world.

Let me have bill for the honey and shoes.

If we come to you for Christmas, I'll bring mince pies. I made some mincemeat. And I want to make Christmas puddings. But now I have to bake! Great success, Graham's bread.

Pup growing huger.

Saluti Buoni

D. H. L.

Now, this made me downright angry. I felt he had gone back on something rare and vital and necessary to us both, and here he was offering to come back—but how differently! Bringing Danes and Seltzers and God knows what not! He was just making use of me. Well, I wouldn't have it that way. *My* will be done.

I answered with apparent regret. I told him I was having a family party only for Christmas—John and Alice and the Hendersons—and that he would surely understand. Also that I had arranged to have Mrs. Harwood take them all in; that she would love to. I made it apparent, I guess, that what I thought they wanted was a house to stay in! I enclosed her invitation. So, with my letter, I cut him off—I threw him away—I left him: to himself and his Frieda and his guests.

It stopped—completely—his newly found enthusiasm for the life up at the ranch, as I had intended it should. He had never imagined *I* would go back on *him,* or refuse him *any*thing.

Del Monte Ranch, Valdez
Tuesday

DEAR MABEL

Your letter just come. I have decided not to come to Taos at all for Christmas. Mountsier remains indefinite, and the Seltzers are no more definite than they were. So I'll have them brought straight out here when they do come: and I must be here to receive them.

No, I don't feel convivial.

Hope you'll have a good time with your festivities.

Yrs,

D. H. LAWRENCE.

DEAR MRS. STERNE

I am enclosing Lawrence's letter and as you see none of our invitations have been accepted. Perhaps it is better this way. I wish you would bring all of your party down for tea on Sunday afternoon. I think a cup of tea would be good before we start out to the Pueblo for the sunset fires. Come early as we should be going out a little before five.

I haven't seen the "newly weds," but we just drove past the cottage and John's car stands in front of the door. With best wishes,

Yours affectionately,

ELIZABETH HARWOOD.

Del Monte Ranch
Valdez, New Mexico
Tuesday

MY DEAR MRS. HARWOOD

Your letter has only just arrived. It was a shame to trouble you about all those other people. I have decided not to come to Taos at Christmas, these arrivals being so indefinite. When Mountsier and the Seltzers do come, I will have them brought straight out here. Your invitation was so very kind, it seems a shame not to accept it. But it will be much simpler as it is. I must look after the Seltzers as soon as they come. Will you please accept my thanks and my regrets?

The Danes too thank you very much, but will feel too shy to come to your house alone.

With all good wishes,

D. H. LAWRENCE.

I had my family party for Christmas. Everyone thought I had finally come back to them after an absence. They had been somewhat distressed at my absorption in Lawrence and had looked on in a kind of terrified amazement when they found me wearing aprons and trying to be a housewife. Far from pleasing them, it seemed to scare them. The Hendersons laughed, but they were watchful. There was possibly a menace in it for little Alice, who was married to John. I do not suppose they figured out what kind of a menace there might be, but they just felt uneasy. I was always incalculable, they thought. I might do anything!

Well, then I was back again. They felt better, but I felt worse. They did not know how the river of life had frozen in my breast and that I had to *make* everything go, that nothing went of its own accord.

I had sent Lawrence a verse one morning in October:

> My soul is a pool of silent sleep,
> Deathly dark and deep
> Until you come, then straight away
> The gold and silver fishes leap!

Well, my soul had gone to sleep again.

Christmas Eve we went out to the pueblo to see the children's dance and I saw the Lawrences walking about in the light of the fires among the other visitors. I saw, from our car, Frieda's foolish grin flashing in the flickering light as she talked to a Dane. I sat tight. Presently Lorenzo saw me and ran up and nervously shook hands. His impulse seemed to me to be merely a conventional one, just a polite gesture. But his face seemed altered. It was very thin and his smile was a grimace. There was an avoidance and an oblique avertedness in his glance. When our eyes met, it was like the flash of an electric light bulb, which, weakened or perhaps broken, goes out almost the same instant that it is turned on.

Willy Henderson stood at the door of the car looking on. He

had not been staying with us while Alice and her mother were there. He had only come for Christmas, so this was the first time he saw Lawrence.

"That's a *mal hombre*," he told me, as Lorenzo scurried away.

"Yes," I agreed.

There was a lapse between us for several weeks. Then I thought I had punished him enough, had hurt him, as I hoped, but that now I might see him again and patch up the breach between us. My life missed him so very much. So I wrote and asked him if they could motor to a dance with us—and whether we might not make a trip, all together, down to Old Mexico. But he was very sore:

Del Monte Ranch, Valdez
Saturday

Dear Mabel

No, I don't think I want to go to San Ildefonso. Neither, yet, to Old Mexico. I don't feel angry. But just that I want to be alone—as much alone as I am—while I am here.

Yrs,

D. H. LAWRENCE.

He wanted to be *alone*! I didn't believe it. He tried to make one think he was well off *alone*, when he had taught me once for all to know what his life was with her. He threw me away, did he? Very well, we would be enemies now. I hated him and I was unhappy hating him. He, too, hated me, and Frieda told me afterwards that she had a terrible time up there with him. His exasperation drove him wild.

"He threw stones at me and hit me!" she said, wide-eyed.

To enforce my own feeling against him, I turned my tongue loose. I told funny stories about him and emphasized all the weak things in him. He was terribly easy to caricature. I wrote a parody about him and sent it to Walter Lippmann, who saw

I was hurt and replied:

"It's your own fault. Don't you know that you can't make a pet out of a snake?"

And not only he and I said these mean things about each other; Frieda too, glad of the breach, very glad, did her share of slandering and slamming me and my people, glad to have them disposed of, misconstrued and misinterpreted everything, and talked all over the village. John did quite a lot of this. He had felt Lawrence's antagonism to him—and he had hated my concentration upon him. Tony, too, went round saying Lorenzo was a snake and poison and a sick man, which last is almost the worst he could say!

At the same time, various people were telling me the things Lawrence was occupied in saying about me!

"He said you tried to make him fall in love with you. He said you tried to take him up on your roof and make him make love to you. He said you have an evil, destructive, dominating will and that it will be the end of you. He said . . . He said . . . He said . . . !"

Life was too much for me. One morning when I was lacing my shoe, I lost consciousness and remained away from myself for twenty-four hours—having a vacation from it all, lying on the bed with a smile on my face while doctors worked round, giving me all kinds of medicine, and Tony sat on the floor praying.

And when Lawrence heard about this, he said it was just defeat! That my will had been defeated for the first time and that it couldn't stand it. It must have been a grand day for Lawrence when he thought that!

Well, I will not tell you in detail all that took place during our separation from each other. He went his way and I went mine. In brief, though he and Frieda joined Bynner and Spud in Old Mexico and spent the spring and summer there, I know little of his life during those months but that he wrote *The*

Plumed Serpent then, and all he knew of Indians and the drum
he had learned from Tony. He simply transposed Taos and took
it down there to Old Mexico. What I had wanted him to do for
Taos, he did do, but he gave it away to the mother country of
Montezuma.

In the spring of that year the Department of the Interior
was stirred up by the efforts Collier had been making to protect
the Indians from the wicked Bursum Bill, which had been a
scheme to deprive them further of land and water. The Department of Justice came into the embroilment. Inspectors arrived to
size up the Taos situation and decided that my house was the
center of disturbance; that I was instigating all the trouble for
the government.

To make a quite long story of intrigue shorter, Jeffers, I will
just tell you that when Tony and I were found living there
unmarried, they tried to use that weakness to quell me, to drive
me away from the Indians and Taos. Tony was a ward of the
government. Very well. . . .

I do not suppose it occurred to them that I was not the kind
they could manage. Tony and I were quietly married. Nothing
could make me give him up, nothing will ever make me give
him up.

Out of the silence between Lawrence and me, my friend
Nina Witt had a postcard from him. Nina had followed me
out to Taos for a visit and had married a one-armed saw-mill
man, a local character named Lee Witt. Lawrence had done
nothing but revile them when he was there—yet here he was,
sending postcards. The card had a photograph of him on one
side, with a most malicious jeer on his face, and on the other a
description of Mexico City in his small, fine writing. It con-
cluded with:

"I hear Mabel married Tony. Why?"

"None of his business why. Don't you tell him!" I told her
angrily, and I stole the postcard from her and kept it.

I went back to my waistless dresses, to my embroidered Mother Hubbards, as he had called them, and I sat there on my hill more or less apathetic, though quite a lot was going on around me.

During the summer Clarence arrived from New York. I must tell you a little about Clarence, Jeffers, because he comes later into the relationship I resumed with Lorenzo. A friend had sent him out to stay with us in Taos and he walked in at the gate one sunny afternoon. It must have been a psychological moment for him, because the instant he saw me standing in the doorway, he fell in love with me, or at least he thought he did. He was a tall, very graceful fellow, with a round, curly head and honey-colored eyes, already in an exalted state from the altitude, I suppose, or the relief at getting away from New York and the noise and grime and confusion of the East. He sat down and plunged at once into a lyrical description of his arrival on the train over at Taos Junction.

"Oh, I feel as though I had come home!" he exclaimed. "While I was waiting for the stage over there, I went into a little barber-shop. There was an old man having a hair-cut. An old man in high boots and a flannel shirt. When I saw all that lovely, soft white hair lying all around him on the floor, I felt: 'These are the kind of people I want for my friends!' "

Clarence himself was extremely sophisticated and exquisite. His silk shirt was dainty and all his clothes were the very last word of fashion. He seemed to me rather effeminate, with his white hands and his pretty smile.

When Tony arrived for supper, he had, apparently, another coup de foudre. He was determined, I think, to love us all! That evening after supper he sat with me under the cottonwood tree by the stream. The moonlight came through the branches, and the water laughed.

"And what are *you* doing here in Taos?" he asked.

"Oh, waiting," I said.

John and Alice had been married months ago and gone to Europe on their honeymoon. When they came back, they came to Taos and we gave them Tony's house to live in. From the moment they entered it, everything went wrong with them. They quarreled with each other and with me. We could not get along together.

"That is a very unhappy house to live in," Alice told me; and pretty soon they went away to Santa Fe to the Hendersons'.

You see, Jeffers, I could make a book out of all that went on there on the hill, but this is just an account of what happened between Lawrence and me, for I want to give you Lorenzo.

I determined to break up the pattern we had—the habit of living with Tony in Taos. We needed a change, and the Colliers persuaded us to take a house for the winter in Mill Valley, across the bay from San Francisco. High up on Mount Tamalpais, then, Tony and I lived in one small house, and Clarence, who came with us, lived in another one close by, along with two Indians we brought with us: my Albidia, who has been with me ever since I went to Taos, and Trinidad, Tony's nephew.

We were a funny collection of people! Clarence so fashionable and fastidious in his modish clothes, Tony and Trinidad in blankets and with their long braided hair, and little Albidia like a Persian miniature with her black hair and long, dark eyes. I suppose one of the queerest sights in the world was Clarence walking down Market Street with Trinidad the day he took him in town to buy him a present!

Clarence was very fond of Trinidad. Indians seemed to soothe him and make him feel good. He liked Trinidad's slender, upright bearing, and his elegant little face, with its closely modeled nose. There was something complete and secure in his whole appearance, the smooth black braids, the striped blanket proudly worn; even his fine gold ear-rings pleased Clarence, and he beamed when he was with the boy. When Clarence asked him what he wanted most of anything in the world, he said he wanted a suit-case! They went into a store. Trinidad looked over every suit-case in it. Suddenly he whispered something to Clarence, and Clarence asked the clerk where the toilet was.

"The one for ladies on the right hand of that door, for gentlemen on the left," answered the clerk. Clarence motioned Trinidad to go to the left-hand door and he started for it.

"*No!*" exclaimed the clerk, hurrying after him.

"But *yes*," insisted Clarence, drawing him back.

"I thought it was your wife!" stuttered the clerk in an awed voice.

Funny things were always happening. . . . For myself, I knew I could not feel right again until things were fixed up with Lorenzo. I had waited and waited, and never a word had come from him. Yet I had been hearing about him right along from other people. Apparently we both kept tabs on each other always, for I learned afterwards that he had known pretty nearly everything about us and what we were doing.

I heard that he and Frieda had gone to New York to sail for England, but that they had quarreled at the last moment and he had let her sail alone. They had been growing further and further apart, I knew that. I knew it from people who had seen them and I knew it out of the air.

Lawrence left her, then, at the dock and she sailed alone. She told me, long afterwards, that she thought they had come to a final separation, and that she cried herself to sleep for three nights on the boat, and then she was over it! She said that when she got to London, everything was so jolly she cabled Lawrence to come. She just cabled: "Come. Frieda."

Meanwhile Lawrence turned and went to Buffalo! He wanted to see Buffalo, he told me, later. I was glad he did. He said it explained so much to him. In Buffalo he got in touch with Bessie Wilkinson again and she took him about. She took him down to Lewiston on the Niagara River to see my mother, whom he said he wanted to know, and *that* must have been a queer lunch-party.

She took him around to a number of old friends of mine, and she ended up with tea at Mrs. Birge's. Mrs. Birge always flattered herself that she knew how to treat artists and writers, which very few Buffalo people did! Lawrence described this visit to me with roars and wry jeers.

"As I turned to leave," he said, "she suddenly pulled a rose out of a vase, with a stem two feet long and thorns at least a quarter of an inch long, and this she handed to me 'wordlessly.' Can you see me carrying the thing out to the street and getting into the automobile with it, held out ever so carefully in front of me so as not to get stuck? Ah me!"

When I could bear it no more, I wrote him a letter. I forget how I knew where to find him—perhaps Bessie had written me. He had returned to Old Mexico in company with one of those Danes. I told him he had hurt me, but that I had to have his friendship. I forget, really, just what I did say. He answered at once:

Hotel Garcia, Guadalajara, Jal.
17 October, 1923

DEAR MABEL

I got your letter here today—when I arrived from Tepic. Yes, I was pretty angry. But now let us forget it. At least I will forget, forget the bad part. Because also I have some beautiful memories of Taos. That, perhaps, is what makes the sting burn longer.—As for reviling you, when I am angry, I say what I feel. I hope you do the same. When John Evans went round saying, "Mother had to ask the Lawrences to get out," then I felt there was nothing to do but to throw the knife back. But now, enough. If it's *got* to be a battle of wills, I'll fight the devil himself, as long as the necessity lasts. But it's not my idea of life.

There, there's an end to the enmity, anyhow.

Frieda is in England, and wants me to go over there. But I don't want to, she'd better come here.

You have striven so hard, and so long, to *compel* life. Can't you now slowly change, and let life slowly drift into you. Surely it is even a greater mystery and preoccupation even than willing, to let the invisible life steal into you and slowly possess you. Not people, or things, or action, or even consciousness: but the slow invasion of you by the vast invisible god that lives in the ether. Once you know that, you will never feel "out of work," as you say. And it's only a change of direction. Instead of projecting your will into the ether of the invisible God, let the invisible God interpenetrate into you.—After all, it's not a mere question of washing dishes. It's the soul's own mystery. And one can make a great, great change in all one's flow of life and living, from the power of output to the mystery of intake, without changing one's house or one's husband. "Then shall thy peace be as a river." And when it comes, like a river, then you won't feel out of work or unliving.

People tell me you are divorcing Tony, and there is another young man, and so on. Probably it is not true. I hope it's not. I don't think it is. Tony always has my respect and affection. And when I say in my book: "one cannot go back," it is true, one cannot. But your marriage with Tony may even yet be the rounding of a great curve; since certainly he doesn't merely draw you back, but himself advances perhaps more than you advance, in the essential "onwards."

Yrs,

D. H. LAWRENCE.

P. S. We rode over the mountains from Tepic and down the barranca and to Matzatlan, and I thought very much of how you and Tony taught F. and me to ride on Granfer and my little Zegua. For that and many things like that, believe me, I am grateful.

D. H. L.

So we were in communication again. I wrote and told him all that had happened while we had been separated. I wished he would come to California, but he could not:

Hotel Garcia, Guadalajara. Jal.
8 Novem. 1923

DEAR MABEL

I had your letter from California yesterday. Don't trouble any more. Let the past die and be forgotten.

Don't trouble about the Indians. You can't "save" them: and politics, no matter *what* politics, will only destroy them. I have said many times that you would destroy the Indians. In your lust even for a Saviour's power, you would just destroy them. The same with Collier. He will destroy them. It is his saviour's will to set the claws of his own White egoistic *benevolent* volition into them. Somewhere, the Indians know that you and Collier would, with your salvationist but poisonous white consciousness, destroy them. Remember, Jesus, and The Good, in our sense, in our mystic sense, not just the practical: Jesus, and The Good as you see it, are poison for the Indians. One feels it intensely here in Mexico. Their great saviour Juarez did more to destroy them than all the centuries of Viceroys. Juarez was a pure Indian.—This is really a land of Indians: not merely a pueblo.

I tell you, leave the Indians to their own dark destiny. And leave *yourself* to the same.

I. I shall not *write* that third book: at least not for many years. It's got to be lived out: not thought out.

I also fight to put something through. But it is a long, slow, dark, almost invisible fight. Yet, little by little, I win. And unless there comes death, or the unforeseen bad, I shall win.

One day I will come to you and take your submission: when you are ready. Life made you what you are: I understood so much when I was in Buffalo and saw your mother. But life put into you also the germ of something which still you are not, and which you *cannot* be, of yourself, and if you go on in the same way. People, lawyers, politics, enemies, back-biters, friends and pseudo friends: my dear, it is all Chimæra and nothing. I will take a submission from you one day, since it is still yours to give. But apparently, not yet.—I was your enemy. But even saying things against you—and I only said, with emphasis and in many ways, that your will was evil masquerading as good, and I should still say that of your will: even as an enemy I never really forsook you. There, perhaps I have said too much. But don't think, even so, you can make a fool of me.

D. H. L.

Frieda and everybody insist on my going to England. And I, I shall give in once more, in the long fight. I may as well go and settle finally with England. But I shall not stay long. A short time only. And directly or indirectly I shall come back here, this side, Mexico. I fight against the other side: Europe and the White and U. S. Before very long I hope to come and see you again. I'll let you know when I go.

D. H. L.

And then, even before I realized it, he had left this continent. His letter reached me when he was on the ocean:

> *Hotel Monte Carlo. Av. Uruguay*
> *Mexico, D.F.*
> *19 Nov. 1923*

DEAR MABEL

I had your letter from Guadalajara this morning. There, you have found your way, the first step. And I am finding mine. Taos was a last step to me, too. On a good day we will meet again, and start afresh.—The end of the old is bitter, but there is the new for us.

I am sailing on the 22nd—in three days—from Vera Cruz to England. Write to me there

care S. Koteliansky, 5 Acacia Road, St. Johns Wood
London, N.W. 8.

I don't much want to go. But I suppose, at the moment, it
is my destiny.

But I shall come back. I like the west best.

Idella Purnell showed me your California poem. I agree
with you, Taos is far, far better than California. I like Jalisco very
much. But Taos is about the best place in U. S. A. I believe
that.

We'll go our separate ways, and see where they'll bring us.—
Mine, I always think, holds the chance of my getting shot. Pues
vedremos. Anyhow we'll meet again and it will be different from
what it was.

D. H. L.

My heart was lightened by being in touch again with Lorenzo.
In another letter he sent me before leaving for England, he
wrote: "Let us keep an invisible thread between us." That was
all I needed, really, an invisible living communication.

The salmon were running from the sea up the river below
us and I wrote him about it and how my need to return to him
no matter what happened between us was like that, like a return
to the source. He didn't reply to it directly, but it was not long
before he wrote an essay about it and I knew he had been struck
by its truth.

Our life on Mount Tamalpais was quiet and peaceful from
that time on. I had been stormy for months and my letters to him
poured it all out and then it was over. By the time his first letter
came back from London, we were all feeling at home in our
little cottages and I had turned to writing some verses and short
stories. Since I do not know how to invent anything, I could
never write about anything except myself and what I saw. I sent
him a poem, called "False Start," that came from his letter about
the tiny germ that was in me, but that was not me. Here it is:

FALSE START

Ask me no more of the full flower's speech,
Tell me no more of the ripe fruit's need,
For I am tired of trying to reach the fruit in the seed.

Leave me awhile, and I will recover
In darkness and night.
It was too soon for me to discover growth in the light.

Bear with my weakness, my failure, my pain,
Grant me this only, this darkness I need.
I sicken from sunlight, but give me the rain, for I am but seed.

I had written several things in an attempt to tell him what had happened during our silence; one was a verse about California:

LAND OF FLOWERS

There is no savor in this salt,
And apples in this country have no tang
At all. The Bay is merely water, just cobalt,
And in my joy there is no joy and in my pain no pang.

The trees here are vivid and glisten in the sun—
All kinds: laurel, eucalyptus, oak, and bay;
All kinds of growing things, but all of them are dumb:
Living growing things without anything to say.

It seems to me upon this hill-side high,
I hang between the happy and the sad
Of life. For in this place we neither laugh nor cry,
Though everyone keeps smiling and no one is good or bad.

And the sun keeps shining and shining,
And if one lies out under it at noonday
Waiting for that certain interpenetrating ray—
Nothing happens!

And another was about my longing for Taos:

I MISS

I miss the Dæmon of that other land,
Where more than meets the eye is in the air
We breathe. Where living is all mystery and
Danger, and death to the soul is our daily, hourly care.

The women are peaceful in these valleys
And everyone moves on a dreamlike blue sea
In white boats. And though it is beautiful,
Oh beautiful, I suppose, it doesn't do anything to me.

But in that lost land where the ether
Is carrying potent spirits of evil and good,
And all things are full of flavor and craft,
Though the women are not peaceful, I love it:
It is the quick of life.

And then these others, called "Tell Me, Master," and "Little
Monkeys."

TELL ME, MASTER

Read this, Master, and tell me what you read:
Once I was like hard soil, rich, I think,
But frozen and bare;
Or maybe life-pressed into a clod,
Iron-hard.
Like earth hard and dry where no growth can be.

But one day a storm broke over this earth at life's brink,
Rending.
And someone dropped a secret into my care.
No knowing, for me, what it is, I am debarred.
Sometimes it seems to me only a tiny thing like a mustard seed,
But oh, precious! for it lives!
And sometimes, oh wonder! it seems God.
But all I can know of it, Master, unless you tell me,
Is that I cherish it—it is my need.

LITTLE MONKEYS

Cageful of little monkeys
And not a smile among you—
For is direst monkeyness never to smile?
Very busy, maybe satisfied, but oh! no smiles.

And among you, my humans,
No smiles either.
Grins and grimaces and gestures a-plenty,
But where is one to see, even to see, the smile,
The real smile?

I know where I have seen once on this earth
The shining glance, the splendid radiant look
That a *man* may wear.
Since then this world, this whole round world,
Has seemed to me only a cageful of little monkeys.

And two others:

BEST TO TELL ALL

Best to tell all.
Maybe earth-cast words will carry away
Desire from this clay.

Wring the tear dry.
Maybe this salt will burn
Lust from this eye.

For over me, forlorn,
Love, old love, hovers still,
Seeking new form.

Wait, soul, for me.
Blood memory lives so long,
Deep as the sea.

Your call to me
Is fiercer than tears or blood
Ever can be.

Oh wait, soul, for me!

GRAY GULL

All the white-breasted gulls followed our ship,
Hovering over it they dived and whirled,
Screaming for food.
Greedy white birds hovering and complaining,
All alike to each other and all hungry for food.

But one among them, one dusky breast, dark-winged,
And this one weaving in and out, solitary,
Eager and unappeased with our morsels:
Eager, uneasy, and peering like a blind thing.

Of a sudden, swift to the west he veered,
And, exultant, he whirled true and straight towards the sun—
Released, he was lost in the light
And my heart blazed and followed in a dim companioning. . . .

After I heard from him again, I felt like a new planet. I tried
to tell him about that feeling, too, in a verse:

I'LL TELL YOU

I'll tell you what it's like to be new:
It's not doing any single thing unless you feel it,
And it's seeing how fresh every morning is,
And it's throwing away words that seem dead
Because someone has chewed the life out of them
As poor old Nina did to the word *consciousness*;
It's to feel a little flame in your heart every day
And not to care whether it rains or shines outdoors,
And it's to love your new dress,
And, oh *happy*! it's to come and go like a leaf in the wind,
A *good* wind that makes your flame *blaze*.

SAPPHIC

All my life long I'd been dancing with God:
Seeking Him all over heaven, I'd beg Him to dance
And He always came and damned gladly we danced.
I took the lead in our forthright measures
And He let me lead Him.

Every year was a leap-year to me then.
And God was the only partner I wanted.
But He wearied of having me do all the asking
And never waiting for Him to seek me out;
Then He threw me down hard!

For quite a long time now I've been mostly a wallflower,
For God is the only One I can dance with.
But lately sometimes when I'm feeling the saddest,
He comes, takes my hand, and together we dance again.
And oh, such sweet dancing!

And I sent him a story about Francesca Alexander who lived on the top of an old palace in Florence and took care of her garden on the roof. She had a wild olive tree growing there that she had brought up from a tiny plant Ruskin had given her when she walked with him long ago in the Tuscan hills. That was all of her life, a few walks and talks with Ruskin when she was a girl; and then long years with her mother high up in the palazzo on the Piazza Santo Spirito. But she was one of the most contented people I ever knew. "It is so wonderful to watch a tree grow," she told me.

But Lawrence was not faring very well in London:

110 Heath St. Hampstead
London N.W. 3
17 Decem.

DEAR MABEL

Here I am, already in bed with a bad cold. And I simply

hate being here. I simply detest it. I shan't stay long: soon I shall go to Paris, and perhaps to Spain for a while: then back to America. I guess I shall be in America again by March. Then we'll see.

I have your story, and two letters, here. The story is good. I shall ask Murry if he would like to print it in the Adelphi. This is a very crucial time for all of us. I feel if we can pull through to 1925, we have saved the situation. Meantime it's hell. England is a tomb to me, no more.—Yet perhaps it's as well I went away from that revolution in Mexico.

But I don't belong over here any more. It's like being among the dead of one's previous existence.

In spite of the bad time you are having, I feel that somewhere you are really happier, and feeling a bit free from the old compulsion. I hope Tony doesn't get a hard life out of it all. I know he feels exiled. The only way to help the Indians is to *leave 'em alone*. We'll laugh last: and really laugh, not jeer. A test of the soul is its insouciance.

Meanwhile I am a diminished specimen, here. But I shall soon rise up again.

When are you going back to Taos? If we are back in America in March, shall we come and see you there? I want, when Mexico is quiet, to go down to Oaxaca. I don't suppose this "revolution" will last long.

Never think of coming to Europe.—But Mexico is another matter.

F. is well and sends *saluti*.

D. H. L.

Like most people, when he did not like what he was doing, he became ill. I couldn't help thinking he had gone back to Frieda against his higher will, but maybe that was only a personal feeling of mine. It seemed to me that the very thing he fought against in me, he capitulated to in her: the surrender of his will. Why was he forever at her beck and call? If her judgment had been good for him, or if she at least carried him to places that were healthful for him to live in, it would not have been so bad. But the woman had no understanding of ill health and she invariably chose spots that put him down in bed and weakened his body still further, and this lessened his resistance to her. I believed she had insisted upon leaving my neighborhood because I backed him up and lent him my force and made it easier for him to combat her. Yet he had called my will destructive even while he had accepted its power. In the reaction back to her, he had called it destructive because, truly, it destroyed her ascendancy over him and undermined their relationship.

But never mind! I need not mind if he called me destructive, for he has called her so in every line, in every book he has written, masking his accusation from her as best he could under many guises so she would let it pass.

I wonder if she knew what she was doing, or if her instinct guided her to draw him, to her advantage and his despite, to the very worst climates and the most depressing surroundings?

110 Heath St.
Hampstead, N.W. 3
19 Decem.

Dear Mabel

My literary agent, Curtis Brown, has a son who has lung trouble and who *perhaps* would like to come to New Mexico to get strong again. He's not very bad. He has a wife and *three* little girls: quite small.

Capt. M. L. Curtis Brown,
　Whitney Point
　　Broome Co., New York.

The question is, could he have a house at about $50 a month in Taos: he's got no money but what his father gives him. If you have anything to suggest, send him a line. If you don't want to let any of your houses—or can't—perhaps suggest another. But *don't* do anything unless you feel quite easy about it.

We seriously think of New Mexico in early spring: and Middleton Murry wants to come along—also, probably, Dorothy Brett, who paints, is deaf, forty, very nice, and daughter of Viscount Esher.

I'm longing to get out of England.

D. H. L.

Lawrence fell back into a great gulf when he returned that time to London. He had learned what life there was in the New World, in the new, unexploited country that is called New Mexico. To go back to that London life was like a dog returning to his vomit. Frieda told me later in the spring about a party they went to. Middleton Murry, Koteliansky, and several of his old friends gave him a dinner.

To understand the unwelcome strain merely of being in England, you must remember, Jeffers, that Frieda and Lawrence had been hounded away from there during the war, when they'd been accused of being German spies in their little cottage on the coast of Cornwall. He has told some of the humiliation and shame of all that time in *Kangaroo*. He had never been back since to face that life. Returning to it must have made it all surge up in him again, the repudiation of his own country, the embarrassment and uneasiness of his friends. He had told me that not one of them had raised a finger to help him—they had all slunk away into corners. And now they were giving him a dinner-party.

He went without enthusiasm—perfunctorily—but guardedly, as though he moved in an uncertain element. Might not the cup be poisoned? But the warmth of their enveloping affection melted him very soon. Aided, no doubt, by the plentiful champagne, they surrounded him with their loving attention. Lorenzo always responded to the least sign of friendliness. He could not help it. He turned involuntarily towards loving-kindness as a plant towards the sun. And now when he found them again, these old-time friends who had been his colleagues, who had striven up by their efforts into some importance, just as he had himself, they not only welcomed him back warmly, but gave him his due. His own people—his own English people—they valued him and appreciated him. He had published some of his best work while he had been away, notably what was perhaps his greatest novel, *Women in Love*, which he said had taken him ten years to write.

Frieda said they cheered him and drank his health. He was as happy and excited as a boy, she told me. Finally Murry leaped up and stood on the table, his glass high in his hand, and gave the final toast: "To Lawrence, the greatest of us all!" And they all stood up to drink it and then threw their glasses to the floor. And Lawrence just put his head down in his arms on the table and cried.

The next day he was simply raging at them in a passion of anger!

"They betrayed me!" he exclaimed over and over again.

His letters grew more disturbed, and he hesitated less to show he needed and must take what he knew I could give him, my strength and my will to create through him some further life and expression of the spirit. He was never more close to me than in those times when Frieda drew him far away. His letters made me glad and I sent him a steady, outpouring stream of power along the unseen path between us.

> *110 Heath St.*
> *Hampstead, N.W. 3*
> *27 Dec. 1923*

DEAR MABEL

Your letters come on safely. I think I have them all. Write whenever you feel like it—I am glad to know you are with me. It is hateful here in England, so dark and stifling, and everyone and everything trying to drag one back. They have no life of their own, and they want to drag one away from the life one would make. I feel the English much more my enemies than the Americans. I would really rather be in America. But anyhow or anywhere it is an awful great struggle to keep one's spark alight and perhaps kindle something new. There doesn't seem really to be anybody.—I'm afraid I don't know much about Wobblies or I.W.W.'s, about whom you ask me. I don't know much about societies and groups anywhere: mistrust them when I do know them.

I am due to go to the Midlands to my people, but don't bring myself to set out. I don't want to go. It's all the dead hand of the past, over here, infinitely heavy, and deadly determined to put one down. It won't succeed, but it's like struggling with the stone lid of the tomb.

I wonder why Seltzer has not written to me—for about six weeks I have nothing from him. I wonder if something has gone wrong with him or his business. Hope not, that would dish me in another direction.

When I can *really* break the clutch of the dead hand over here, so that its grip is broken in the world forever, I think I shall go to Paris. And I really hope to be in America by March: apparently Murry does want to come, but I don't altogether trust him. Can't rely on him *at all*.

Remember I am depending on your spirit at the back of me, over there, no matter what there is over here. I am glad when I hear you feel relieved of the old tension, and happy apart from taking thought. That is how it should be. Perhaps it is because you are learning to *give* your life into the creative future. For a woman, the greatest joy, I think, is to give her spirit and know it is not in vain, that the gift is needed. Which it is.

I shall tell you when we move. I wish it might be soon. How much I would rather be in Taos than here.

Remember me to Tony.

D. H. L.

You can see in that letter, Jeffers, that Lawrence had.a belief in an almost unlimited power that it was his destiny to wield for the destruction of the old modes, the evil, outworn ways of the world, as well as the new, equivocal, and so-called aids to life called the inventions of science. This was a belief that he had frequently talked of to me. He really thought he was able to deal death—to destroy and to create; and that he was here on earth for that purpose; that if he could overcome evil and destroy it, he would have fulfilled his destiny. But he knew it was a struggle in which he might fail—the Satanic powers could destroy him if he were not everlastingly vigilant and alert. These deathly and backward-plunging powers worked through people in whom they embodied themselves. So the gods ruled, he believed, using men and women for their instruments. And he was on the right side, he believed; on the side of the great, dark gods that would destroy and overcome the enemies of life, all those enemies of life that strengthen themselves with machinery, with all mechanics, whether of steel or of brain. He believed the intrinsic acceptance of machinery was a hampering of life and a subtle temptation of the inimical spirit, just as he thought that most of the mental systems—all forms of thought and intellect— were schemes of the Devil to put life in chains. And he spent himself opposing this subtle tendency that masqueraded as modernity, but was in reality both murder and suicide. He was allied with the old, dark gods of life, the undisclosed, impenetrable gods who live in the living and remain forever unnamed.

So, Jeffers, life for Lorenzo was a fight to the death, and the world was a battle-field for him. Do we dare to call his conception of his rôle on earth pure fantasy, a poetic avoidance of the real problem, which lay, really, within himself? I wonder.

He was so canny, really, that he never committed these ideas about himself to paper, although he often spoke of them with one. I do not remember his ever again referring to it as openly as he did in the letter you have just read. Something held him back. Perhaps Frieda? When he talked about these things and she was there—"Bosh!" she frequently exclaimed!

Anyway, Jeffers, he was slowly destroying an old and, as I now believed, an evil attitude in me. Truly I had tried to seduce his spirit so that I could make it work for me instead of doing the work myself. Now I only longed to pour myself out to him and let his will be done as he would have it done. I submitted my will to him and told him so. I luxuriated in submission for a change and hoped I pleased him by it. But he, who always found a flaw in every expressed desire, flung me back and would not have, in words, the earnest consciousness of endeavor. He simply loathed *conscious* endeavor, do you see? I asked him to find out about Gurdjieff and the Fontainebleau Institution, and this made him mad.

> *110 Heath St.*
> *Hampstead, N.W. 3*
> *9 Jan. 1924*

DEAR MABEL

You certainly are an egoist, and your letters are egoistic, as you say. Soon you must learn to forget yourself. You must learn *not to care*, not to think, and simply to laugh. Poco a poco.

I have heard enough about that place at Fontainebleau where Katherine Mansfield died, to know it is a rotten, false, self-conscious place of people playing a sickly stunt. One doesn't wonder about it *at all*. One knows. Now call into action your common horse-sense, of which you have your share, as I have mine, and use that. Don't go back on your common horse-sense. It is the centaur's way of knowledge. And if we come back into our own, we'll prance in as centaurs, sensible, a bit fierce, and amused. I am sure seriousness is a disease, today. It's an awful disease in Murry. So long as there's a bit of a laugh going, things are all right. As soon as this infernal seriousness, like a greasy sea, heaves up, everything is lost. And it was so with us at Taos. If only we'd kept up an *honest* laugh. Not a dishonest laugh: but an honest laugh: then the vileness of 1923 need not have been. Now it takes far more courage to dare not to care, and to dare to have a bit of a laugh at *everything*, than to wallow in the deepest seas of seriousness. The thing I admire most about you is your dauntlessness. Be dauntless in this, then. Not any forced will of your own, nor any forced submission, but a certain *real* trust, and the courage *not to care*, and the power to laugh a bit. Do this and we'll have a good time among ourselves. One's got to put a new ripple in the ether. And one can do it only by *not* caring about any of the old things, by going beyond them all with amusement and a bit of jolliness, and having a bit of stark trust inside oneself. Stark trust in a Lord we have no name for, and also stark trust in one another. Instead of a recklessness of defiance and mistrust, a recklessness of trust, like a naked knife.

I find that here in London they all *instinctively* hate me: much more so than in America. But that too, in the end, only makes me laugh. My gods, like the Great God Pan, have a bit of a natural grin on their face. Nous nous entendons.

I am still planning to come west at the end of February or in March, with Frieda, Murry and Brett. I hope you are looking forward to it. But on your honour, Mabel, no seriousness. The seriousness of the Great God Pan, who grins a bit, and when he gets driven too hard, goes fierce. You are one of the very few people in the world at the moment who are capable of this: this fierce recklessness, based on trust, like the recklessness of Pan; trusting deep down to the springs of nature, the sources: and then the laughter.

The old communion was in seriousness and earnestness. The new is in fierceness, daring, knife-like trust, and laughter. Bien entendu.   D. H. L.

Oh, dear! How could I believe in his daring, when he was still so enslaved? He continued to make that plea for unconsciousness, for insouciance, for *not* knowing and not formulating.

110 Heath St.
London N.W. 3
22 Jan. 1924

DEAR MABEL

We are leaving for Paris in the morning—stay there about a fortnight, then a while in Germany—and by early March I still hope to be in New York; and in New Mexico by end of that month.

I think I have had most of your letters—but none yet to say you have heard from me. And I sent a line as soon as I got here. Let us know your plans.

London, England wearies me inexpressibly. I cannot tell you how this winter in England wearies me, and the people. But it will finish.

Let's try and be really sensible when we meet again—and laugh and send most things to the devil. None of the strain of insistence. Why insist.

Yes, I liked Fairytale. And your poems do amuse me. But I am not going to think of you as a writer. I'm not going to think of you even as a knower. You know and write whatever you feel like, of course. But the essential you, for me, doesn't know and could never write: the Eve who is Voiceless like the serpent, yet communicates.

But let us above all things be able to laugh and not care, and not scheme and insist, and not, in a tight way, exclude. One can ignore so much, and it is so good. The last days of life are for living, not for knowing or insisting.

Let's have an open, careless heart.

D. H. L.

Yet his gradual influence upon me was, to my evident improvement in health and in joy, to make me more conscious,
more careful, and more understanding! I was writing in these
days, painfully, yes, but how it helped me to clear up in my
mind the turgid and unexpressed volume of energy that was so
hard to carry along! I sent him more poems: "Fairy-tale" and
"The Ballad of a Bad Girl," which were written for him.

FAIRY-TALE

On the hill there, I reigned in my castle of steel and pearl,
There I reigned!
And the slaves willingly build up my strength,
For my power saved them,
Saved them from themselves.
And all day the sun shone on the walls of silver and steel,
But within, the turquoises were growing green.

And nothing could shake our castle down!
Nothing.
Until one day a queer red god came to that place,
And just with his words he made the walls shiver and fall,
With his words and his glance.
And all the impregnable defenses fell down,
And the slaves shivered and fell down, too.
And they called him enemy and covered their faces,
For he took away all my power
And left them bare.
But I do not call him enemy!
I do not call him enemy!

For he came and delivered me of my power.
He made the turquoises bloom.
And I am alive again!
I am alive!

And pretty soon I wrote "Change of Life," that thing that was
so difficult to write and was distilled out of months of slow
perception.

One day when Tony and I were lying on the grass outside our house, we heard a shout and a loud "Hallooo!" We turned and saw a queer fellow coming along to us. He was wearing a long cape, his shirt was open at the neck, and a blue béret clung to the back of his head. He said his name was Jaime de Angulo and that he had heard there was an Indian living on Tamalpais, so he'd walked over from Berkeley to look for him.

So began our acquaintance with Jaime! It was he who told me all about Jung, with whom he had been working in Zurich, and I began to see life all extraverts and introverts, with energy like arrows going to the sun, and arrows coming from the sun, and what not! It was awfully interesting to me, too. I wrote Lorenzo all about it and he was up in arms at once. More attempts to know and to understand! More systems and more consciousness! All he wanted was the *flow* and not the knowing about it! He was longing to come back to Taos, and planning about it, though he spurned the idea of a *plan* about anything. I had begun to feel the weariness of running my big house in Taos. He wrote then:

> *Care Frau Baronni von Richthofen*
> *Ludwig—Wilhelmstift*
> *Baden-Baden, Germany*
> *7 Feby. 1924*

Dear Mabel

We have just come here. I find two letters from you.

It would be good if we could make a bit of life at Taos. The only thing is to try. I think it would be a good idea to run the big house as a guest-house. But henceforth in the world I count on nothing. Things will have to happen in their own way. No good trying to *make* anything. Yet of course one has to provide for the hour, even if one looks no further. So I think it quite a good idea to make the big house a guest-house, and the rest of us dispose ourselves in the others. Frieda must write to you too. Which house would you choose for yourself?

We are due to stay here two weeks: then we go back to Paris and London. It may be necessary for me to be in New York by March 10th, to pay my income tax. If Seltzer will see that it is paid for me, we may not come until beginning of April. If we come early, we might come on to Mill Valley. Quien sabe!

Your long letter about extraverts and introverts! You know those classifications mean so little to me. No classification whatever means much to me. But it seems to me, the life that rises from the blood itself is the life that is living, while the life that rises from the nerves and the brain is the life that is death.—As for washing windows—we called at that Fontainebleau place. The Russian there believes entirely in going against the grain. He would make you wash windows and scrub floors eight hours a day, and the viler your temper the better he would find it for you. Get your energy out of reaction and out of resentment. The fine fury of resentment. His idea.

But as for me, I am no curer. At least I am not extravert enough for that. Please yourself whether you wash windows or whether you don't. Myself, I don't care much for washing dishes or windows any more. But, in these cities, I would be very glad to be cutting down a tree and sawing it up, or cutting the ice in the stream, as in those months at Del Monte with the Danes.

I am awfully sorry about Granfer. And my little Zegua— what a tartar she'll be by the time I see her again!

If being an introvert means always drawing in, in, in to yourself, and not going bravely out, and giving yourself, then for God's sake wash windows also and go out to them, if only savagely.

Que vamos hacer? Quien sabe!

D. H. L.

Best write to London.

Before I had time to get this letter and remember how he disliked analysis of anything, I had written him more about Jung, to which he replied:

Baden-Baden
9 Feb

DEAR MABEL

Now don't you keep on going on to me about introverts and extraverts and insides and outsides. It's all in the head, and no good will come out of the head. I can feel you going like a terrible clockwork when you write those letters.

And wash just a few windows and dishes, till you can do it rhythmically and with a grace. It's good for you. But no need to condemn yourself to any of those things. Only don't condemn yourself further to headwork. It's just *futile*. You must learn to abstain from that vice of "knowing," when knowing is mere nothingness, not even an end in itself, because there's no end to it, like a bottomless pit: which swallows every human relation. Worse than sensation.

I read *Demian* in German when it first came out, and have almost forgotten it. But the first part interested me. The last part I thought *sau dumm* with its Mother Eva who didn't know whether she was wife or mother or what.

Germany is queer, though. Just changing, making a great change. Very interesting. Things might happen here, and people might be as one wants people to be.

We are going to Munich for a few days.

I rather hope Murry won't come to Taos. Don't trust him very well.

D. H. L.

Life on Mount Tamalpais was going on slowly but surely. There was nothing exciting about it, rather something deep and quiet: wherever Tony is, there, for me, is always a certain amount of reality. He makes a *real* feeling in the air. Of course, sometimes, I get terribly restive with him, for so much of his life is beneath the surface and I, like Frieda, was what Lawrence called a dynamic woman. Dynamic women like to move things about with their momentum, see things happening, have something "going on." And one can't work on Tony that way. There would be long periods when he would not even *say* anything, and I did so need to talk sometimes. Once in a while I blew up and let out my accumulated impatience. There was one evening when we were alone just before going to bed, and I flew out at him:

"I can't stand living this way, Tony. You never talk to me. You forget I am here. There you are, right near me, and you pay no *attention* to me. *I* have to talk, and have the feeling that *something* is going on! Sometimes it seems to me I am carrying a dead load around with me."

Tony looked at me with a terrible, wounded look on his face and walked to the door.

"Tomorrow I go back to Taos," he said. I didn't care. I went to bed and started to read. Between the paragraphs I thought to myself: "It will do him good to be shaken up a bit. He sinks down more and more inside himself." But I couldn't fix my mind on my book. His look, quiet and hurt, kept coming back to me and finally I jumped out of bed and hurried in the dark into his room and rushed into his bed and held him close.

"I didn't mean to hurt you, Tony. But it's so hard for me, sometimes, when you don't talk to me for days."

"It seems to me my heart is talking to you all the time," he said. It was. It was. I knew it. How ruthless we are when we live on the surface of life!

Jaime became a frequent visitor, and Clarence hated him at first. The latter had been out on the mountain the day Jaime strode into our garden calling "Halloooo!" and when he came back and found us around the fire, he stood a moment and looked at Jaime with a look of astonishment and rage and ran out of the room.

Although Clarence was gentle and effeminate, he had a curious violence that arose in him sometimes. Rages passed across his delicate face—thunderous looks and blackness. He was an inner ruin; he had been demolished in his childhood. He had no control of his forces and no will to take a hand in his own behalf. He lay back upon Tony and me like a child for whom everything is done, and anything that threatened his ease was inimical to him. Perhaps he knew, intuitively, that Jaime was destined to become a factor in his life—for at supper that night he told us:

"When I came into the room and looked at that man, I knew I had seen the Devil."

Little by little, Jaime won him, however, by the interest he took in him. Clarence was very vain, which is often another name for being uncertain of oneself; don't you think so, Jeffers? Jaime thought Clarence was in a very dangerous condition. He said that Clarence had almost wholly identified himself with his feminine side, which Jaime called his "anima," and that this was the image of the woman that all men carry with them and that they search for in the world outside. Clarence did not look for her outside, but within, and, finding her in that half of himself that was female, and letting go his manhood, he had become wholly feminized. This explained his reluctance to fend for himself and to take on himself the responsibility of his own development. Jaime made me understand that what Clarence craved for in me was the male that was so strongly evident! In fact, his anima was after my animus!

This new drama with its new vocabulary fascinated me! To have Clarence loving the man in both myself and Tony explained why, apparently, he came to cling to us both. Jaime had opened up a new world!

"Have you seen the monsters yet?" he asked Clarence one day soon. He explained that at a certain stage in a psychic degringolade, inanimate objects reveal themselves for what, possibly, they are. The inner, invisible life of things opens up. Rocks and trees and other forms show their monstrous reality; losing their immobility, they are seen to move. The earth becomes alive, nature's secrets are told. This is to experience the collective unconscious. It is to cross what is called in the *Yi King* the "Great Stream," or what William James and Frederic Myers termed "the threshold." It has always been a well-known experience to occultists who have had methods for developing it, and it has been well known to psychiatrists in the past who have sought to check it and hold individuals back to what they called the norm.

Jung, it appeared, went further than the old-school scientists and, allying himself more with the occult schools, asserted that the great world beyond the senses held the total experience of the cosmos, animal, mineral, and vegetable, and from the amœba to the highest, man; that it might be safely entered with the proper guidance, and that therein were to be found the answers to human fate. Apparently Jung himself, according to Jaime, was a kind of personal conductor into these realms; he was provocative, and induced by his presence, during an analysis, the border states of what we have learned to call madness.

Clarence wasn't sure whether he had really seen the monsters before he saw Jaime, but he certainly saw them afterwards! We all began to see them. That is, Clarence and I did. Tony thought it was a play and only laughed. I thought to myself, he has always seen into the different worlds and taken it so much for granted that he really doesn't know what we are talking about. You know, Jeffers, how he is about the earth and the sea and the sun? He said to me the other day:

"The ocean is asleep, and the sound you like—that is his snoring!"

"Will he wake up some day?" I asked him.

"Perhaps," he said, "but it will be too late. Everything will be over then."

Small events, then, on Mount Tamalpais began to take on a deep significance. Life was a series of symbols. Everything was not only what it *was*, it became highly significant and full of inner meaning. The furniture was perceived to group itself in curious patterns, easily read and quite terrible when we understood them; and every single thing anyone said was fraught with import. In fact, we had quite a little madhouse there on the hill!

Clarence's left eye, always slightly out of focus, slanted more and more away from his nose! By this time the younger Indians had returned to Taos for ceremonials they had to take part in, and we had a Chinese cook, named Wong. Wong lived in the cottage with Clarence. He was a compassionate Chinee and quite sorry for the boy, but he would not go to the station in the automobile if Clarence was driving it.

"Boy got the accident eye," he announced to me, solemnly, pointing a slender finger to his own left one. "But I help him. I make him midnight tea every night."

I liked the scarey, exciting world of Jung and Jaime. I sent for all Jung's books and read them, but was disappointed not to find more thrills in them, so I had to depend on Jaime for the more esoteric portions of the new system.

Our dog Lorraine had puppies one day. They were darling little black French bulls. Lorraine I loved with all my heart and she loved me. I loved her in the way people love animals when they are unable to love their own kind. I was unable to love my own kind. I loved no one except Tony and Lawrence. Before I knew Tony, I had never loved anyone. He awakened my heart. But even after it awakened, it did not answer to anyone but him. Lawrence I did not love with either my senses or my heart—but with another unnamable faculty.

So I loved my Lorraine, and everyone knew it, and Clarence knew it. When she had her puppies, he begged me to give him one. He put an enormous amount of what Jaime called "libido" into his wish for a puppy, and when I gave him one, he chose a female and called her "Anima"!

Now Jaime analyzed this in the most fascinating way! It seems that Clarence was trying to help himself, albeit in rather a roundabout way! He identified Lorraine with me, the puppy with Lorraine, and, calling his puppy "Anima," he identified himself with the puppy and in this fashion, turning me into a woman, sought at last to love the feminine image outside himself!

Well, he loved it and loved it! He grew perfectly maudlin over it and nearly killed it with *kindness*, until one night he went out in the dark to give it some hot milk the last thing before going to bed. . . . Tony and I heard a scream that sounded like a demented woman, and Clarence rushed into the house with Anima in his hand, her little body limp, her head hanging over.

"Look! Look! I have *murdered* her!" he moaned. "Oh! Oh! I loved her so! She was so sweet! She was beginning to know me!"

"What happened?" asked Tony. I couldn't ask anything. It all made me feel somewhat sick.

"I *killed* her," repeated Clarence. He was crying now, like a girl. "I had a piece of wood against the door to prop it open, and my foot struck it and knocked it over. It hit Anima on the head and *killed* her! My foot *meant* to do it! Oh! Oh! What shall I *do*?"

He was upset all night long, and when Jaime came the next day, he took the accident very seriously indeed. He said that Clarence's own anima was fighting against his regeneration, and that this might be the beginning of worse trouble!

"I wish you could get over and see Jung," said Jaime. "You need more help than I can give you."

I determined to help him go to see Jung. For one thing, I had begun to feel that all this was repulsive. I wanted to get rid of him. I have those sudden volte-faces sometimes. I bought a steamer ticket for him and in a trice he was gone! This hampered my life a good deal, but when I want a change, I want it so much I will make any sacrifice to get it.

The night before he left our little house on Tamalpais, he was very, very sad.

"Oh, Tony! How can I live without you and Mabel?"

"Clarence, I tell you little story tonight. When I was a boy, I ask my parents to let me go on a trip to Trinidad with two, three friends of mine. We was not very big. About *so* big. And we never been away from home before. And it was winter. It snowing hard outside and the snow was *deep*. My father look at me and then he say:

" 'Yes, you go.' But my mother she cry a little bit. But she gave me a sack of bread, and us boys we started over the mountain. We feel very good because we going away from home. We going to Trinidad to dance and sing and maybe we make some money.

"So we walk through the snow and we *walk* and *walk* and pretty soon it get to be night. Dark. But we walk, and our feet they feel so cold and we all wet. By and by we couldn't *stand* it and we stop and make a *big* fire and we put branches on the snow and we lie down with our feet towards the flame. Then we eat bread and pretty soon we sleep.

"The next day it was the same. One boy he want to go back. He want to see his family. But we say no, we go on now. We go to Trinidad and dance and sing and maybe we make some money. So he had to come too. All day we walk in the snow, and we sleep at night in the snow on branches, and next day we ain't got no more bread to eat. We ate our bread too quick. We just little boys! But we keep on and we keep on, and pretty soon we get to Trinidad. Bi—ig town! We so hungry and tired now, but we got to do something. We got to dance if we want to eat! So we go to a big light place, lota men, and we try look happy. We ask if we can dance and sing and the men they say sure. So we dance and sing and they pay us. That night we eat meat.

"So we stay in Trinidad three days and we get some money. Then we decide to go home to the pueblo. We so happy! We find our own way out of the pueblo and we make money and now we go home see our families. We decide we have big supper in the woods, and we buy a *bi—ig* piece of ham. Nearly a whole little pig. That night we cook him on the fire and we sing and dance just because we so glad.

"But pretty soon we eat too much ham! We just little boys! I have a terrible stomach-ache! We don't sleep none all-l-l night. Aw-ful! And all day next day we go so slow, we feel so sick, but we keep on, keep on. By and by we home. No matter how sick we got, we feel good when we look down from the mountain and see the pueblo. So we start to run and we run all the way home. When I come in the house, I give my mother the money I made. That made me feel fine. My father laugh and say:

" 'You man now! You take care your mother.'

"No matter we make mistake, Clarence, and eat too much ham, we *did* it, what we went out to do. That makes a *man*. You must make yourself a man, Clarence. *You* see, you try and pretty soon you feel good—like that. . . ."

Clarence threw himself impetuously down by Tony's knees and seized his kind brown hand.

"Oh, I understand, Tony! I *will*, I *will* try!"

And so he left us. While we are on the subject, Jeffers, I might as well tell you that he never got any farther than Paris, and when his money was finished, he came back to Taos—and you will hear about that later.

I began to wonder what Lorenzo would think of Jaime and whether or no Jaime would be a help to him. I wrote and asked him if I should ask Jaime to Taos for the following summer. But my tales of Tamalpais frightened him and put him off and even plunged him again into uncertainty about life.

You know, Jeffers, Lawrence *had* to have one or two people

completely with him, with their attention undivided, flowing with sympathy along with him, backing him up, being *there for* him. When he had a sympathy with Frieda, then he did not need me, but in Europe he did not have her as he had her, for instance, in Australia. He lost her. She went in other directions. She was naturally interested in others; she went out to her mother and her other relatives. This made Lawrence feel stranded. You know how he says in his article: [1]

"The fact remains that when you cut off a man and isolate him in his own pure and wonderful individuality, you haven't got the man at all, you've only got the dreary fag-end of him. Isolate Napoleon, and he is nothing. Isolate Immanuel Kant, and his grand ideas will still go on tick-tick-ticking inside his head, but unless he could write them down and communicate them, they might as well be the ticking of the death-watch beetle. Take even Buddha himself, if he'd been whisked off to some lonely place and planted cross-legged under a bho-tree and nobody had ever seen him or heard any of his Nirvana talk, then I doubt he would have got much fun out of Nirvana, and he'd have been just a crank. In absolute isolation, I doubt if any individual amounts to much; or if any soul is worth saving, or even having. 'And I, if I be lifted up, will draw all men unto me.' But if there were no other men to be lifted, the whole show would be a fiasco.

"So that everything, even individuality itself, depends on relationship. 'God cannot do without me,' said an eighteenth-century Frenchman. What he meant was, that if there were no human beings, if Man did not exist, then God, the God of Man, would have no meaning. And it is true. If there were no men and women, Jesus would be meaningless. In the same way, Napoleon on St. Helena became meaningless, and the French nation lost a great part of its meaning without him in connec-

[1] "We Need One Another," *Scribner's Magazine,* May 1930.

tion with his army and the nation; a great power streamed out of Napoleon, and from the French people there streamed back to him a great responsive power, and therein lay his greatness and theirs. That is, in the relationship. The light shines only when the circuit is completed. The light does not shine with one half of the current. Every light is some sort of completed circuit. And so is every life, if it is going to be a life.

"We have our very individuality in relationship. Let us swallow this important and prickly fact. Apart from our connections with other people, we are barely individuals, we amount, all of us to next to nothing. It is in the living touch between us and other people, other lives, other phenomena that we move and have our being. Strip us of our human contacts and of our contact with the living earth and the sun, and we are almost bladders of emptiness. Our individuality means nothing. A skylark that was alone on an island would be songless and meaningless, his individuality gone, running about like a mouse in the grass. But if there were one female with him, it would lift him singing into the air, and restore him his real individuality.

"And so with men and women. It is in relationship to one another that they have their true individuality and their distinct being: in contact, not out of contact. This is sex, if you like. But it is no more sex than sunshine on the grass is sex. It is a living contact, give and take: the great and subtle relationship of men and women, man and woman. In this and through this we become real individuals; without it, without the real contact, we remain more or less nonentities."

Lawrence was so strongly individual that he couldn't mix with others. He felt singular with most people. The most he could do was to avail himself of the power, in very rare cases, of another woman. I suppose he merged with the energies that Frieda contained, or that I contained, and felt strengthened and able to do his work and live.

"When *two or three* are gathered *together,* I will grant their requests."

When we are reinforced by others, we are able to answer our own prayers. The psychoanalysts call this an exchange of libido; and other modernists are trying to organize the sum of several streams of energy and understand its power so as to be able to direct it. The latest social form lies in the new group idea that grows, synthetically, out of the tribal or unconscious group activity and tries to avail itself consciously of the united streams of thought and feeling that rise and flow together involuntarily when several people are united.

Orage, in his advanced groups, worked towards this. It was demonstrable that several people could think better and feel more deeply when they did it in unison. The vibrations seemed to be raised. This has naturally always been true, but it has not always been done purposively, with awareness and under observation. It is the only step forward, so far as I know, for one who can no longer be just one by himself, and who cannot *count,* forever, upon his mate. It is more daring, more difficult, and more what is called divine than the love of mates. Lawrence never reached it, though I believe he had an intuition of it. Had he been able to take this step, he would be alive in the world.

He wrote me petulantly when I suggested a new element for Taos. The idea of Jaime did not allure him. And he was too much of an artist to endure the psychoanalytic rigamarole I had been sending him. And, besides, it had enough applicability to himself in it to cause his complexes to duck and hide their heads!

Baden-Baden, 19 Feb.

DEAR MABEL

I can't answer about those diagrams and Jung introvert stuff—it really means nothing to me. I don't really like the mental excitation of it all. Nor the sort of excitation that comes out of de Angulo's letter, and that business of Clarence and the puppy and the "anima." It all seems to me a false working-up, and an inducement to hysteria and insanity. I know what lies back of it all: the same indecent desire to have everything in the *will* and the *head*. Life itself comes from elsewhere.

As for inviting de Angulo to Taos, do as you like. It doesn't matter much, either way.

The little story of Tony is nice: but the road is more difficult than snow and ham.

That *Men Beasts and Gods* seems to me a good deal faked. Anyhow that oriental stuff is a fraud. The middle of Asia there is the old evil destructive center, now about to rouse again and work on us—particularly Europe.

But we have no real faith unless we can see through all that stuff, and then ignore it. Also all this poking and prying into the Indians is a form of indecency.

I feel very unsure about everything,—Taos and everything. Everything seems to take the wrong direction. Why do you send me those clock-face diagrams and ask me to draw you? Can't you see the effect that has on me—makes me just completely skeptical.—However, one just fatalistically makes a move—like Tony's going east.

By the middle of March, I expect we shall be in New York —then we'll decide the next move. Frieda wants to come to Taos.

D. H. L.

I read Arabia Deserta long ago, but shall like to read it again.

Frieda wrote me also from Baden-Baden, a good-natured, cheerful letter reflecting her poise and health. Reflecting also the fact that Lorenzo had shown her my letters, my so intimate letters, sent him to Old Mexico when we became reconciled. I couldn't help squirming at the thought. Yet, on the other hand, she was so jolly and generous at the moment she wrote, one couldn't help liking her and wanting to see her again. There's no doubt about it, Jeffers, Frieda was somebody. Somebody real, hearty, and full of meat. What she lacked in spiritual insight of the kind Lawrence had, she made up for in a volume of zestful enjoyment. She was good company. I could have enjoyed life with her, had it not been for him. In fact, I did have fun with her sometimes, but he always broke it up.

Ludwig Wilhelmstift,
Baden-Baden, 18-II-24

DEAR MABEL

I read Tony's story, which I think is really charming. And you send us lots of interesting stuff. Don't be so terribly energetic. I think, after all, it must be a great strain on you. Don't overdo it, this San Francisco life. Well, we really will appear in Taos. I have a feeling that the Indians did not like us living on their land. I loved that little house and always thought it so nice of you to take so much trouble for *anybody*! as to make such a complete thing! But I would, we both would rather live in the other house, the two story house, and I think Murry and Brett will come too. I am looking forward to it all—and then Old Mexico. We must soon be in New York because of income-tax. I can't write any more because the family sits and rattles.

Love to Tony and you. No, we haven't heard from Nina since we left—

And Lorenzo wrote soon before leaving Europe—preoccupied with the everlasting worry over publishers, whom he never trusted. There always had to be someone he didn't trust; he was so full of suspicion, it had to be directed somewhere or he couldn't have contained himself.

Garland's Hotel,
Suffolk Street,
Pall Mall, S.W. 1
29 Feb. 1924

DEAR MABEL

I think we shall sail on Wednesday, 5th March, on the Aquitania, arrive in New York by 12th March. Send a line there, care Curtis Brown, 116 West 39th St., New York.

I am still having trouble with Seltzer: do hope he's not letting me down altogether.

Dorothy Brett is coming with us: but Murry not yet.

I look forward to Taos again, to space and distance and not all these people.

Greet Tony—Frieda sends her excited greetings.

D. H. LAWRENCE.

Publishers were always a great outlet for his mistrustfulness and he talked frequently about them, relating various horrifying and scabrous anecdotes of his sufferings in the past and his apprehension for what was to come. He had never had a penny from Mitchell Kennerley, who had apparently published *Sons and Lovers* in America in a popular edition. I forget the various complaints he had against the others, both English and American. But one thing should be recorded, and that is that he never seemed to have any real contracts with any of them. Either he was too timid to arrange them, and Frieda was too ignorant of business, or else he simply hoped and trusted that everything would be all right and let it go at that. I know that, face to face with anyone, he was always smiling and polite, for he was afraid of men. It was only behind their backs that he slew them! Certainly where his interests were unprotected, some publishers have taken advantage of him, and he was badly cheated—as, for instance, in the pirated editions of *Lady Chatterley's Lover.* But I do not know that there is anyone to blame but himself, since the world is run by contract, and everyone is supposed to know it.

A last letter from Frieda, and they were ready to sail for New York:

Baden-Baden
10-ll-24

DEAR MABEL

I want to be in Taos by the end of April. We never saw the spring there and I want to see that. And I don't see why, with some good will on all sides, we should not live near each other. Not quite à la Fontainebleau: a community *forced on* us from the *outside*, but we have all reached the same point as far as the world is concerned, and we *must* go *on* further together; nobody else will. Personally I always feel happy these days. Lawrence also is happier here and in Paris. England is really like an unboiled pudding at present.

It would be fun to stay at the ranch, too, for a little while in the spring.—And poor old Granpa dead, that grieves me.—We won't have a friendship like A., "small beer" won't do. You must have had a hard and lonely time, but it's good for one and you have Tony. It must be so difficult to understand each other, you and Tony—such a gulf, it's wonderful, really!

I am looking forward to our new life! Your washing dishes and hating it made me laugh! You don't know how lazy I have been sometimes. Just as one feels!

All good to you.

FRIEDA.

Now the time was come to leave California and go home to Taos; to leave a mild, moist atmosphere, perfumed with mimosa and bay leaves, for the hard, high air of the upland valley where everything is a challenge and where one must be strong to face the sun without wavering.

Change

*Change**

I. *Transition*
    Languidly dying month by month,
    Recedence of life in every cell
    And along the nerves.
    Gradual fatigue of the pigment
    And departure! Departure everywhere!
    Absence.
    O God! Nobody home.

    Motor-power growing fainter,
    Yet, cruelly, enough to keep life
    In this body.
    But not love-life and the love-juices.

    And what is a *body*
    Without love to go on?
    A misery, a doubt, a panic fear.

    The sweet life of the blood
    Has gone out like a tide,
    Leaving the living organism
    Without flow and without flavor.
    All this river of lovely wisdom
    In motion, left to become still
    And to blanch slowly.

    Scarlet days fading out to white,
    What shall I do in white days, God?
    All my years have been
    Crimson, scarlet, and orange;
    How shall heart beat on in this dawn pallor?

* Published in *Palms: Poems*.

157

Heart! Of you no words tell,
Save only:
That where once blood sang,
Now white tears fall here
Onto dry sand.

(Ah! God! Can't You stop
This change?
Can't I stay in my body?)

Even remembrance seeps out.
Remembrance of life
In this way.
Dripping slowly away
Like an inevitable, irreparable leak,
Receding, receding of life
From these centers.
From this precious and lifelong neighborhood,
Uprooting,
Leaving a fluttering fear in the nerves—
Where before ran a brave flame,
A low throbbing along the nerves,
A slow heavy patter is this lessened vibration
Lowered to pain.

Soul gone from the body,
Deserter!
Leaving this congeries alone and in danger,
Utterly gone on an unknown errand,
Leaving a naked and helpless vulnerability.
Death! Come and preserve me!

II. *Intimation*
Be still—be still!
This is not all the truth.
A change is really here,
And not just a leave-taking.

Be still, frightened and shaken one,
The hardy blood was never

Photo Theodore Merrill Fisher.

GATE TO THE BIG HOUSE

More true than now.
Penetrating the new spaces,
Carrying along all that is living
From the old concern.
Breaking camp!

Blessed change!
You see, my own, how the heart opens
To the new occupation?

The magnanimous mountain of the heart
Breaks open to embrace this influx,
Offering freely its eternal fire.
Here in this place, my own,
You receive at last
The power of the virgin.
This is the happy time.

Part Four

Part Four

Taos in the spring is full of a tender excitement. The water that has been turned off all winter from the irrigation ditch runs by the house again, rapid and sparkling. The willow branches along its banks and bordering every creek and river are turning from scarlet to green, and the soft gray buds swell into furry nubbins, while overhead the great cottonwood trees are all a pale blur of young leaves.

There is a south-west wind that blows over to Taos in the spring, and it varies from a kind of pensive, enveloping embrace, wrapping everything in warmth, to a fierce, urgent hurricane thing that drives all the dust up into the air and beats against the trees and the house in a mad invocation. This is the wind that shakes the leaves loose from their buds and that calls to the flowers beneath the earth. The sky grows bluer and more blue, and great white clouds hurry overhead. The Indians are plowing their fields, and the rich, dark earth is turned back in steaming furrows. Everyone is gardening—even the most house-imprisoned women come out to plant some little seeds, marigolds or sweet peas, beside the door.

And all the young animals! Why, Jeffers, every way one looks, one sees the new life. The foals beside their mothers, the lambs and the calves, and, most adorable of all, the tiny, fluffy burros, with enormous, long-eared heads and mild, unsuspecting, dark eyes! Every Indian and Mexican keeps burros to pack wood on in the mountains. They can clamber up the steepest and narrowest trails and carry down a load of split wood of their own weight. It is packed and roped around them in a semicircle and they come swaying along with vastly pregnant shapes.

The air is so sweet in the spring! Do you know that before they break the ground, one can smell the violets and hyacinths? Then, all of a sudden, the hard, wooden branches of the wild plum burst into white flowers, and every narrow road and lane throughout the valley is bitter-sweet with their lovely odor. The Indians' fields are separated from each other with wild-plum hedges, and, looking down from the mountain side, one can see their land mapped out in white-bordered squares. This is the first flower we bring into the house after the winter. Thorny, harsh twigs and branches covered with the small, white blossom, filling the rooms with a fragrance that pierces the heart and makes it rise and fall with a sudden quick emotion. We throw out the dry red and yellow leaves we brought in the fall to fill the jars in the window. It is spring again and the wild plum is in bloom!

Frieda and Lawrence, with their new friend Brett, reached Taos from New York the day before Tony and I came home. They were staying in the big house, and when we rolled through the gate, blowing the horn, Lorenzo came running out to meet us. It was six months since I had seen him, and I had suffered from the separation that began in anger. Somehow he had overcome me. I came back to him willing to be as he would have me be, more gentle and unwillful.

"I *will* be as Frieda is *not*," I thought. "I *will* be gentle and unwillful." Determined to please him, I assumed a chastened mien and instantly, I believed, became like Mary before our Lord!

He opened the door of the car and I saw he was breathless and shaking a little, and his eyes were black with excitement. Our hands fumbled a greeting.

"Hello," we each said.

Frieda came along behind him. I don't know how to describe

to you, Jeffers, the hearty sounds she gives out. Shouts and shrieks, but muffled ones, blasts of energy with her big, wholesome mouth open and her white teeth shining.

I was not so glad to see her, but, springing out, I seized her by the shoulders and planted a kiss on her hard, pink cheek! She started back, green eyes surprised, smile gone. She was not wanting my kiss. Lawrence, who was hauling my bags out of the car, giggled the same faint, small giggle I had heard so often before, and then Frieda and Tony were shaking hands. There was something equal to each other between these two, as they stood shoulder to shoulder, solid on their feet, both real, though differently so.

We made our way into the house. I felt flustered and overcome by the assault of all the impressions that were coming at me from all directions. Tony and I had been away for months on our first long absence from Taos; and on returning to the familiar living-room, with its chests and chairs and pictures that I have lived with for years and years in Europe and New York and New Mexico, everything looked strange and unknown. I live so completely in the moment wherever I am that all other places and things are forgotten, blotted out. When I see them again after an absence, I come back into them with a shock. There is nothing matter-of-fact about it. So I stood there among my things and they were all speaking to me, crying and shrieking to me for notice. And Lawrence was fussing about and saying little things, being polite to Tony, asking him about our trip, and Frieda, recovered from my kiss, was exclaiming something about "the Brett."

"Wonder what you'll make of her."

"Where *is* she?" I asked, looking round.

"She's painting a rose back on the bowl we have for you!" screamed Frieda, laughing heartily. "We bought it for you in Mexico—a wooden bowl. But we used it, and all the pattern came off it. We had it in Europe. But we brought it back to you!"

At this moment a tall, oldish girl came into the room. She had pretty, pink, round cheeks and a childish expression. Her long, thin shanks ended in large feet that turned out abruptly like the kind that children draw. She was an amusing and an attractive grotesque, and her eyes were both hostile and questioning as she came slowly up to me, examining me, curious, arrogant, and English.

She shook hands with me with one limp, pumping motion, and silently handed the wooden bowl to Lorenzo. To be sure, it had a large, pink rose in the center!

"Here you are! Be careful, it's wet."

Brett had stuck a brass ear-trumpet into her ear and was eagerly turning it in all directions to pick up scraps of conversation. Almost always it was pointing at Lorenzo. It had a bland-looking, flat, dipper end to it that seemed to suck into itself all it could from the air, and this had the effect of inhibiting all one's spontaneity. Because it was not a jolly, sociable ear-trumpet that longed to be a part of everything else. No. I soon saw that it was an eavesdropper. It was a spy upon any influence near Lorenzo. Inquisitive, pertinacious, and solitary, it was forever between Lawrence and the world.

He didn't seem to mind it. In fact, he told me almost at once that he had brought Brett along to be a kind of buffer between him and Frieda. "It's a little *too* hard, alone with her," he said. He felt her deafness prevented her from being so altogether present as servants are, overhearing and speculating upon their masters. But he was wrong. She was more present and pervasive than the air around him, for the air at least leaves one alone, while she perpetually swallowed up the life of others, living vicariously upon the misconstructions of her wishes.

Do you think I liked it when I saw that brass dipper swallowing up Lorenzo's talk to me? Good heavens! It was worse than Frieda's restraining presence! She saw my restiveness the very first evening and said, laughing:

"You mustn't mind the Brett. She doesn't count. She helps Lorenzo. She plays piquet with him and types for him." Frieda trying to comfort me for feeling that my relationship with Lawrence was inconvenienced by Brett was a new, strange turn of things!

"My God! I can't stand that brass dipper always between us," I groaned. And Frieda shrieked with laughter.

"Where ever did he pick her up?" I queried.

"She was a friend of Katherine Mansfield's—at least Katherine *used* her. When she died, Brett turned her devotion onto Murry. She had a little house in London and let out rooms in it to Koteliansky, Murry, and others. She was always saving Murry from some designing woman! Murry made use of her, too. We thought surely Murry would come along with us— Lorenzo persuaded them *both* to come. But Murry backed out. She *amuses* Lorenzo. And she's a great help, really. . . ."

In a day or two the Lawrences moved into the Two-story House across the alfalfa field from us, and Brett was given the studio a few yards away from them. The wide double door faced their house, and in it Brett sat all day long, apparently sketching the view of the Truchas Mountains, but in reality watching every move of Lorenzo to and fro between our houses.

We all breakfasted under our own roofs, but they all came over to us for lunch and supper unless it rained or they felt like being by themselves. And so our second effort to live a kind of group life started.

It seemed to me that I never saw Lorenzo alone any more or had him undividedly. I simply detested the kind of group life that had any more elements in it than Lorenzo and me or, at a pinch, Lorenzo and me and Tony and Frieda. The addition of Brett made it richer for Lorenzo, but poorer for me, it seemed. She paid all her attention to him, just as I did, and this is not the way to live a group life. In that way of life all the flow is to a common whole so that each one may share it all at any time; and we were each of us trying to live exclusively, while on the surface we had an appearance of communion. I wanted to flow along alone with Lawrence in the sympathy and understanding we had together. And each of the others, of course, wanted the same thing! He really did not object to a number of sympathies coming his way. He only began to object when Jaime and Clarence appeared on the scene and changed, somewhat, the combination.

Lawrence and I had a few horseback rides again together. The new, strange submissiveness that had come into me affected my courage all the way through and I felt uncertain, as I had never before, of the horse and my control of him. Although I rode my old horse, Contentos, just as before—and he so light and fleet-footed that it was marvelous to be on his back—still I felt quavering and uneasy and timid. Contentos knew me and liked me. He was balky and flashed a wicked red eye at any man who tried to mount him, but he always stood meek as a lamb for me. Once Lorenzo tried to get up on him, and Contentos fought him and wouldn't let him mount at all, and Lorenzo always disliked him for that. He couldn't brook hostility or criticism from man or beast!

Lawrence stood at the horse's head, encouraging me gently as I trembled. My limbs seemed turned to water.

"I am not the same as I was!" I murmured, ashamed. Lawrence grinned. He seemed to like my weakness; was that his idea of feminine charm, I wondered. Once I was up on the horse, we rode decorously away across the desert; no more wild riding with me in the lead and he tearing after me!

Brett watched us enviously. She had never ridden in her life. Her father, Viscount Esher, had kept a racing stable, but he never let his daughters learn to ride. The nearest they had come to horses was staring at them grazing in the pasture when, as little girls, they and the horses were together at the country place.

Now her greatest wish was to have a horse and ride across the desert with Lorenzo; and pretty soon she had her desire and he was teaching her to ride. He taught her to have an imaginative relationship with the horse, to feel she was sympathetically en rapport with it, to feel "the flow" between the horse and herself; but he never did teach her to ride well or to know how to *manage* the animal. She was always afraid of it.

It has been my experience that to the best horseman a horse is a horse, first and last, with no unusual, human traits. It takes a lively imagination to see in a horse what Lawrence saw in St. Mawr, for instance, and imagination interferes with horsemanship.

People seem to be divided into two groups regarding horses. The first group, taking no thought, believing the animal to be inferior to themselves in intelligence and will, just get up and ride, dominating easily and in a matter-of-fact way the little spirit that animates the large bulk of flesh and blood beneath them. The other group innocently imagine that the spirit of the horse is commensurable with his size and his flashing eye; for them power is ponderable and they are secretly unable to conceive how they can ever control a force so much greater than theirs. These people never get over their longing to subdue this creature of their imaginations. But as their conception does not include mastery, they are obliged to take their pleasure vicariously. Hence the enormous popularity of the "Western" movie with its splendid horses: animals with great flanks, rolling eyes, and swishing tails, that are the true heroes of the drama, saving their masters (who by superb command have bent their indomitable wills) from death and disaster, by hair-trigger judgment at the instant of catastrophe. A movie horse is the friend of man. Moreover, he has a godlike power and discrimination, and a fidelity not met with anywhere else. He prefers to have his master on his back rather than not, and he never, never lets one down.

That is the way most people *wish* horses were. Personally, I think horses have their preferences among people, whom they judge more often by their odor than by anything else; but I believe that almost any horse will not hesitate to try to scrape his rider off where the trees are close, because he likes better to go free than to carry a weight. Then, of course, some horses are meaner than others, and some more generous, but *all* need *riding* and riding awareness.

Lorenzo was an anomaly with a horse. While indulging in every conceivable imaginative fantasy, endowing it with his own sensitive reactions, he, with no past training or experience, rode fearlessly, if uncertainly, and had at all times both courage and will. It was as if he combined in himself the two kinds of peoples I have just told you about, Jeffers. While full of imagination, and the kind that lessens one's prowess, too, he yet rode as though he had none.

You see, that was how he was all the way through! He was and he was not; he had it and he didn't have it! He was always double—split in two. He was forever two! He was born on the second of the month and he died on the second of the month. He was the Son—the second person of the Trinity—but (God help all women!) though we tried to overcome and possess him, yet secretly we always wanted him to be the Father!

And, poor darling, his struggle lay between these two rôles. Begotten a son, it was his destiny to raise himself to fatherhood. I imagine that was what he was here on earth for. He perpetually strove to adopt for his own the difficult and lonely rôle of Father, and as often he slid back to the shelter of the Beloved Son. Everything conspired against him. The women who loved him seemed to be impelled to hold him back, even while they themselves most greatly needed his attainment. The vacillation went on forever.

If anyone asks you why he died, Jeffers, tell them that this struggle wore him out. And yet sometimes it is my fancy that he overcame himself. That, as he wrote me, he changed. And it is also my fancy that when he finally succeeded in making that change in himself, he had no more work to do here in this world, and he was let off. Though he loved some things here very much, the flowers and the earth and the little animals, yet most of man's life wearied him. He didn't like it. I think he was glad to be through with it all.

And this story I am telling you, Jeffers, is all about how we all tried to drag at him and wrestle with him and prevent him from having his way. Whichever shape he took, that shape, it seems, we tried to demolish. But there it is! We were, ourselves, like the rocks of your tower, turned and ground against each other and against him by some vast preternatural Sea that gives us our final form and may yet shape us for use in a "Tower Beyond Tragedy"!

Can you conceive, Jeffers, of a happy, humming, active life with a number of people who have, consciously or unconsciously, a sense of *place?* Do the electrons which compose the atom shove each other about and try to displace one another? Does each and every one want *first* place? Or is each one always equidistant from all the others and satisfied to be where it is? It must be so, for had they not some satisfactory law holding them in place, they would all rush upon the atom and smother its life out. As we did Lorenzo's.

What holds the stars firm in their constellations, able to withstand the awful magnetism that must attract them to each other? They abide by their pattern. Why cannot we do so? Shall we ever learn to live in an active, happy, humming group, keeping a pattern and remaining content? Do you agree with me, Jeffers, that this is the next step, and that until we learn it, we shall jostle together and bruise ourselves against one another in our partial freedom, that still is greater than star freedom—but less than what it will be?

When he gave himself up to one, Lawrence enjoyed it. I

remember how he sat in the center of Brett's studio while I
pranced round him, cutting and trimming his red beard. He sat
meek and good like a little boy, a white towel tied around his
neck, and the red bits of hair fell around him on the floor. I
simply adored cutting his beard. There must truly be an old, old
reality in that legend about the power centered in one's hair.
And he luxuriated for a moment in passivity; giving himself
up to it always soothed him and made him temporarily bloom.
Such ease in relaxing, such ease! He smiled, and his eyes were
soft and blue like lupines. There are very few memories of
him so.

Evenings were varied. We always had to be doing something.
Lawrence couldn't bear to just sit, as I told you before. Now we
played mah-jongg, a new game I had brought from California.
Brett and he and Frieda and I played together.

I cannot describe to you my increasing irritation at Brett's
ridiculous ways. She had an annoying habit of employing the
diminutive for anything she could; it was her insatiable and un-
satisfied maternity, I suppose. She wanted to have everything
little. And she talked incessantly, thinking out loud, naming
everything: her feelings, her wishes, or the names of the little
blocks with which mah-jongg was played. With little shrieks,
she would exclaim: "*Oh!* a li—ittle flower-pot!" until I was rolling my eyes and finally imitating her, sotto voce, which amused
Frieda and made Lawrence sore.

One evening when I needed my hair trimmed, I mentioned
it, saying how I hated the town barber. What I really wanted
was to have Lorenzo suggest that he do it for me. I *longed* to
have him shear me. But he didn't say anything, and instead
Brett said, brightly:

"*I'll* do it! Run along and fetch me a little shears. I always
snipped Katherine's for her."

I made a face for Lawrence's benefit that she didn't see, and
brought the scissors and sat down, grim. Lorenzo hovered

round and began to direct her, and Brett slashed into my hair. I could hear her panting a little. She slashed and slashed and suddenly cut the end of my ear off!

The blood ran down and Lawrence palely offered me his handkerchief. I looked at Brett in amazement and, I must admit, in some admiration! She was half snuffling, with tears in her eyes, and laughing too.

"Why, you cut my ear off!" I exclaimed. I couldn't get over it. Jeffers, she hated me, and she was deaf, and she tried to mutilate my ear! That seemed so interesting that I forgot to be indignant. However, I didn't forget to make a good deal of it to the tender-hearted Lorenzo.

The new little Pink House down in the alfalfa field near the orchard was finished and ready to be painted. Clarence had started to build it the summer before, for himself, but when I found that he was having most of my men do the work, I got impatient and wrenched it away from him and said he couldn't have it and that I'd finish it for myself.

"Besides," I said, "it's in Tony's field and would belong to him anyhow, legally." Clarence was blighted and made a great story out of this when he turned against me. Well, anyway, I had finished it. I was getting it ready for Alice Sprague, who was coming to visit me in June.

Lawrence said: "Let's all paint it. We can make some nice decorations on the doors and furniture."

So there we all were with pots of pale-colored paints: pink and light yellow and so on. Lorenzo first painted the brand-new pine-wood toilet that stood off at some distance from the house. Had it been done in green, as I had planned it to be, it would have faded into the landscape and been unnoticeable. But what do you think he did? He gave it a coat of cream-color to make it stand out more than before, and on it he made an enormous design! In the center, coil on coil, and swaying upwards, was a great, green snake wrapped around the stem of a sunflower that burned and shone like the Taos sun. On either side of it he painted a black butterfly as large as a plate, a white dove, a dark-brown bullfrog, and a rooster. Whom all these were supposed to symbolize, I will leave it to you to puzzle out. Certainly they were not just fortuitous forms.

This toilet became a scandalous landmark. It was known far and wide. Tony hated it, particularly the snake, and wouldn't go near it. Finally it faded. One can hardly see the sunflower any more! But, strangely enough, the dove is more clear than ever, in contrast with its faded neighbors.

In the house Frieda was doing an old walnut chest of drawers that had for handles bunches of grapes and leaves. She painted the chest a light pink, and the fruit was purple, with emerald-green leaves. It may sound dreadful, but it looked lovely against the pale adobe wall.

"Oh, it's such fun putting a dot of high light on every grape!" exclaimed Frieda.

"Now on this little round door," said Lorenzo, "I'm going to put the Phœnix rising from his nest of flame." I knew what he meant. I had heard him talk often enough about the Phœnix. He identified himself with it. It was himself he wanted to place there—his sign manual on that house. Well, he put that blithely on the upper part of the door, and Brett was carving out some figures for the lower part. They put their heads together and created a Garden of Eden, an apple tree with red apples on it, a *huge* serpent, and a brown Adam and Eve on either side of the tree. They both liked *doing* things with their hands and I hated to—so that was that. I was just swishing paint round on window-frames and places where I could go fast and furious and where it didn't matter, and I was getting mad. I felt out of it. The others kept up a running comment, Lorenzo giggling and Brett excited.

"Here, put a smile on the serpent," he said, chipping at it and nailing it on the door.

"Here's Eve—the bitch," Brett said, viciously, "*cause* of all the trouble. Here, let's give her a good fat tummy."

And Lorenzo answered, responsively: "Yes, the dirty little bitch with her sly, wistful tricks."

Now, maybe this needn't have made me mad, but it did. I was Eve. I got up and solemnly walked out on them. I was covered with paint, so I went home and washed it off myself and put on a clean dress. When they came over for supper, I was cold and *digne*. I paid no attention to either of them and gave myself all to Frieda.

Lawrence began to frown and cast dark looks in my direction, while Brett jerked her head to and fro like an alert bird, watchful of every move. We finished supper and moved to the table for our game of mah-jongg. I kept myself to myself, cold and stagnant inside, until Lawrence was able to bear it no longer. After two games, he rose and said quietly, but frigidly:

"I don't care to play any more tonight. I think I'll go over to my own house." And he left the room.

In a flash I was after him, opening the door and closing it behind me so swiftly that I found him still on the threshold out in the warm darkness. I put my hands up on his shoulders and leaned up to him in a flood of yearning.

"Oh, *don't* be mad," I breathed. He bowed his head over me until I felt his beard brushing my cheek, and he put his arms about me in an instant's silence. Then:

"Nay, nay, lass," he said, in a voice ever so gentle and low. "I am never really mad any more."

I went into the house and he went on home.

The next morning I awoke in a jubilant mood. As I sat up in my swinging bed on the porch, I looked out on the shining world and thought it was the weather. Below the house the orchard was breaking into bloom, a pale ocean of pink and white flowers; the water ran merrily in the ditch that encircled it; blue-birds flashed by like little rockets in the sun, and meadow-larks sang on every fence post. Oh, life was wonderful, Jeffers, almost too beautiful to be borne! I saw Tony's eyes on me from his swing in the corner. He was lying there calm and meditative.

"Oh, I feel wonderful!" I exclaimed, throwing my arms up over my head.

"Maybe too wonderful," he answered.

"How they want to pull us down!" I thought, angrily, as I jumped out of bed and ran into the house to dress. Usually I waited for Albidia to bring me my coffee on a tray, and I drank it there in my swing and ate my slice of toast and honey while I looked over all our place and saw the life of it going on. Over across the alfalfa field was the barn, and the big corral where the horses stood munching their morning hay while José, our tattered Mexican, ambled round, feeding the pigs, watering the sheep at the trough by the well, or harnessing the team up to the wagon to go off on some errand or other.

Near to the barn stood the little cottage, empty now, but soon to be occupied by Clarence, and next to that, only separated by another small orchard, was the Two-story House. From my perch I could see Frieda come out on her upstairs porch and vigorously shake a blanket over the edge of the low adobe wall, or Lorenzo, as he went to the well for a bucket of water, his shoulders always bent, his eyes on the ground.

"There goes Lorenzo, looking at his feet," the Indians used to say.

Next came Brett, always hovering near her wide-open doors, forever watching Lorenzo—*forever!* Below me, as often as not, an Indian was riding into the *placita* and tying his horse to one of the hitching-posts.

"Hello, Geronimo. How are *you?*"

"Fine!"

Fine!

One day Lorenzo began, for the first time in his life, to write a comedy: a Taos comedy. He laid the opening scene in the morning in our house, with the usual anomalous mixture of people. The guests straggle into the big kitchen, one by one, to breakfast, and Mary Austin is keeping her promise to make us waffles.

"Oh, good morning, Mrs. Austin. How are *you* this morning?"

"Fine."

"Hello, Mabel. How is everything?"

"Fine."

Ida strolls in, looking tragic.

"Hello, Ida. How do you feel today?"

"Fine."

And the young bride and groom join the others.

"Well, how did you like the cabin?"

"*Fine!*"

A tap at the door, and a smiling Indian face peering in.

"Oh, it's Juan. How are you, Juan?"

"Fine."

"Fine—fine—fine! That's all Americans have to say about themselves!" Lorenzo had scolded one day. "I'll show them." And he started to write it. But he never went on with it. Too bad.

Yes, usually I lay there swinging gently to and fro and watching things, but this morning I was too full of energy to be still. I ran right out of the house and over to the Lawrences. The alfalfa field was still wet with dew and full of blue butterflies. I was so dizzy with the life in me that I could not keep to the narrow, board path and I kept stumbling off into the wet grass; and my skirts swished over the wet stalks and gathered up the dampness.

Frieda and Lorenzo were sitting at a small table in the shaded porch, eating their breakfast; and I rushed in and fell into an empty chair beside them.

"Oh, I feel so *good* this morning!" I exclaimed.

"Humph," muttered Lorenzo. Had I not been so dazzled with my inner excitement, I might have noticed how cross he looked. He frowned and averted his eyes from me as though I were a most repulsive sight to him. Frieda, too, continued to eat, holding herself to herself, unsympathetic and distant.

"Well, I do," I went on. "I just feel marvelous—as though I could move the world."

"Well, that's the time you had better look out for yourself," answered Lorenzo, emphasizing his words with sideways nods in my direction, but still not looking at me.

"Hah!" burst out of Frieda—an unfriendly ejaculation.

"Well, what ever is the matter, anyway? Can't a person enjoy good health or *what*?" I retaliated, catching the contagion of ill temper.

"No, not that way," he responded, his eyes on his plate. "You think it's good health, but it isn't. You think it's *good*, but it isn't. It's just sheer unrestrained ego, that's what it is. It's the destroyer. It's the thing that causes all the trouble."

"Oh, my goodness!" I thought. "How they all want to pull one down!" But I didn't care for the moment. My life was burgeoning in me and I didn't need any man's approbation. I raised my eyes and rolled them in a way I knew was infuriating, and strolled over to Brett's. She, of course, had been sitting in her doorway trying to absorb this scene, which, however, had been slightly out of her range of vision, as the Lawrences' porch was sheltered by the wall of the house.

"Isn't it a wonderful day?" I screamed into her ear-trumpet.

"What?" she screamed back, always unable to hear a word I said. "Hay? Is José cutting hay?"

"No!" I bellowed. "You *idiot*," I added in a lower tone, "I said, isn't it a wonderful *day*!"

"Oh! *Day*." She frowned, looking bored and supercilious.

"Well, what of it? What about the day?"

"Oh, *shut up!*" I snapped—and turned homewards.

Tony was making his way majestically towards the garage to take out his car. His black hair was smooth and shining in the sun. He had a white sheet wrapped about his loins and he was the picture of well-being. When he saw my face, he paused and said to me:

"Guess you better ride horseback this morning." Then he got into the car and drove slowly away down the hill; and there was I all alone with my rare good feeling all going wrong inside me.

Yes, we had our ups and downs. And we had, too, some talk from Lorenzo from time to time that made up for all the rest, when his dæmon took possession of him and he became a mouthpiece for the buried life within him.

What a pity that I cannot tell you what he said at such moments, Jeffers! But, strangely enough, all that bright, high eloquence is lost to me. Perhaps there are others living who can remember his words at such times, but I cannot. I can only remember how he elevated one and keyed one up to higher and higher reaches of vision and understanding. I can remember the *feeling* of it, but not the fact, the unsustained elation that was like a wave that leaps beyond its usual range and breaks over a dry and untouched crag.

No, I can remember the funny little everyday ups and downs that made our sparkling uneasy life on the hill; it is for someone else to record the superman that spoke with Lorenzo's lips. But there was another speech he uttered all the time. His flesh and blood were a kind of speech; and to be near him was to be destroyed and, possibly, re-created—though this last was by no means assured to one.

And since I have not registered in memory the words of his mouth, and since it is not description that will contain and define the creative, living Word embodied in him, my hope is, Jeffers, that somewhere in these pages you will discover what he was and what he was doing: the implicit Lawrence with his cherished involuntariness, his spontaneous and undefeatable power.

When we went to the Plaza sometimes to buy meat or groceries for them (because they had no telephone in their house, and, besides, Frieda believed in "picking it out" herself), Lorenzo would hesitate at the door of the car.

"Come along with me, Frieda."

"I suppose I must!" she would sigh, and whisper aside to me: "It scares him to go into new places, like the butcher's, by himself; I always have to go too!"

I shall never forget the time I saw him naked for the first time. It was over at Manby Springs, which is fifteen miles away from Taos and down the steep side of the mesa that supports the upland valley. There one descends again to the Rio Grande River, which is running rapidly in a narrow bed between the two mountain sides. It is a strange place—far from people. One sees nothing living there but the birds—the eagles are soaring far above, and the hawks—and an occasional flock of sheep whose shepherd has come down from the high mountains with them and pauses on his way to a new grazing-ground to take a hot bath and, as Tony says, to leave his whole skin behind him in the water, like a snake. The days the shepherds are there, we turn and climb back up the mile or two of steep trail and go sadly home, feeling thwarted!

The hot water rises bubbling from a sandy surface right beside the river. Old Manby laid a claim to it years ago and built a rock-walled house over it: a room to undress in above, and steep ladder stairs leading down to the steaming pool. The only light in the water room shines down from a small window high in the rough stone wall, and the side where the ladder descends is made of a pile of natural rocks themselves, heaped dark and harsh, one on top of another.

The water itself, Jeffers, is the most wonderful water in the world. Hotter than blood-heat, and so buoyant that it is difficult to keep oneself below the surface! One goes over there keyed up, tightened beyond the normal pitch, by the altitude, aching from the stiff descent from the top of the hill, and, groping one's way down the rickety ladder, one sinks into the dark, grateful spring. Oh, there is nothing in the world to compare with it! "Untied are the knots in the heart," Jeffers—that is what it feels like. When it was analyzed in Denver, it was said to be "highly charged with radium." That is what we need more of on this earth, Jeffers. Radium. My instinct tells me so.

Sometimes in the spring the river outside is swollen from melting snow and ice, and it rises until it reaches the outlet of the spring (for it is rising and flowing out all the time), but the radium water is too strong for the river and holds it back: it hardly makes its way into the pool at all.

It was a most peculiar experience to go over there to that hot spring. The whole thing was like entering a different world and a different epoch. The curious appearance of white bodies shining luminously, pale and green, in the mysterious water, the moist rock walls, one's swift response into an altered being in this real aqua viva—there was something primeval and archaic about it that took one back to other times. The very earliest Greek baths must have been like that.

Perhaps most strange of all, Jeffers, outside the stone house there were two great rocks with faint but indelible incisions on them. On one was a fragment of the Greek key pattern, six or seven inches wide, soft and blurred, but unmistakable; on the other, close beside the entrance to the water, was the symbol of that oldest of human wishes—the dot within the circle, the sign of eternal life.

Our local legend from the Indians is that the people who lived near the river long, long before the Spaniards came, took care of this spring until the white men appeared and heard tales of it; then the Indians tried to hide it from them lest they, too, bathe there and live forever. The Indians wanted to live forever, but they did not want the white men to! So they covered the bubbling water with sand as best they could and, to mark it for their own kind, they cut the sign into the rock—as if to say: "Close by this stone is hidden the way to eternal life."

You can imagine, Jeffers, how Lawrence loved this hot spring. He was at home with all natural, earthy things like that. We used to go over there once or twice a week to bathe. The women would go in first, while the men waited on the sandy little river brink. While we undressed and went into the water, Tony would make a fire and we could hear it snapping and crackling outside as we lay in the soft hot water.

Frieda and Brett and I looked quite nice in that dim place, without our clothes. I was the quickest and always the first one down into the water, and I loved to see Frieda come cautiously down the shaky stairs and reach the flat rock at the bottom. Her Renoiresque body looked like a great pink pearl veiled in the gray mists steaming up in the twilight depths of the cave. Brett was shapely, too, long-limbed and white. Her hands and feet and head were over-small, though, and seemed merely vestigial, like those of a race that is lapsing away.

We luxuriated in the water, which relaxed us to itself and then stimulated us in a different way. Sometimes we heard the strangest sounds coming through the rocks that lay against the mountain side of the pool. From immeasurable distances, far, far into the depths of the mountain, faint, weird, rumbling groans came through to us. These sounds, escaping from some subterranean scene of fire and flame, both awed us and charmed us! We loved the sense of rock-bottom contact with the earth's life.

One couldn't stay long in that water. Five minutes of it and one had reached the peak of efficacy. Any longer than that was a loss of strength. But just enough—and we issued forth into the daylight feeling made over and, in fact, looking smooth and new. We sat drying our hair, that now was soft as silk, by the sweet fire of sage and driftwood, while Tony and Lorenzo took their turn.

I never saw them together in there, but how strange a contrast there must have been between those two men! Tony broad and brown, like a bronze Pharaoh, as Lorenzo called him, square shoulders and shapely thighs; and Lawrence like a thin, white blade, topped with his flaming red beard.

When I first saw him on the beach after he bathed, and he came, clad only in bathing-trunks, to dry himself by the fire, I was struck with the meaning of him. His body was as white as lard and translucent, and one easily saw the bones of the shoulder-blades and the ribs and the thin muscles binding them. His shoulders were high and his long shanks looked somehow swift and very tenacious. That body—it did not seem frail. It seemed, rather, indomitable, with a will to endure as ivory endures, sinewy and resilient.

"Why, what does he look like?" I thought, baffled for a moment. "That tousled head and red beard and eyes like blue stars." His nudity seemed to separate us from him and keep him alone, like a picture or a statue or an allegorical fantasy. He ceased to be merely Lorenzo, and he stood there, a fleshly Word we did not understand. He stood for something. What was it?

Then it came: John the Baptist! Not Peter and not Paul. Certainly not David or Sampson—nor yet Jesus Christ. But John the Baptist—oh, yes!

"I am the voice of one crying in the wilderness. . . ."

Quite suddenly Jaime arrived in Taos. He strode in one day on his rope-soled sandals, his small Spanish feet twinkling in wide, Mexican trousers, his blue béret far back on a head of long, crinkly hair.

Jaime was prepared to worship Lawrence as a hero, and he was determined to impress him. But perhaps Lawrence was prejudiced against him in advance. Although at first Jaime flattered him by attending to him every instant, after a very few days Lawrence was scolding and snubbing him. Of course Jaime, like most other people, had misinterpreted Lawrence's writing and he attempted to please him in the very way Lawrence couldn't endure!

Lawrence himself was outspoken enough, to be sure, but he didn't like other people to be so; particularly he disliked uncouth language from other men. So when Jaime called women bitches, Lorenzo just squirmed. And when Jaime tore off his shirt in the dining-room one day after lunch and strutted up and down, showing what fine muscles he had in his back, Lorenzo looked quite pale and sick and ran out of the room.

"He's not quite all right," he told me, presently. "You must keep an eye on him. Next time he'll rip his trousers off, I wouldn't wonder!"

We all went soon to the hot springs together. When the men came out, Tony was laughing and Lawrence was in one of his rages again, while Jaime was oblivious of both of them. He was declaiming about the magical atmosphere down there, and he said:

"As soon as I entered, I recognized the Power . . . the collective unconscious."

"What's the matter?" I whispered to Lorenzo at the first opportunity.

"He started saying his *prayers* or something, in the water!" replied the incensed Lorenzo. "Closed his eyes and stretched himself out and began to murmur! 'It's the sacred Indian word,' he explained, opening one eye and then relapsing into it again. it's insulting! A man has no business to be so indecent in a nice hot spring like that!"

Lorenzo was simple. He demanded that other people be as simple as himself and never expose themselves as Jaime was always doing, both inside and out! Probably he felt the wonder of the place even more than Jaime did, but it was unthinkable to him that anyone should forget himself and let his ordinary everyday behavior be replaced by an outré impulse to pray! I think you can understand how he felt about that, Jeffers. He was always not only outraged, but pained if anyone acted *queer*! And he felt so sorry for anyone who hadn't enough sense of humor to prevent himself from being ridiculous that he hated him!

Jaime began to resent Lawrence's treatment after a while, so then he turned his attention to Frieda; and she, nothing loath, responded with crescent-shaped smiles and began to primp herself. Lawrence couldn't bear it!

One night after supper when Spud and Tony and Jaime were all there and Ida was up from Santa Fe on a visit, Lawrence jumped up from his chair and ran up to Frieda, who was joking with Jaime, a cigarette dangling from the corner of her mouth. And he began to shout invectives at her, calling her a bitch and so on. And he so out-Jaimed Jaime that the latter was speechless for the rest of the evening. The next day he told me Lawrence was a red fox, and that, after all, Frieda was much the more important of the two, much more of a person.

"None of you people around here appreciate her. You're all *hypnotized* by Lawrence. He's nothing but a neurotic!"

However, he couldn't bear to give up. He ceased to try to impress the man and began to compete with the writer. He produced pounds and pounds of paper and arranged a writing-table in the wide window of the log cabin, where, from the el that juts out from the main, long house, he was in plain view of everyone coming or going. There he sat, bent over a typewriter all day long for days and days. When we went out, we saw him, and when we came in, we saw him. He would lift a pale face and glare balefully out at us without a sign of recognition.

It kept Lorenzo giggling. He called Jaime "your captive

author," and, indeed, he looked like a poor imprisoned devil who had so many pages to do before he could be freed. At meals he scarcely spoke, but stared at his plate in silence.

"He is acting like a writer, I suppose," tittered Lorenzo once.

Finally Jaime came in one night with a roll of manuscript.

"I should like to read it to you," he said, in a low, even voice, with an air of "I don't need to say anything; I can let it speak for itself" about him. We were polite. We grouped ourselves around the fire in comfortable chairs, and Jaime started to read.

I suppose it was autobiographical. And it was meant to be awesome. There were dark pools at the bottom of the garden; there was a monster, half man and half toad; and it went on for pages and pages. My mind wandered and I watched the others. Lorenzo was playing with Lorraine's ears; Frieda was smoking and knitting; Tony was asleep; and Ida was staring at Jaime with a puzzled glint in her large, horn-rimmed spectacles. What was it all about? Would it never end?

"My mother! Oh, my mother!" wailed the monster in Jaime's Spanish voice; and Lawrence flecked me a little look as much as to say: "The *preposterous* fellow!"

The fire was out and the room was cold when he stopped reading. To this day I don't know what he read. I never listened less to anyone, and that is saying much! Jaime was confident he had hit a bull's-eye.

"Well," he said, getting up and trying not to look proud of himself.

"Yes, my dear Jaime, but is it not rather long?" queried Lorenzo.

The last of him was seen the day we all went to the dance at Domingo. He had bought an Indian serape, broad, dark-blue and white stripes. He said he was going to walk home from there to Berkeley. Just like that—he with his new serape over his shoulder!

I am sure he never believed we would let him—but we did.

Towards sunset he started west when we turned eastwards to
Santa Fe: a tiny figure on the broad highway, with his blue
béret and his rope-soled sandals, looking so solitary and yet
with a kind of courage and panache about him.

"How could you, Mabel! He never meant to do it!" cried the
tender-hearted Lorenzo.

A few rods behind our house the Penitente Morada crouches
in the desert upon a piece of the Indian land the Mexicans have
leased or borrowed from the Taos Indians. To the east of it
runs the road they call Calvary, with a great, stark cross at the
end of it, and a pile of the bleached and weathered crosses lie
on their sides outside the door, ready to be taken up and borne
along the painful path.

At various times during the year the Penitentes meet in the
Morada; and inside the room without windows, they beat themselves until the whitewashed wall is flicked with blood. And
besides performing their religious exercises they meet to discuss
political questions. The ruling vote in that part of the country is
a Penitente one.

In the dead of night, dressed only in short white cotton
drawers, they drag the crosses along the road to Calvary, some
singing the strange old agonized tunes of their Order, some
whipping themselves with the flails made with bundles of cactus
at the ends, and one of them playing a wooden flute that rises
above the wailing song in a wild, outlandish, primitive lament.

Most people who come to stay on our hill are fascinated, or
at least interested, in our proximity to this medieval survival.
It is always eerie to be awakened at night by the voices of those
fanatical men ringing out between us and the hills: weird, despairing, lonesome, the shrill notes of the flute rising higher and
higher, and the slap-slap of the flail punctuating it all. . . .

But Lorenzo didn't like it. He rarely took a merely intellectual or literary interest in anything. Either he liked things or he
didn't, and his responses were as instinctive as a peasant's. He

heartily revolted from the Penitentes, and thought them a nasty drawback for our house. He slept inside the Two-story House with the windows closed so as never to hear them, though most people sleep out on the upper porches. He was like the Indians in this. They don't like the Penitentes, either. Yet something drew Lorenzo to the Calvary Road, and frequently he ran over to it and walked up and down that trail, bordered on each side by the sweet sage.

The summer was not coming along very peacefully. Almost all my "submission" had faded away and I was full of impatience and irritation a great deal of the time. Brett annoyed me beyond words. She sometimes had a paranoiac glare in her eyes, directed upon me, whom she quite plainly detested; and I, I fancy, turned upon her an obvious derision that must have been trying.

Frieda and I put our heads together to crab about Brett. She was not "real" enough to get by with either of us, for whatever illusions *we* had, they were not those of grandeur or of persecution. Frieda and I both took directly what we could get of what we wanted. Brett, on the contrary, sat in the doorway of life with her mouth slightly open, like a paralyzed rabbit, and imagined herself in rôles of power and importance. People, in this world, are either hated for going out and helping themselves or detested for fooling themselves into false beliefs of success. Of the two, I think Frieda and I were both content to belong to the former class.

Lorenzo, however, quite liked Brett's devotion. He did not seem to mind her sitting at her studio door watching him. Now, why should he like *her* attention and dislike mine? Every time I showed any particular emotion towards him, he drove it back into me, and this was making me feel rather weak and ill at times. I tried to probe him about her one morning when we were out together on horseback, and he seemed to be in an amenable mood.

"What *is* it about Brett you like?"

"I don't know. Somehow I feel that she has something of a touchstone about her—that shows up things. . . . I can't explain it exactly."

"Something like a Holy Russian idiot?" I asked with seeming innocence, but with inner rage.

"Perhaps," he answered, but with an inattentive voice that forgot what we were speaking of; and with an intense blue look in his eyes, he rode his horse alongside me until his thin leg and thigh brushed against me. I was satisfied for the moment about Brett. I knew he would never do that with her, that he would never, with sudden forgetfulness, unconscious of himself, need, like Icarus, to reach out and replenish himself from her life.

Lorenzo seemed to have these involuntary impulses once in a while. I have seen him, forgetful of the tug of war between them, sometimes suddenly look at Frieda (who might be knitting or doing some other thing, quite oblivious of him) with a concentrated expression and begin to sing softly:

> Au-près de ma blon-de,
> Comme il fait bon, fait bon, fait bon!
> Au-près de ma blon-de,
> Comme il fait bon dormir!

Conversely, if I walked past him in a certain way he hated, or raised my eyebrows, or rolled my eyes, he would hum, and never know it:

> Malbrouk s'en va-t-en guerre!

I was always trying to get him to dance, but he would not. Or was it that he could not? We others—whoever happened to be there—often danced in the evening either over in Brett's studio or in our big room. I loved to dance until the sweat ran down over me. But Lorenzo railed against dancing. He called it an indecent tail-wagging, and he used to spring up in a fury and imitate the motion of the one-step, making it, in truth, quite indecent, but not like our way of dancing.

We never once, any of us, could get him up to dance. Frieda danced, I danced, and even Tony danced, majestic and remote and with his perfect sense of rhythm. But that darling Lorenzo would sit there, alone, with a disgruntled look on his face, and his eyes averted as though he could not bear to see the disgusting sight; or companioned by Brett, who looked at us with Lawrence's expression of disgust, but who was far from realizing that in reality he was longing with all his heart to be merry and carefree and able to let himself go. I *always* knew Lawrence wanted to dance. There were lots of things about him I was uncertain about, but not that! It was too bad; it would have done him so much good.

Something has reminded me of what fun we had doing charades. *Then* he could let himself go! He loved to act and was perfectly unselfconscious about it. We used to imitate each other in the syllables we were acting out and I wish you could have seen him and Frieda being Tony and me in the front seat of the car, Jeffers! We used to laugh until we were tired. One night we acted a scene that represented me taking Tony to Buffalo to introduce him to my mother! Lawrence was my mother, Ida was I, and Tony was Tony! Spud was my stepfather, Monty; and Frieda was "a guest." That was so funny we couldn't finish the act! Tony, wrapped in his blanket, very seriously making deep bows to Lorenzo, who was dressed in a shawl and a big hat, flourishing a horrified lorgnette. . . .

We really did have fun—such fun as none of us will ever have again, I suppose!

By this time Brett had evolved a costume for the West, consisting of a very wide-brimmed sombrero on the back of her pin-head, high boots, with a pair of man's corduroy trousers tucked into them and, in the right leg, a long stiletto! I suppose this was somehow reminiscent of a Scottish dirk for her. It seemed to give her great satisfaction, for she had secret fancies about assault. As a matter of fact, the natives were all afraid of *her*, and one old Mexican refused to drive her up to the ranch, later on.

"Señorita with dagger very dangerous!" he told Tony.

It wasn't long before they began to talk of going up to the ranch to stay, the ranch I had given John several years before. He had named it "The Flying Heart," and it was like that, somehow. The two little houses came to rest on the high flank of the Lobo Mountain as though they had settled there to rest for a moment only. Behind them the pines, climbing up and up and up; before them, first the alfalfa fields, and then the pines; and below to the east and south and west the shimmering valley of Taos, stretching away to the dark crack that showed the Rio Grande canyon, with the river in its bottom. On the opposite side of that was the dry farming country called Carson, reaching to the railroad, thirty miles away; then the whole rim of the horizon sweeping up into blue hills, with the peaks of the Sangre de Cristo range to the east, the Jemez mountains to the south, and the Colorado Rockies to the west.

The little one-story white cottages seemed to have flown over from New England. Surrounding them was, actually, a white picket fence to keep the animals out, and there was one tall pine tree in the yard! You have read all about it in *St. Mawr*, haven't you, Jeffers?

Lorenzo was uneasy down in Taos. It was so plainly to be seen that he longed to be up on the ranch that one couldn't help wanting to put him there; but I was terribly regretful to have him go, and in some ways I felt he needed to stay on our hill. I told him this, and he nodded.

"I can come and see you all the time," he said. "It will be easy to ride down for the day—maybe it will be better so. We can talk. . . ." I know what he meant, loath though he always was to put anything that was between us into words. As it was, we were scarcely ever together without either Frieda or Brett or both, and my irritation at this kept me constantly bad-humored, so the "flow," as he called it, that could go running between us whether people were there or not, if all was well and harmonious—this flow was interrupted all the time. Things were not going well—and it was his instinct to make a change.

Very well. I helped them. I persuaded John to trade the ranch back to me for a buffalo-hide overcoat and a small sum of money! Then I gave it to Frieda. I wanted to give it to Lorenzo, but I knew he would rather I gave it to her, so I did so. They moved up.

Lawrence had a new toy to play with. He loved getting the place all in order, building porches and an outdoor oven. Almost as soon as they arrived there, Frieda sent me a note to say she had written to her sister in Germany for the handwritten manuscript of *Sons and Lovers* because she wanted to give it to me for the ranch. Of course I was thrilled to have that coming to me, but something in the way Frieda put it to me had a sting in it: it was as though they didn't want to be under any obligation to me and sought to balance my gift with another. There was something cold and distrustful about Frieda's gesture—something that really spoiled the whole exchange.

I never altered my opinion about this, or ever cared for that manuscript, once I had it. Too bad that people can't do things more beautifully. I cared so little for that great bundle of finely written pages that Lorenzo had sweated out long ago that two years later I gave it to Brill in payment for helping a friend of mine. I suppose he still has it. I never asked him.

Jeffers, have you ever read Lawrence's essay about being "out of touch" and our need to find our way back to human, warm contact? I think it came out of our dancing there before him in the evenings when he had been locked out of it—barred out by his inhibitions, while probably longing for the simple unrestraint of blood and muscle that we others were showing him. He

was entombed in his recalcitrant body. But I will tell you about
how he found his way out, with the Indians, and once, later on,
after Clarence came, with me.

Sometimes we invite a couple of dozen Indians to come down
for the evening to dance and sing. We light a big fire on the
square, canopied hearth of the studio and perfume it with burnt
cedar and osha root. The Indians ride down in the dusk, wrapped
in their white sheets, on the pattering ponies, and tie them to
the hitching-rails outside the house and go into Tony's room to
change into feathers and bells. Off come the boots and corduroys
and shirts. Moccasins on their feet, loin-cloths and beaded vests,
feathers on their heads, and bells about their knees—that is all
they wear for a party! Their brown bodies are beautiful, for
every inch of them has a gleaming awareness as though their
flesh is wholly awake. One sometimes sees this happy resilience
in a young bride, among us, but it is usually a fleeting thing, for
our bodies are deserted. We do not live in them and they are
like abandoned houses. Of what avail to fly like eagles beyond
the clouds, to count the ranges on the moon, or to talk, over
the sea, to London, when here and now in the flesh we no longer
note the voices that travel across the deep sea of the blood, and
the nerves are silent save in pain, and of the ranges and valleys
of our own white bodies there is nothing to tell?

You see, Jeffers, life, with Indians, is not all in the head, with
the occasional shriek of an orgasm to break the numb silence of
the flesh. No, life is diffused over all the surface of them. They
are forever bathed entire in the flow and wash of it, so that their
limbs have a radiance, and an expression as vivid and speaking
as a smile. Yes, they talk, those brown bodies, and laugh. And in
sorrow and anger their very backs and bellies are more eloquent
than the speech of our lips.

Figure to yourself, then, the magnetism they have that is not
sexually local, as so often with us. It is more powerful than that
and more attracting. It is like a call to awake and to come back

to life. When anyone comes within the radius of the vivid effluvium, the tissues know and react to it even though the obstinate mind tries to hold out against it.

I do not know anything more irresistible than a roomful of
Indians dancing to the drum. The air is filled with life and joy.
And there Lorenzo found his holiday. You should have seen
how he flowed off into it, Jeffers, dancing step, step, with a
dark one on either side of him, round and round in a swinging
circle for hours. We all danced. We danced until we were
fresher and more fresh, lighter and happier. At midnight everyone was joyous with lightened hearts.

You cannot conceive a greater contrast to an evening of this
kind than the usual ball-room entertainment with a tired cynical
orchestra in white shirt-fronts, and the stoical masks of the
anæsthetized dancers dreary and more dreary as the hours pass
by. No, one is communion, and the other is—well, I hardly
know what to call it, for it seems almost like the despairing
ratification and acknowledgment of inexplicable doom.

The bodies in a ball-room, speechless in their nudity or silently
masked in the comic black and white habit of the male, all
seem to betray involuntarily their plight and at the same time
their inability to escape it. *I* don't know what is the matter: do
you, Jeffers? But it is something terrible.

There were two cottages opposite each other inside the whitey-
gray picket fence up at the ranch, and Lawrence and Frieda
went into one of them while they cleaned and painted up the
other. Brett was given a tiny hut near the other outhouses, just
large enough for her cot bed, a small table and chair, and her
trunk. Up there one didn't need house-room, for the mountain
side was like a home. The tall, friendly pine trees stood pro-
tectively around the clearing of alfalfa fields where our horses
grazed. We had kept them there when we were not using them,
and some we kept there all the time, the aging ones and the

colts, and Lorenzo said they must stay right on.

The spring was up above the corrals, and three times a day they solemnly and slowly marched themselves up there in Indian file to drink. The wild flowers were so luxuriant! Mauve columbines, two inches across, and the small red and yellow ones, cobalt-blue lupine, and that strange-smelling yellow daisy the Mexicans call "the angel of death." Lorenzo planted some pansies.

How such a vast and noble neighborhood could have such a cozy atmosphere is a curious thing. But that is how it was: very secure and spacious at the same time. Lorenzo immediately changed its name from the "Flying Heart Ranch," first to the name of the mountain it was on: "Lobo," which means wolf, and then to "Kiowa."

The plan we had was that as soon as their cottage was scrubbed clean and the paint dry, they would move into it, and then Tony and I would do the same to the one they left, and we would have a bed and a few things there and our own stove and cooking things and come up whenever we wanted to. They were to keep on the Two-story House, leaving their trunks with their winter things in them along with most of their good clothes, for at the ranch they only needed corduroys and wash dresses.

They had some Indians camping on the rise behind the cottages, to help get the place in order: Trinidad, and his wife, Rufina, soon called The Ruffian by Lorenzo, she was so hard to move, like a piece of heavy, carved oak-wood, obstinate and stolid, with shining eyes; Geronimo, stocky and virile; and Juan Concha. Sometimes Pondo came up to help with the building and adobe-making, and sometimes Candido. They had Pablo Quintana, the dignified Mexican drunkard, who was an excellent carpenter, for a couple of weeks to make furniture and do the things that were too hard for Lorenzo to manage— though *he* was quite good: he put a porch over the kitchen, supporting it on some carved posts which poor Clarence had intended for *his* house, and he worked on the roofs, reshingling them.

One night when Pablo was very drunk, he called Frieda "Chiquita." Frieda was amused, but Lawrence didn't like it very much. Pretty soon they got rid of him.

The Indians made adobes and laid them in neat rows to dry in the field. It was like a little picture out of the Bible to see them. Frieda scrubbed the floors and windows, and occasionally she came to the door to take a deep breath and look over her domain.

"Oh, Lorenzo, isn't it lovely!"

Lorenzo scurried busily up and down, with Brett behind him. When he hammered, she stood at his side handing him nails. Frieda and I soon started to call her his handmaiden, for that was what she was. As Lorenzo said, Brett was the perfect servant, happy in serving; but it irritated us to see her attending him. She ignored everyone except Lawrence. When he and Frieda had their rows, she always took his part, sitting by with an indignant face, whether she heard what was said or not. It was in their first days up at the ranch that Frieda began to lay off me and to get annoyed with Brett.

There were frequent squabbles over small things. Frieda wasn't very practical—Lorenzo was trying to be. Everything mattered and had an issue in his eyes. Things must be done *right*. In spite of himself, Lorenzo was really very *serious* and it was not easy for him to be insouciant, as he counseled and commanded me to be. But when the evening came and the supper things were washed and put away, if he was not too tired, he could be simple and gay. He liked to sit on the steps and look up at the stars and sing ballads with Frieda or with anyone who knew them.

Up in the Indian camp in the evening a big fire flamed, lighting the upper branches of the pine trees, and the Indians sat around it and sang their songs. So it was peaceful and complete. The full, sweet air fed one, and the silence calmed, and one always had a feeling of occupation, even if one were sitting idle. I used to say that the climate was a career. I suppose it is, because the altitude makes everything in one work a little harder, and one has the illusion of functioning. Certainly the Mexicans, sitting on their haunches at the corner of the Plaza, forming what the Americans call the "Sun Club," have quite a significant feeling of being fully occupied.

After Frieda and Lawrence moved into their house, Tony and I, camping above with the Indians for a few days, patched up the other cottage. I hung a swinging bed between two trees and slept there, and in the morning we cooked over the open fire: good camp coffee, with bacon and eggs. The blue smoke of our fire was sweet in the sunshine that slanted down between the big trees. Happy.

A few of Lorenzo's notes to me at this time supply all there is to tell about these days:

Lobo, Monday

Dear Mabel

Geronimo came up in a carriage—milordo!—so the coachman will bring you this note. I do wish I'd thought to ask you if we could have the adobe tools for a week—we ought to begin 'dobying in the morning, and we want to begin cementing the chimney now, but no trowels or tools.

Later we shall want whitewash—or alabastine or whatever it is—and white and turquoise paint—and brushes.

And a packet of tin-tacks and another pound of putty: hinges for cupboards and screws. These things whenever anything is coming up, on wheels.

Thundering like the devil, and fierce rain. Good you're in shelter. Ponies neighing, trees hissing, Pablo scuttling.

Candido is very nice—he enjoys doing things. We chinked

the end room this morning, it is all ready to plaster. Now we want to build chimney—going to get sand as soon as rain holds off.

My article—Pan in America—will, I think, have to have two parts. I'll see if I can finish first half this evening, and send it to Spoodle to type, if he comes.

Remember the address is Del Monte Ranch, Valdez, N. M. Was that what you gave the postwoman? We've had no mail.

Hope you're feeling better, and *very* comfortable, by way of contrast.

A rat and chipmunk and squirrel-enlivened night.

D. H. L.

And the loan of the little grindstone.
I wish Contentos was sold—he spoils the other horses and he'll never be good to ride any more.

[Poor Contentos! Poor Lorenzo! After these years Contentos is still alive, but blind and old, and Lorenzo is dead!]

Monday Evening

Like a fool, I let the man go without this letter. Send it to post.

Ask Tony if anyone in the pueblo will let me have a sack of fine straw—almost chaff—for plaster. But don't bother about this—I'll manage with the rough, unless the other turns up easily.

More rain—but hot again.

Been a very busy day—very satisfactory.

D. H. L.

Wed. noon

Dear Mabel

Sending this by Pablo—he is just leaving—not quite finished shingling, but near enough.

We will come down on Saturday if you wish it and if you send the car. Trinidad and Rufina say they want to go down for the week-end—and in that case we can't leave Brett. But if they stay over Monday, Brett will stay here.

We have washed and painted the other house—looks a different place. Thunder and lightning and deep hail—very cold. The devil's in it.

No news this end—nothing happened.

Hope you are feeling well.

D. H. L.

Extra things ordered in today's letter (by post to you)

  20 lbs potatoes

  1 tin bowl

  1 lb putty

  dressed lumber: 2 planks 1 x 10, 3 planks ½ x 6" or by 8"

Monday

DEAR MABEL

Of course I forgot a bit of my list, in this rush: baking day, too. If not too late, will you ask Gerson's to send these things in the wagon. And, as you come, if you feel like it, will you call at Wayne's and bring me 3 doz eggs! It's the low cellar-like house on the road between Seco and Hondo, about ¼ mile out of your way, when you come by the Whiskey Distilleries— about ¼ mile straight forward along the road to Hondo, where you leave it at that little sign 5 miles to Del Monte Ranch— the turning you take to bring you to the top of the Valdez canyon.—A long, low white and black shanty on the right.

And would you mind asking the bank for a book of cheques for me.

Don't bother about the eggs unless it amuses you to see that place, with all its chickens.

D. H. L.

Lobo, Wed. Evening

DEAR MABEL

Your mail came—thanks for Delight Makers—yesterday—

so sorry the pains—we felt uneasy about you. Best keep warm
and still. Frieda too had pains today and spent a good deal of the
time in the camp hammock. She's better this evening. One has
days of discouragement.—I wonder what Clarence will really
be like! I think we shall like him. Jaime is simply an imperti-
nent, through and through. No more of him, no matter what
works or doesn't work inside him. I'd rather have heard from
Ida.—I think the Spoodle is really nice, in the last issue.—I
know the Brett is a terrible sloven—but don't bother. Another
letter from Murry—still putting up little catty defences—
leaves me cold. Letter from Seltzer, saying business is still very
bad, and I am to be careful with my money, not spend much.
But the advice would sound better from a different source.—
John Concha must have been mad with us all to have neglected
those mares. I feel mad with him. I always like my three Indians—they try to do all they can for me, so nicely. The walls
of Jericho (the log cabin) are re-built, and chinked and chinked-
plastered outside, and inside end room. But alas, lute is rifted,
they couldn't get on with the chimney, rocks were too lumpy,
not flat enough. So I had to send Trinidad for William's wagon
with more straw, and we've started making adobe bricks—34
made this late afternoon—look very nice, lying in rows in the
field. It rained on them a bit, just to show that even a 'dobe is
a naked dog. Pablo was rather tiresome for two days. I wished
him anywhere but here. Today he's "good" again.—Lamp glass
has just cracked.—I think the man's drawings are good. I don't
feel myself competent to do anything at all serious. Don't talk
of more houses—what with Jericho and Rattenheim, I feel I'm
deep in. But heaven knows what we'll do in the future. But for
God's sake, let us be our best selves, and be friends. When we
are our best selves, we *are* friends. I haven't finished the article
yet—too many things to do, till late evening. But I had said the
things you wrote about the Indians, differently. At present I
feel a trifle discouraged, don't want to write. We shall be ready

by 10 o'clock Saturday to come down to Taos, but if the motor-car is any bother, we will ride horseback.

D. H. L.

Candido says he'll stay the week-end all alone, and then go down to the Pueblo on Monday. We might like his brother. Geronimo doesn't like to ride horseback. I said, if you sent the car, he could go down with us. He *arrived* in a little carriage. Tony might tell the man of the little carriage not to come, if Geronimo is going down in the car.

And this from Frieda:

I looked for you to-day, a very perfect day. Sorry you felt so ill. I also did think the Lord wanted me higher up, but am better! I think Lawrence gasped at the idea of another house, no, lend us one of the others. Nice to get such a fat mail. We are looking forward to coming on Saturday—the change and getting away from the work. I lay in your hammock all afternoon in the sun. My mother writes *sadly* that we are so far away! Well, Haime can keep *his* sanity all to himself! Last night we went for a beautiful walk and heard the Indians singing far away! Pablo was horrid but has recovered. I *like* the different attitudes of the Indians towards work. Not so efficient, but a game and life in it, that's why adobe looks so pleasing.

Much love and get better.

F.

You see those words about my feeling ill? Every time he slipped away, I had a queer relapse into psychic emptiness as though the bottom had fallen out, and the queerest feeling of dispersal, as though my elements were "just a pack of cards," as in *Alice in Wonderland*, and Lorenzo had let them fall and scatter. It made one feel quite weak and inadequate for a few days.

Meanwhile Clarence returned to Taos. Debonair and distressed, with shining waves in his ash-blond hair, agonized eyes above his white silk shirt, Clarence was so graceful and intelligent that one had to forgive him for being neurotic. He was amusing, Jeffers, and his imaginings were as ingenious as De Quincey's.

He became inflamed with the idea of Lawrence before they met and, I think, attributed to him in advance those characteristics that belong to either the Hero or the Devil, according to the angle from which one views him.

As our cabin was in readiness, we could go up any time. I had made a present for Lawrence, a contribution to their new house. I had turned the studio, where Brett had been, into a carpenter shop, with a long table and all Tony's shining tools: saws and chisels and planes. And there on the floor of the large room I wrestled with two-inch boards until I finally manifested a great chair. It was more or less like our Spanish arm-chairs, only much larger. It was wide and deep and it weighed pounds and pounds. I carved it a little and cut up a fine old blanket to upholster it, with shining brass nails. It was intended to become Lawrence's very own chair. I fancied him always sitting in it and always writing in it. One of those dedicated pieces of furniture that would slowly become associated with him.

When Clarence came, he found me in the studio. I was lying on the floor on my back, and the chair was on top of me. The sweat was running and I was panting, he said, when he described the scene afterwards.

"I thought it had thrown her down and was stamping on her," he said.

Anyway I conquered it. Then I painted it pale pink, for the blanket was that color, and I put a few touches of green in the carving. I can see it seems perfectly frightful, Jeffers, but really it was attractive, and, strangely enough, it was a perfect portrait of Frieda!

Finally it was finished and we hoisted it up on a wagon, where it loomed and swayed like the seat of honor in a triumphal procession, and José drove it up to the ranch, pale and majestic through the dark trees!

Well, Lawrence took an immediate dislike to it, called it "The Iron Maiden," and quite soon had it moved over to our cottage!

Clarence's first experience of Lorenzo set an impressive seal upon his mind that he never got over. Tony and I hadn't been up to stay at the ranch house since the Lawrences had been there, so now that the cottage was ready, we decided to go for a few days and to take Clarence. So we got our groceries and blankets together, and Tony took his gun and we motored up.

Now, although Lorenzo wanted us to use that cottage and wanted to see us and wanted a group life and wanted us to be peaceful and gay all together, the minute he saw us arriving, he hated it. He was not smiling and eager, he was nervous and frowning. My heart sank and died in me. Oh, dear! That wasn't going to work, either! Tony calmly unloaded our things and carried them into our cottage. He was imperturbable enough, goodness knows, for one who had been as extremely mad as he had been when I confessed I'd given away the ranch and really had no more right to pasture our horses there or let the Indians go up and stay there when they were hunting. No, Tony was philosophical. He dumped all the things on the floor of the cottage and took his gun, and "with deiberate speed and unperturbed pace" he descended into the trees to hunt porcupines, for he had pointed out to me on the way up the damage they were doing. They eat a band of bark right around the tree, Jeffers, and that kills it. That's the way we lose our pines in this country.

As I put our things away, I heard a shot, and from the window I saw Lorenzo staring off down the field with a dark, angry look on his face. Presently Tony came up smiling and chewing pine gum. He had his gun over his shoulder and in one hand he carried a porcupine, head down, with all the quills hanging over backwards.

"Shot a porcupine," he announced, with satisfaction.

"I don't want any shooting here," said Lorenzo, angrily. "I *like* the porcupines."

"They going to kill all the trees if you don't keep 'em down," said Tony, stubbornly. He took the porcupine and climbed up to the camp above on the side of the hill, where the Indians were already cooking their supper. He wouldn't go down again that night. He and Clarence put up a tent and got it ready to sleep in, while I had to sleep below in our cottage.

Well, in fact it was much pleasanter up there with the Indians. The fire made a bright, warm neighborhood, and the happy Indians chatted and sang in their joyous ease, while down below, one felt a constriction and a gloom. Not a sound reached us from them. We were as separate as families in apartment houses!

I mulled it all over in my mind, understanding, but not liking it. Lorenzo was proud in his spirit—noli me tangere—at home on his own bit of land—proprietary. No one had a right to assume anything or to take things for granted without asking first, certainly not to shoot the animals on the place. What if they did kill the trees? They were his trees now; he had not asked anyone to save them for him. Better to lose all the trees than to have one person invade the strict privacy of possession and be too much at home in the radius peopled by his spirit. No one must be able to arrive like that and walk in and be at home on his place—no, not though he had said to come. Thinking about it was different from having it happen. Very different. No one shall open that gate and walk in and be at home. No one. He brooded on the fate of the porcupine and finally got it out of him in an article, "The Death of a Porcupine." Only he had himself shoot it, not Tony.

Clarence was looking portentous in the firelight. Tony was laughing at me from time to time. That night we all slept well, but I woke up angry and unassuaged. As I dressed, I felt angrier and angrier, and by the time I left the cottage in the high, early sunlight, I was furious. I stepped off the porch and stalked up the path. As I passed Lawrence's window, I walked with my head up and my starched pink gingham skirts swinging from side to side.

"*Ridiculous* creature," I shouted to myself. "Simply doesn't *know* how to behave! One just can't *bother* with him! Life's too short!" I flounced by, radiating independent angers of my own, not caring if he saw me, hoping he did!

After breakfast up there, I began to feel better. That is, more easy. Carrying along the customary inner argument, I was advising myself to be more lenient with poor Lorenzo. "Remember he is nervous and troubled," I persuaded myself, indulgently.

To Clarence, I said: "Go down and fetch Lawrence up here. I want to talk to him." Clarence looked scared.

"My *dear*!" he said in his careful voice. "Do you *really* think I'd better?"

"Certainly," I answered loftily. "He must be feeling terrible. I'll *fix* it."

"Well, I guess I go hunt some more," said Tony, getting up. His one idea was to escape that fixing scene! Clarence walked gracefully off, picking his way daintily among the flowers. He came back almost immediately, wringing his hands, his face white and solemn.

"*Well.* That man is *terrible*!" he exclaimed. "Do you know what he said? He said: 'You tell her if she wants to see me, she can come where I am; if she doesn't want to do that, she can leave!'"

I sprang to my feet like a battle-horse when it smells powder, and rushed down to Lorenzo's house. There he was, puttering among the breakfast dishes, while Frieda was looking smug, and Brett was the picture of righteous indignation.

"Will you please come over to my house?" I asked Lawrence in even tones, standing before him with my hands folded. "I have something I'd like to say to you. Alone." He nodded. I turned and led the way and he came along. When we got inside the room, I slammed the door and, crying in a loud voice: "How *can* you treat me like that?" I burst into loud weeping and flung myself down on the unmade bed.

Well, I wept and I sobbed and I cried. The tears flowed like rain-water and I shook the solid bedstead. Lawrence sat by my side on the tumbled sheets, bent over, his hands clasped between his parted knees. He couldn't get a word in edgeways for quite a while, but when the worst part of the storm had subsided, he said:

"Well, I can't stand a certain way you walk. As you went by my window this morning . . ."

"Oh! Oh!" I interrupted, sobbing at him, "you want to *kill* me, that's what you want!"

"No—o," he replied, in a hesitating voice. "Not exactly."

I can't tell you all that was said, Jeffers. I don't remember. I remember the pleasure of the strong struggle and the pleasure of breaking down, and the pleasurable luxury of weeping myself away until nothing remained but a weak, childish bundle on the bed, and a crumpled sheet soaked with tears. We both enjoyed our morning, I think.

After quite a long time had passed, Frieda came in and looked over the situation. Lawrence was still sitting with his head down and the waterfall passing over him. I was sobbing energetically. Neither of us paid any attention to her. She looked quizzical, but seemed rather to like it, too, for she stepped gently out in an uninterfering way, as one who would not poke herself into a death-bed scene. She left the door open, and after that nearly everyone walked by and took a good look into the room.

It was quite an event. No one had ever heard of me weeping, much less had an opportunity to observe it. The Indians went by, Brett went by, and Clarence went by. Tony, of course, did not.

The whole morning passed. Work was neglected, for no one had anyone to direct him, but it didn't matter. It was a great gift I made Lorenzo that day. I knew it at the time, as I know it now. I kept my sobs jerking up long after they had naturally subsided. I really made the most of it. When I couldn't cry any more, no matter how I tried, I got up and washed my face.

"Oh! I feel *wonderful*," I exclaimed, in a weak voice, though I knew I might be setting him off again with those words. But it was different.

"A little is good for her—any more might be bad," he said, tenderly.

"Oh!" I thought, indomitable still, "no matter what it costs, I *must* keep this going."

We drove home to Taos, and that was the first and last time we stayed in the cottage. It was soon turned over to Trinidad and the Ruffian and the chipmunks.

Clarence was simply dazzled by Lorenzo's power. He had had an idea that I was an immovable object since the day he first came to Taos, but now he had seen me dissolved. He began to long to be victimized himself by Lorenzo, for he felt instinctively that *Lorenzo's* power gave promise of greater persecutions than mine.

Poor Clarence! Something in him was always looking for trouble, though he thought he wanted peace. He came to Taos, he had told me bitterly the summer before, to find peace, and what he found was torrential!

"People who want peace," I'd replied to him, "shouldn't try to moor their boats in mountain torrents."

Lawrence liked Clarence. He told him that he always judged people by the backs of their heads, and that he liked his round

one, with its short, waving hair like a wet spaniel's! And
Clarence began to turn all his attention upon Lorenzo. When
they came down for the week-end, as they usually did, the two
of them rode off alone into the desert together every day. I saw
them come riding slowly back, walking their horses, their heads
close together in confidential intimacy.

And now Clarence began to get silly. He invented a little
dark-red velvet coat with full sleeves that he had made by the
village dressmaker, and he trimmed it with Navajo silver but-
tons. Although it was quite becoming, at the same time it was
perfectly revolting. Instead of opposing Clarence in this fool-
ishness, Lorenzo appeared to like it; and Clarence rode off by
his side, looking as sumptuous as a figure from the Renaissance.
That was in the days before anyone but Navajo Indians wore
velvet in the desert. Now, of course, everyone does. Poets, Harvey
couriers, chauffeurs, flappers, newspaper men, and shopkeepers
—they all wear velvet, and the Navajos are beginning to prefer
white shirts and leather coats!

You can imagine how much any of us liked to see these two
going off into an exclusive tête-à-tête all the time! There was
another woman there now besides us three: the friend that had
sent Clarence to me in the first place. It was dear little Alice
Sprague, who had come to stay in these early summer days. She
went into the Pink House and every morning she walked across
the alfalfa field in a full-skirted, white muslin dress, and with
her graying hair parted and smoothed down, and her uptilted
smile under her round brow, she looked like a drawing by Da
Vinci. She was one of those who determinedly see only the best
in anyone.

Clarence was in the small cottage directly across from us that
came next to the Lawrences' Two-story House. He had arranged
himself neatly in the tiny rooms, with his typewriter on the
table, and an ample pile of paper. He always meant "to write."

Lawrence was like the rest of us in his inability to be inclusive.

He couldn't sweep a number of dear ones all at once into a wide embrace. It had to be *this* one or *that* one or t'other. Someone was always left out in the cold. Now several of us were out in the cold, formidable ones, too! Yet for a while we maintained the pattern of a group. We continued to go places and do things together.

One of these excursions was a horseback trip from the ranch to Taos by way of the waterfall. Over above the village of Arroyo Seco, high on the side of the mountain, there is a rocky cave. We had to leave our horses and climb up by a trail that is nearly obliterated, through pines and cedars and tall grasses, by a thin stream that would lead anyone to the spot if the trail were lost. Winding in and out and finally rounding some huge rocks, we came to the opening. It is a place the Indians feel very strongly about. They will not camp near it, for, they say, there are bad spirits there.

The vast, pelvic-shaped aperture faces the west and yawns upward to the sky; and over it descends the mountain water, falling thirty feet across the face of the entrance to form an icy pool below. We skirted the waterfall and entered the cavern; chill and damp and dark it was, too! Here there are holes hollowed out in the rock walls where Tony says the bears sleep in the winter; and at the right-hand side of the back wall of the place there are a number of rude climbing steps that lead up to a shelving ledge. Above this altar-like ledge there is a faint sun painted high up to the east of it. One by one we climbed to the high altar, and, looking before us, we saw the clear fall of water across the opening, green and transparent.

It is an ancient ceremonial cave, Jeffers, and truly it is full of strange influences. Once I went there with an archæologist, who wanted to make some notes about it. I had been there several times before that day and had always been conscious of the faint, far-away echoes of other times that are encountered in the dim, queer atmosphere of the place—but nothing out of the way had happened. But the day I went with that professor, all of a sudden I became conscious of unfamiliar fragments of impressions that were striking into me, awesome and terrible, but incomplete. Half-thoughts that were not mine collided in my brain with the remainder of consciousness that was my own. Terror and doom struggled to overcome my quite legitimate and conventional wish to remain my natural self and not to seem queer to a stranger. He was talking to me, and his voice echoed in the domed rocks as he noted the painted sun, the altar, and the waterfall cutting across the far-away western horizon. I wanted to tell him how, at the winter solstice, when the water has turned to an icy column, as the sun turns to go south, it shines through the erect, transparent pillar of ice and falls precisely upon the altar. But I could not tell this thing. I had forgotten my own language—completely and definitely. I could almost think in English, but I could not remember the sounds of the words. Instead, another language was in my mouth. I could have spoken it, but that was the last thing I wanted to do. All I could manage was to keep quiet and occasionally to nod a response.

It was not until we were home again and at lunch that my accustomed speech returned to me. It was more than aphasia, for I believe with that there is only blankness, and this was a positive experience of something dim and unfamiliar, something strong and terrible and not to be forsworn, a floating relic out of the stored past that haunted, yet, the walls of that place. I never can go back there without a shudder. Of course I had told Lorenzo all about it, and that was why we went there that day. We had a beautiful ride home through the dusk. The sky was pink and gray.

Still we danced in the evenings and still I tried to make Lorenzo dance with me, and always he refused, angrily. Clarence danced beautifully, and Frieda sometimes glided about with him, though Lawrence couldn't bear that at all. It usually precipitated a scene. Little Alice Sprague sat among the lions like a protected saint. She continued to smile and smile and to consider Lorenzo an avatar, and Clarence a potential genius. Frieda she considered a beautiful woman, and of me she often said that I had "great power."

I wonder just what a visualization of her conceptions would be like. How near do these blessed creatures come to the truth? She was certain something wonderful was coming out of the summer with all of us together. She believed intuitively that we were all gathered there for a reason greater than our separate wills could devise.

We drove up to the ranch quite often, though we never stayed the night any more. We went up for tea or to bring the Lawrences down for the week-ends.

One day I found Lorenzo had made a copy of "The Man with the Sunflower," quite a good little copy from a colored print of it. It seemed to me an emblem of himself. I saw him so, and I knew he saw himself so. I wanted it and he said I could have it.

Then, lo and behold! Brett, who had been watching this little passage, quietly removed it from my side while I was drinking tea on the porch, and hid it somewhere in the house! Of all the impertinence! I was off in a tantrum as soon as I discovered it. I rushed into the house and overturned things until I found it behind something on the chimney-piece; but Brett pursued me and snatched it away again.

At this point Lawrence came into the house looking embarrassed and pained at this unseemly scrimmage. I didn't care. I couldn't *bear* to have anyone try to oppose me—particularly Brett, for whom I had all the contempt that a realist has for a sleep-walker.

"Come, come," murmured Lorenzo, looking worried.

"Well, what do you *think*!" I exclaimed. "I suppose I'm not going to let that *hag* decide things!" I fled after her and caught her as we circled the house.

Their life up there was nice. Lawrence wrote in the morning
after he had finished the chores. It is to be admitted that Brett
did all she could to help. After they had all worked hard to
clean out the spring, they had to carry pails of water from there
to the houses; and there was wood to be chopped and washing
to do. Frieda sewed a great deal. She embroidered a tapestry to
cover the back and seat of a chair Lorenzo made, a delicate,
decorous chair compared with the Iron Maiden!

He used to go down and sit under a pine tree and write on
his knees—a small, neat, clear handwriting, with hardly a change
on the pages. In the afternoon he worked along with the Indians, who liked him very much. Brett worked with them, too.
That is, she did what she could. When there was nothing else to
do, she handed things. While he wrote in the morning, she typed
out his previous day's work, or she painted rather thin pictures
of the desert. Once they all collaborated on a large picture of
the ranch with the desert below, and all the animals on the
place, and themselves flying along on horses. They had fun together and I envied them, because they liked to *do* things!

Once in a while *I* could do something, too, though. I painted
a picture of a procession of melancholy, bowed-down Penitentes,
carrying great crosses along to Calvary in the moonlight. A pale
moon over the shadowed foot-hills was half obscured by hurrying storm-clouds that took the forms of great women with
their heads back, exultantly galloping over the sky on white
horses! I entitled it "The Heroes" and sent it up to Lorenzo. He
smeared the women out (with a wet forefinger, I guess) and
hung it in the other cottage! I don't know why, but all *my*
inspirations were satirical. Of course, some of his were, too,
weren't they? That Adam and Eve—and that toilet!

Lawrence was growing more and more confidential and intimate with Clarence. I probed the boy and removed many poisonous bits about myself from him. Apparently Lorenzo was always complaining about me.

"He says your will is on him," Clarence told me. "He says when he is up at the ranch, he can feel you sitting down here *willing* him!"

He was all for Lorenzo now. He sympathized and took his part against me. I couldn't adjust myself to these constant changes, and my spirits sank. Still I kept my head up and hoped for a happier day. It was true that my will was upon him, but not, I thought, for evil, but for a longing that he cease vacillating and shifting and become steady. A steady flowing of sympathy and good feeling was what I wanted, so that my own feeling could flow out to it in response. No one could dam me up like Lorenzo. On the other hand, no one could, with a word or a look, release the living stream like him.

I tried to explain and clear it by letters, *patiently*. I tried to forget how disloyal I felt him to be to something that I knew he, too, reckoned precious. I put aside the realization that my letters must be read by Frieda as well as by him, and I brought right into the open the fact that we needed to keep alive for both our sakes the little bit of reality between us. While I was at it, I wrote what I thought of Brett, too, and her ludicrous attitude towards him.

"We have to have our Bretts and our Clarences," I said, "but we need not take them too seriously."

He replied instantly:

Lobo, Thursday

DEAR MABEL

Your letter about "flow." Anyhow, how can one *make* a flow, unless it comes? To me it seems you always want to force it, with your will. You can't just let it be. You want evident signs, and obvious tokens, and all that. On Saturday evening, you can't just let one be still and let the flow be still. You want to "do things" to me, and have me "do things" to you. That isn't flow. I only wanted to sit still and be still on Saturday evening. Must I then exert myself to dance or to provide entertainment. I never ask you to exert yourself. I wish to heaven you would be quiet and let the hours slip by. But you say it's not your nature. You'll say it is your nature to "do things" to people, and have them "do things" to you. That wearies me. Even you apply your *will* to your affection and your flow. And once my own *will* is aroused, it's worse than most people's. But I do assert that, primarily, I *don't* exert any will over people. And I *hate* the electric atmosphere of wills. You'll say it's because I just want my own will to predominate. It's not even that. It's that I want my will only to be a servant to the "flow," the lion that attends Una, the virgin; or the angel with the bright sword, at the gate. That is all I want my will to be. Not a rampaging Lucifer. But in you, even your affection is a subordinate part of your everlasting will, that which is strong in you.

If the problem is beyond solving, it is. Who knows. But there's the problem. How not to arouse these bristling wills of ours—they're in all of us the same—and admit a natural flow. The moment *one* exerts a will, the whole thing rouses in all the rest of us. And hell to pay.

And of course it's so much easier to flow when one is *alone*, and the others are just thought about. As soon as two are together, it requires a great effort not to fall into a combat of wills. Even wrestling with one's material.

As for the apple-blossom picture, the symbolism, the meaning, doesn't get me, so why should I bother about it.

D. H. L.

I know that the only way to life at all, is to accept the invisible flow. And the flow should be manifold, different sorts, not exclusive. As soon as you try to make the flow *exclusive*, you've cut its root. Only one has to guard against false flow—which is *will* in disguise—like Lee Witt or Bynner. Even with Brett, if you'd take your will off her, she'd be all right. But you won't.—It's no good *insisting* on "flow." The minute anybody insists, on anything, the flow is gone. And I *know* when the real flow is gone there is nothing left worth having. And perhaps I have a fatal little germ of hopelessness. Because, of course, your letter stops Frieda's flow, and her will starts up in a fury—as yours about Brett. And what then? Then my will is up in arms, and it's only a fight—useless all round.

This letter did nothing towards increasing the harmony. I felt it was unjust and without his usual insight and I decided to stay away for a while, so I tried to put them all out of my thoughts, and Alice Sprague and Clarence and I motored about together and tried to be happy. But nothing was as vivid as when Lorenzo was in the neighborhood! Life seemed more commonplace without him, and after a few days had passed, I wrote to him again and said they must come down for the week-end. I told him in that letter that it was no fun to rattle up to the ranch for tea and back, and that it wasn't worth the trip; that I liked hours and days or else nothing.

Lobo, Thursday

DEAR MABEL

Has your Mrs. Sprague come? If she has, do bring her up here to see us.—I wrote and asked Bynner and Spud to come for a week, to try how it is.—Soon I want to come to Taos too —but not for the week-end. Think it would be better *not* a week-end. Sundays are better away from civilisation. How are you? —Time passes quickly and quietly here. I ride every day, if only for the milk. Brett has walked off to Gallina to try for fish. I began to write a story. Am getting used to this place and its spirit, then one likes it. F. is dozing—she had a cold. I'm just riding down with this to catch the mail-man.

I hope you are well. Come and see us if you want to, but whatever you do, don't "rattle up to the ranch and back." As you say, no more of that. But it needn't *be* that.

Greet Tony and Clarence.

D. H. L.

Geronimo isn't a man of his word—he has never turned up to build the oven. If you are coming, I know you won't mind bringing the goods from Gerson's. If you are not coming, Ted Gillett will bring the things up. Don't you bother in the slightest.—But come and see us.

I missed the mail—bad luck. Ted Gillett won't be going down again—he's gone today—but Louis Cottam will be coming here on Monday, he'd bring the things.

No, I didn't want to go and see them. I wanted them to come and stay in Taos. So I just sent the things they asked for, and again I urged them to come for the week-end.

Thursday

DEAR MABEL

Many thanks for sending up the things. The saddle will do very nicely—only it's *hard*. I'll send a cheque when I've got one—my book is empty. We forgot to ask for Frieda's brown trunk: someday when you're coming alone in the car and sitting in front, would you perhaps put it in the back. The weather is calming—and the raspberries coming ripe—if you come up, we'll be quite quiet and peaceful.—F. has got the diarrhœa—seems a bit of an epidemic—so we won't come down this week-end. Emilie's sister came with the wagon—her husband—nice people—stayed the night. They'll bring you this note.

D. H. L.

Finally one morning they sent word they were coming late

Saturday afternoon. That same day George Creel arrived in Taos
to spend one night and I had to ask him to dine. I had known
him quite well in the old days in New York. He was married
now to Blanche Bates, the actress, and he had with him a young
Englishman who was Blanche Bates's leading man at the moment. Very attractive, but one of the nameless kind who simply
remain "Blanche Bates's leading man" in my memory!

George Creel had crinkly black hair, snapping black eyes, and
the hard, white teeth of a public man. He was on his way to
Mexico. He had been a sort of messenger from our President to
the Mexican President at one time and he knew everyone down
there. Now, I had heard Lorenzo say that he wanted to know
Calles when he went back for the winter. Calles and Gamio and
other people, too. It seems to me he had to know them for
that *Plumed Serpent*, that he had not finished it yet, perhaps.
You must overlook these vaguenesses, Jeffers! You understand,
though, don't you? I just can't remember that kind of thing.
Anyhow, I remember feeling the old New York glow at the
thought of putting two people together and having something
come out of it. Lawrence would get some letters from Creel,
Creel was ever so anxious to meet Lawrence. In a trice I was
Miss Fix-it again!

Now there is an altogether different rhythm in this inward
flurry and fuss of social pie-making from that in the grave sim-
plicities and delights of the life of a hermit-thrush like Lorenzo,
and apparently I could fade from one to another as easily as a
chameleon. Not that I was conscious of the change at the moment, of course. It was only afterwards that I realized it, and
it was always Lorenzo who made me aware.

Well, I sent a note over to the Two-story House to be pinned
on their door to say there were two men from New York coming to dinner; and I dressed up a little for the occasion. I put on
a low-necked gown and over it a splendid Chinese coat that
Clarence had given me, made of vermilion satin embroidered

with gold and many brilliant colors.

When Lorenzo came over the bridge, I was a Hostess. Creel and his friend radiated an air of the outside world, with their urbanities, their faun-colored spats and their easy vivacities; and Lorenzo, with his two women behind him, hastened, a little late for dinner, into this unaccustomed atmosphere. He himself had changed from the usual corduroys and blue shirt into the gray town suit, and Frieda had on her Spanish shawl, while Brett had met the exigency of the moment by a short, paint-spotted dress. You must realize, Jeffers, that in those days of difficult roads far fewer guests arrived on the hill, so they made a decided difference when they came.

I stepped forward to meet them and gather them up and float them into the circle that was already gathered there on the terrace near the front door. Lorenzo was looking furious and outraged; he wouldn't look up, and it made my heart waver for an instant; but Frieda looked pleased. Brett was unsmiling, but self-possessed in a hauteur that sought to chide me for annoying Lorenzo in this way. I passed easily over the bumps, and, murmuring all their names to each other, I led them into the dining-room.

Now, naturally, Jeffers, I had to put those men on either side of me. Tony was, as so often, away, and I asked Frieda to take his place at the end of the table. Instantly Lorenzo jumped into a chair on one side of her, and Clarence jumped into the other, so that Brett and little Alice Sprague came next to the two strangers and formed a complete insulation between them and the Lawrences, who should, for social purposes, have been nearer our end of the table.

I shall never forget that meal! There I was isolated, with Blanche Bates's husband and Blanche Bates's leading man making one group, while Lawrence and Clarence and Frieda made another, and those two, Alice and Brett, effectually separating both contingents by their deafness and dumbness. Alice Sprague continually smiled, but that was not enough to fuse the intractable elements: Clarence and Lorenzo kept their attention directed upon Frieda and ignored the rest of the table.

I don't know whether such things matter much or little, Jeffers, but in those days I would have a sense of failure after a party like that. I had reverted that evening to the pleasurable anticipation enjoyed by one who had been called in past times a catalyst. I had expected things to mix because I brought them together, forming new combinations out of which significant things might come, while I sat there smiling.

Creel and the agreeable one on my left kept up an animated chatter. They reminisced; they spoke of the old days of the salon in New York; Creel reminded me of this occasion and of that; the Englishman interpolated, frequently: "Did you ever meet So-and-so . . ."; and together they re-created the past so that they could be secure in it; and, taking me back into it with them, they succeeded in leaving the antagonistic ones stranded in their own uncertain present.

You know how cruel such defenses can be, Jeffers! But Lorenzo had set the example of apparent exclusiveness. He had remained separate, and refused to mingle, and the others had defended themslves by making their own neighborhood lively and impossible to enter: a small repetition of what happened to the Jews in the more distant past!

The evening was warm and fragrant, the table was softly lighted with candles, and the food was good. There was no reason why we shouldn't all have been having a good time together. "Why, the wild animals who gather at a water-hole know better how to make a truce than Lorenzo," I thought angrily.

Well, he never made one move to speak to us or even to look in our direction, and when I finally stood up at the end of the meal, instead of leaving the dining-room with us, he made a bee-line out through the kitchen to the desert behind the house,

Clarence after him! With the ridiculous and unnatural custom
of not taking notice of anything unusual, no one appeared to see
these actions. Alice Sprague, lifting her gentle voice, asked us
all to come over and sit in her cottage, and we strolled across the
cool fields in the dusk.

Before we went, I took a hasty look over the desert from the
window of the big room, and I saw Lorenzo pacing rapidly up
Calvary towards the cross, and Clarence, ridiculous creature, as
rapidly moving towards him from the opposite end! I heaved a
sigh and joined the others.

Frieda was charming to the two men; and an easy hour of
talk passed about Mexico and Gamio's work there, his aims and
his obstacles, about Calles and the future. We must have been
well into the second hour before Lorenzo came back. He stepped
up into the room and sat down with an air of confronting Creel.
He was ready to fight, I knew.

But Frieda, paying no attention to his mood, exclaimed: "Oh,
Lorenzo, Mr. Creel can help you in Mexico City. He says . . ."

"Frieda, you *know* I don't want any help in Mexico City. I
want to know Mexico, not the oddments floating on her surface."

"I should be glad to give you letters to Calles and to Gamio,"
began Creel.

"I want no letters. I distrust the whole self-righteous, opinion-
ated brand of uplifters and reformers. Thinking they're going
to do Mexico 'good'! Trying to 'help' them! No. They'll do
more harm than good in the end. Give them injustice and oppression—more and more oppression. That's the only thing
that's likely to help Mexico!" He relapsed into a gloomy silence.

Creel smiled and shook his head, and Frieda looked a trifle
discouraged. She wanted to live easily and smoothly with pleasant companions, and Lorenzo made it so hard. Why did he
have to oppose everything? Why not take things as they came,
instead of making an issue of everything. Alice Sprague smiled

and beamed in the lamplight. Perhaps she felt an unaccustomed sparkle from the friction in the air, different from the somnambulistic conversations in New York drawing-rooms. "Lorenzo makes everything seem real," perhaps she thought. "Mexico seems more real when he speaks of it, and not so far away."

Clarence had followed Lorenzo into the room and sat glowering near the door. He didn't have the least idea what it was all about, and certainly he didn't care. He liked Lawrence's line and he followed it. It made him feel more significant to rush out into the desert like Lorenzo than to sit and drink coffee out of little cups.

After a while Creel and his friend took leave. They said they'd enjoyed the evening very much. As he shook hands:

"If he changes his mind, just drop me a line. I'll be glad to give him those letters," Creel said. He couldn't believe that Lawrence really didn't *want* to meet Calles and Gamio. And perhaps he was right.

It was not possible to forgive and forget and to have a merry time that Sunday. Lawrence, always so keen to the shades of feeling in the people near him, kept away to himself, and Clarence joined him.

Frieda and I were sitting together under a tree, chatting together, but we were watching the two men, who sat at some distance from us on the floor of the porch of Clarence's house, talking in low tones. They were completely engrossed and all the rest of the world was shut away. I saw Lorenzo make a wide gesture with his hand over the desert. What *were* they talking about? When Frieda could stand it no longer, she exclaimed:

"They have done enough *schmarming*! I'm going to stop it!" And she rose and joined them. They both looked extremely guilty and avoided her eyes like two dogs that are discovered with a stolen bone. I was consumed with curioisty and did not rest, after they had returned to the ranch, until I had extracted from Clarence Lorenzo's conspiracy.

"Will you *swear* not to tell, Mabel?"

"Absolutely. You *know* I never tell things if I say I won't."

"But this is too important to have an accident with. Are you certain you won't forget?"

"Of course not! Now what *was* it, Clarence? You *know* I have to know about things!"

"Well, Lawrence is planning— Oh, dear! I'm *so* afraid to tell! I don't know *what* he would do to me if he knew I were telling you this!"

"Clarence, if you don't go on and tell me, I'll go and tell him you told me anyway—then you'll see!"

"Oh, dear! Oh, dear! This is a *terrible* responsibility. Well, Lawrence is planning that pretty soon he and I are going to ride off into the desert on horseback and never be seen again!"

I gave a loud hoot!

"Well, I'd just like to *see* that happen! And who is going to take care of Lorenzo? You? And who is going to take care of you? Lorenzo? What a *perfect* idea!"

"Well, he just feels sometimes that it's the only thing to do. To get away from the women, and the strangers, and all the world of things he knows."

"And where, pray, do you intend to go?"

"Oh, off. Maybe towards Old Mexico. Anyway, it will be the last *you'll* see of us!"

"Well, that's splendid. . . ."

Now, of course I felt that it was my duty to tell Frieda about this, just as one would if a child confided he was going to run away with another child. Would one promise to keep his secret and let them run? Hardly.

When I got her into a corner later in the day and told her, she seemed to increase in stature right before my eyes. She was tall and broad and rosy, and very mad.

"Just let them try it!" exclaimed the Queen Bee, with her hands on her hips. "The idea! Lawrence would be back inside a week with his head hanging," she said, certain of herself. She did not say anything to Lorenzo, but she was on the alert after my warning.

I was feeling shattered of late. Every time they came down, I felt ill afterwards. Yet I couldn't give up. But I thought I'd leave them alone for a while—to keep Clarence and Lawrence apart for one thing. I wrote to him after a week or two passed. Spud was going up and I thought I might stay up a day or two myself. I told him I had decided to go to Croton-on-the-Hudson for the winter and rent the Finney Farm that I had had years ago with Maurice Sterne.

Lorenzo's letter in answer to mine showed him still quivering from Creel's visit. Can you sympathize with that, Jeffers?

Tuesday

DEAR MABEL

Did you get my letters, ordering things from Gerson's? Hope it's not a nuisance. In the second letter—gone today—I asked for these few extra things.

Yes, come up, and for God's sake let's be peaceful. I hate my nerves being jolted: and strange people weary me—only a sense of hospitality carries one through, and one becomes more and more estranged from strangers.

I think Spoodle can sleep in the barn—he won't mind, I'm sure—if you are in the guest-house. Bring only a very little meat—the Hawks have killed a pig and we can eat some of that. And never mind about the eggs. But do bring me a book of cheques, please, from the Taos bank.

We'll talk about tripping when you come up.

A little too much thunder lately, in the sky. It wearies one. But not so badly as people.

D. H. L.

And this added from Frieda:

DEAR MABEL

Thank you for photographs, letter and books. Today I scrubbed the guest-house for you. If Spud can stay a day or two, order a camp-mattress for him. Bring him if you like, and Tony. The big farm-house near New York sounds rather jolly. Yes, I am *sure* you want to be alone. I die inside me if I don't. I want to come to San Domingo, just my days. I don't know if I will.

So we expect you. Bring Lorraine, if you like.

F.

I did not stay the night after all when I motored Spud up to the mountain side. I think Frieda was growing tired of us all and our interference in her life. That is the only way I can explain what happened next, and it has never been wholly cleared up, for we none of us ever spoke of it to each other.

Again they were down in the Two-story House, and once again, for the last time on this earth, Clarence and Lorenzo were confabbing together. Supper that night seemed serene enough. Alice Sprague and Lawrence talked together quietly. He liked her, for she did not molest him in any way. She merely waited to *understand*, as she was sure that, some day, she would. She had an interesting feeling that a vast drama of unseen forces was playing itself out around her, though she couldn't imagine what it was all about.

Tony drove out to the pueblo after supper, and the rest of us strolled over to the studio. All of a sudden Clarence and Lorenzo disappeared for half an hour while the rest of us were playing the Victrola—and we didn't know what had become of them. Frieda and I joked about it, but we watched the door. Presently the two of them came in. They both looked quite gay and excited, and Lorenzo produced a bottle of moonshine from his pocket, much to our amazement, for we never had anything to drink; it was difficult to get and not good when we got it.

They ran over to the house for ice and glasses and ginger

ale, and presently we were cheerfully drinking each other's healths. As the unaccustomed alcohol ran through our veins, we all drew together, feeling more convivial than usual, more cosy and reassured. Clarence and I began to dance. Dancing was easy. Easy and enlivening. Frieda was begging Lorenzo to dance with her and he was snappily refusing her. When we stopped, Clarence seized Frieda, and together they began to circle in a dignified, dreamlike way, around the room. I took Lorenzo's hand.

"Oh, come, Lorenzo—just this once. Try it." And there we were dancing! Frieda did not notice it at first. She had her eyes closed and an ecstatic, small smile on her face; and when she did see us, apparently she took no notice. Lawrence didn't know how to dance. Actually he had no sense of rhythm at all! Not any! But I led him round and round in a one-step, and he bobbed and jerked about with an intensely concentrated look of doom upon his face. Brett, after her high-ball, was dancing alone. If one can call it dancing. She, too, bobbed. Alice Sprague sat on the couch smiling and smiling. When Lawrence and I stopped beside her, she exclaimed, with a gesture towards Frieda and Clarence:

"Isn't that a *picture*? They dance so beautifully together! That beautiful woman and that tall, lovely boy!"

Lorenzo seized me, this time of his own accord. We spun a little faster around the room in the wake of the more romantic couple.

When the Victrola ran down and we all stopped to pour our-selves more high-balls, Frieda was glowing with life. She ap-peared extremely attractive and very self-sufficient. She didn't speak to Lawrence, but she was smiling at Clarence, who was looking rather superciliously at us others, with one eyebrow raised. And there began to rise between us all that feeling of di-vision and comparison that is so odious. Particularly odious to those who are not shining as brightly as they wish. Brett's brass trumpet was held out hopefully in our midst, but no one was saying anything!

The Victrola started another meretricious but irresistible dance record, and we all four involuntarily sprang into the same couplings as before and paced off into the candlelighted room. Poor Brett! She and the ear-trumpet went round and round after us!

Now a fiercer and more sinister emotion had sprung up between the two couples. The real dancers, Frieda and Clarence, glided round and round in an evident trance of self-satisfaction. Their feeling of superiority showed in every move they made: two unusually beautiful human beings enclosed in a pattern of motion and harmony! How different they were from Lorenzo and me—both odd numbers joined in a frenzy of expostulation!

That night for once, and for only that once, I was able to join to his all my physical energy, and my will, destructive or not, in a mutual effort against the outside world. This was no deep, invisible "flow" of life between us, reinforcing each the other. No, it was his use of my strength for a battering-ram. That was what our singular "communion" had come to.

Frieda and Clarence, shielding their harmonious exhibition as best they could from our onslaught, pretended not to notice us, while Lawrence and I flew, circling the room, bumping into them as hard as we could at every round! We gathered speed and momentum as we went, and each bump was heavier than the last. Brett, not quite catching on to what it was all for, spun around too, and endeavored to crash into *me*, and at the same time to avoid shattering Lorenzo.

Round and round we went. Can you imagine it, Jeffers, and conceive it as a picture not quite ridiculous and somehow very ominous? Lorenzo kicked Frieda as often as he could.

The sweat ran down my face and I rubbed it against Lorenzo's shoulder to wipe it out of my eyes. As we swept past Alice Sprague, I saw her still smiling sympathetically. I was having a grand time, for there I was, clutched by Lorenzo, united at last, one will, one effort, to break, to crush, to shatter if we could, the ease and beauty of those two others.

The music stopped, and left us panting. We had effectively interrupted the others' pleasure and doubtless bruised them along with ourselves. I know I found I was covered with great black and blue marks the next day.

But although that was the end of dancing, it was not the end of that evening. Frieda and Clarence, whispering to each other, melted out of the wide door and disappeared into the night. I couldn't believe my eyes. That was simply not done among us. I mean, no one ever went out of sight of all the others. What one did we all did. There were no tête-à-têtes, no dialogues, nothing that was not in plain sight of all the others.

I realize that you, Jeffers, are one of the very few who can understand what a shock this sudden departure from our tacitly accepted custom was to us who were left staring at the empty doorway. Everyone is so free and easy nowadays that there is not very much significance left in anyone's going out or coming in. But with us every move counted and was a symbol of an inner activity. Was it all very foolish and overstrained? Perhaps. And yet the days had their value.

As we stood there, Tony came in from the pueblo. He noticed the absence of the others right away and he said:

"Where is Frieda and Clarence?"

"Oh, they stepped outside to cool themselves," answered Lorenzo, conventionally. "Well, I'm off to bed," he added.

"What a *beautiful* evening it has been," sighed little Alice Sprague.

"Humm, yes!" affirmed Lorenzo with a very grim expression.

We all went out into the soft moonlight, leaving Brett to go to bed there in an atmosphere that must have been jangling with violence and discord, had she had the eyes to see it.

"I will fix your door for you," offered Lorenzo, politely, to

Alice Sprague. This was usually Clarence's job. The little woman
required a log of wood to be propped against her door on the
outside. Sleeping alone there, with a door that would not lock
properly, and where three steps downward from her bed led her
into the alfalfa field, she felt more secure when she was thus bar-
ricaded, and no one ever shook her confidence in this method of
defense.

Tony and I strolled the few feet from the studio to the Pink
House and waited a moment while Lawrence stood the heavy
log up on end against the door and afterwards slipped up on the
adobe bench under her open casement window.

"You're all safe now," he assured her. Then he joined us.

"Where do you suppose they are?" I asked him in a nervous
voice. My heart was beating fast. I could feel the restrained
anger in him.

"Ah, youth and middle age!" he exclaimed with a light, nasty
laugh. He was peering into the black shadows under the apple
trees.

"Well, good night," said Tony, marching homewards. I was
dying to stay with Lorenzo until the others came back, but that
was not the way we did things, so I went along home behind
Tony, furiously conjecturing.

He and I went to bed on our upper porch. The moonlight was
so bright I could see everything on our hill. The two great cottonwood trees dark and motionless over the stream, the glim-
mering alfalfa field, and all the little houses across the way
showed their clear outlines. A light in Lorenzo's downstairs
room burned yellow in the milky night, and not a sound was
to be heard save the rusty mocking-bird that always summers in
the depth of the orchard.

Tony was silent and asleep in his swinging bed in the corner
and I lay wakeful in mine, swaying it back and forth a little
in my excitement. Wherever *could* they be, those others? The
moments passed. How long? I do not know. But after a while

I heard a low murmur of voices away down the road. The air is so clear there, Jeffers, that when it is windless, sounds carry great distances, especially at night.

They were coming! I held my breath and watched them, two tiny, indistinct figures, enter the lower gate and walk up past the corral. When they reached Clarence's cottage, they stopped and sat down on the corner of the porch. They continued their low hum of conversation. By this time I was simply shaking with excitement and curiosity. I felt I had to know what on earth they were talking about, and I felt terribly out of it. It went on and on; would they never finish? A low, continuous, insistent mumble reached me in the high porch. Tony continued his even breathing, with an occasional snore in it. I felt alone on earth, suspended between the upper and the nether millstones.

Finally I couldn't endure it another moment. I got out of bed, clutched my thin kimono from the chair, and, without making a sound, crept, on bare feet, into the house, down the stairs, through the dark living-room, where everything that was disclosed by clear patches of moonlight looked unfamiliar and frightening.

Out through the big screen door that stays unlatched all night and across the open terrace I tiptoed, with my heart in my mouth. My caution turned my action clandestine, an unusual and breath-taking experience. Never mind, I had to get over and join those others and hear what was going on. If only Tony wouldn't wake and miss me—for he would stop me, I knew, disapprovingly.

I reached the wide white lake of alfalfa, and when I was right in the middle of it:

"Come back here!" bellowed Tony in the most terrible voice —a voice I had never heard from him before. I looked back over my shoulder as I hurried along, and I saw him standing there looking down at me over the low adobe wall between the pillars. I tried to make a gesture to him that would say, all in one sweep, that he mustn't mind, but that I just had to go on over to Clarence's house and find out about things, but I fancy my gesture must have been totally inexpressive. I couldn't help myself now. I was compelled to go on. Nothing would have turned me back.

But when I reached the blue well at the end of the board walk I had crossed, I saw that those two had left the porch! Frieda had gone on to her house; Clarence, I saw, was just inside in his bedroom and I could see him taking off his clothes in the patches of moonlight.

"Clarence! Clarence! Come out here!" I whispered as loudly as I dared. He came to the door in his shirt and trousers and, seeing me, stepped out into the quiet night. He didn't say anything at first, and neither did I; we just stood there by the well under the plum tree looking at each other, and there was the sternest look on his young face.

"What *have* you been doing, Clarence?" I said at last.

"I have been learning the Truth!" he answered, portentously.

"What!"

"Mabel, something has to be done and *I'm* going to do it," he interrupted, sternly. "Mabel, do you know that that man is determined to *kill* you?" He turned me faint. He really succeeded in turning me scared and faint, he was so stern and convinced and, for once, so strong and convincing.

"Oh, *Clarence!* What *do* you mean? Oh, dear, *what* a night! What have you heard?"

"Frieda has told me *the Truth!*" he said in a lower but more passionate voice. "She has told me many things. Many. But what concerns *us* is what he is doing to *you*. She says he has *told* her he will destroy you, and every time he comes down here he goes a little farther with it, and every time you are a little weaker and more sick after he has left. She says she is *scared*. Do you realize that, Mabel? *Frieda* is *scared!*"

I was shaking all over—trembling with the shock and the strangeness. It sounded true. It *was* true.

"You have all believed Frieda was the strong one," he went on. "You don't *know* that man's power. None of you know what he has done to her. . . ."

I was cold. My teeth chattered. I longed to hear more, but I feared to have him go on talking. As I stood there before him, my hands clasped tight, I heard a familiar sound from the other side—from our place. It was the sound of a car starting.

"Oh, *heavens!* That's *Tony!* Where is he going? Oh, I must go and see. . . ." I turned to go, but Clarence, paying no attention to the noise of the car, stepped nearer to me and said, violently:

"And I am *not* a Brett, Mabel."

"Good gracious, what does *that* mean?" I panted, and turned and ran as fast as I could across the field. But, oh, sickening sight, I had hardly gone half-way when the headlights of the car flared over the tops of the apple trees and disappeared rapidly in the direction of the pueblo.

Nothing mattered to me now but the fundamental reality of my life: Tony. And he had gone away. I knew he was not one to play and pretend, to make a threatening gesture and to revoke it. No. He had awakened to see me creeping away in the night, and when he had summoned me back from a flight that must have appeared to him in one light and one only, I had disobeyed him and gone on. I knew then, as I should have known when my compulsion was carrying me over beyond the boundaries of custom, that he would not stand for it.

Now I knew, but it was too late. I was in an agony of bereavement. Lawrence? He was a dim and unimportant chess-man in a game I had been playing to occupy my days. Tony was real, and nobody but Tony counted. I flew back to Clarence's house and found him still standing beside the well, silent and menacing.

"Oh, Clarence, Tony has gone away! Will you go after him and fetch him back? You *must!* Take the other car and go after him. Tell him I only wanted to come and see what you and

Frieda were doing! *Will* you? Please—please . . ."

"I don't *blame* him for leaving!" answered Clarence, like a judge.

"Never mind. Go *get* him. Will you? You can make him understand if you only will! He's *got* to come back!"

"Very well. I'll go on one condition," answered Clarence. "If you promise me that you'll send these people away from here and *never, never* see that man again, I'll go. Will you promise?"

"Oh, *yes*. But why? Oh, *dear*!"

"I'm going to save you, somehow," he said, "if it's not too late. As it is for Frieda. Will you promise never to see him again nor even to write him?"

"Yes," I said.

I went back to the house and lay down on my swing. My heart hardly beat at all. I suddenly felt the silent emptiness of our big house. I was alone in it as I had never been before in my life, though I had often been there alone. The very life and heat of it seemed to have gone with Tony, and it was like being alone on the moon.

I couldn't stay there. Whatever had gone on between Clarence and Frieda was secondary to my need to be near another human being, and I rose once more, and once more I ran barefooted over to seek her and have the comfort of another woman's presence. I stole into the house and up the stairs to where I knew she slept. She was still dressed and lying on her bed. I told her in a few words that I had come running over to join her and Clarence, and that Tony had waked and called me back, and that when I had not paid attention to him, he had dressed and gone away and that now Clarence had gone after him. She looked thrilled.

"Lawrence is mad, too," she whispered. "He frightens me, he is so angry in his sleep. Do you hear?" I listened and heard a faint, submerged roaring noise from the room below that reminded me of the subterranean groans that came through the rocks from under the mountain at Manby Springs.

"Come and look at him," she urged. Shaking with a nervous chill, I followed her down and peeked into the moonlighted room. True, Lawrence was mumbling and groaning in his uneasy sleep. We went back to the upper porch.

"Where *were* you with Clarence?" I queried—just to say something.

"We just walked down and around the Plaza. The village looks so strange asleep. There was no one but ourselves about." . . . We stood on the lighted porch and looked toward the pueblo.

"Oh, he'll come back," she said, reassuringly. Of course that had been her experience, but would it be mine? It had been quite a long time now since Clarence had gone. The moon was soaring along across the sky, and everything seemed peaceful enough, with little Alice Sprague asleep in her Pink House, guarded by the log of wood, and Brett silent in the studio close by. Frieda and I were the only ones awake in the night—like the Valkyrie women in the Penitente picture I had made for Lorenzo, we mingled with the moonlight, but only one of us seemed to be exultant. She was as robust and cheerful as ever; a strong woman, Frieda.

I don't remember what we talked of or if we talked any more. The interval fades in my mind—until Clarence was standing below us looking up. I rushed down to him.

"Tony will come back in the morning," he said. "He is at his mother's house. And when he comes, he and I are going to have a talk," said Clarence. Oh, yes, he had full command of the situation!

Towards morning I got up and wrote these lines:

INEVITABLE

Alone! Alone in the upper room in the night—
Or is it early morning I have wakened to?
From the window by my bed

The eastern hills show black against the dim sky.
Is it the before-dawn time, or the light from the veiled stars?

Oh, *why* am I here in this unrevealing land?
I do not know this unavailing country;
It is strange to me yet, after these five years.
I was born beside a wide lake.
This air is stranger to me than God.

What aloneness it is to awaken in the night
Away from native air and earth!
The heart is appalled by the eternal alien and everlasting
Unknown land.

I am not here in my body—
I am unflowing—into this night.
How deliver myself from this shrift?
I am split into hard crystal atoms—
I cannot bring all of me together into my body.
My blood has gone out of me or I have gone out
Of my blood.

Oh, if I were but in some common room again!
Some room terribly familiar and used,
Like a sleeping-car, or at my grandmother's house
Or some old friend's house!
Then my heart would beat naturally again.
Anywhere *away*! Away from this other-land, other-air!

And you! You alien! You perpetual stranger for whom
I so completely give up all else!
Are you there in your room under the porch?
Are you there in your dark, deep sleep?

Or are you leagues away?
Are you off in the night, winding a silent trail
Up the mountain to the never-forsaken shrine?
Are you hidden with your brothers in some dark cave,
Sitting before a cedar fire in the secret, forbidden peyote rites?

Ah, lost! lost to me in other worlds,
Wrought by the mystical subtle peyote dreams!

What incomprehensble aloneness for the white woman
Who crosses over into the Indian heart!

The light behind those hills is paler now.
Sleep, come to me for an hour before dawn!
Come—blot out this intolerable hour!

I cannot lie like this any longer.
My warmth does not warm me inside.
Cold—cold—this empty room—this maybe empty house!
I must know if I am alone here on the edge of this desert,
Or I shall flicker out—out like a fallen star.

Oh, unfriendly! unkind, that dawn wind!
My feet recoil in disgust from the wooden floor,
From contact with the dirt roof.
The blanket does not shelter me from my loathing
For this moment.

"Ohé! Ohé! Are you there, are you there?"
"Yes, I am here."
"When did you come?"
"I came at midnight."
"What time now?"
"It is dawn."
"Come up!"
"I am coming."

Oh, light heart! Run back to the warm bed!
You are not alone. The stranger is coming again
As he has come a thousand times before!

That soft bare step on the stair that carries the big body so gently!
Flow, happy blood filled with light,
So benign and essential a lover is coming!

I can feel the color of the red and purple blanket rather than see it,
And the dark body that is more known to me,
To my eyes and nostrils and all my ways of knowing,
Than the body of my mother or my son or the husband I left
For this.

When my feet, delighting in his warm, friendly feet, come alive,
My whole body feels long and slim and complete.
And when his soft, hard subtle hand rests on mine.
I am in perfect balance.

Grow, heart! Swell fuller, fuller!
That is why we are here.
Drink, heart! Drink that dark draught,
And learn the secret the brain cannot fathom.

(How often in the night or in the day
Has this past-ridden mind made the brain to shake as in a great
     earthquake
At the sudden sight of that dark skin
And at the thought of that dark, unknowable blood!
Alien! Alien forever to this mind of mine,
But somehow transfused into my blood
So that you are no stranger to my heart!)

Now, blood, you travel your own road evenly again!
Heart, you are full blown like a rose!
Just to lie in the ambient of this man restores me to myself.
To lie within this arm against the ungiving wall of that chest and
     belly
Is health come back.

No security for me like the certainty of this unknowable man.
He is more than father.
No child in all the white world has the freshness for my cheek
That his dark face radiates in the night.

Thank God! Never again to live with unaired people
In safe, familiar, outworn places!

Sweet light in the east over the dark moist hills!
Sweet, sweet sage-brush breeze over the eastern desert!
I am at home.

The next morning Tony came and went into his room down-stairs, the middle one that opens on the long portal, and I ran down there. He just looked at me as he brushed his long, black hair.

"Oh, Tony! Everything's all mixed up!" I cried. "Did Clarence tell you anything?"

"I guess Lawrence pretty sick man," said Tony. At this moment along came Clarence with a set face. He came in to talk to Tony, I saw, so I left. I went over to the Two-story House. I was so tired after the night of alarm that I felt as though I'd been in a terrible storm. A peaceful lethargy was all through me. I didn't care what happened. I sat down by Lorenzo, who was eating his breakfast. He looked exhausted.

"Tony's back," I said. Frieda stuck her head in at the door.

"Well, you've all had quite a *schmarm*," said Lorenzo, with a black, lowering look at Frieda. "I've decided to go back to the ranch this morning," he continued. "It's too upsetting down here. I want to get on with my work."

"Shall I really *never* see him again?" I thought.

"I will bring my story over to show you before we leave. Will Clarence be able to drive us up this morning?"

Oh, heavens! Would he? I couldn't help wondering at Frieda's apparent unconcern. Did she have such confidence in Clarence that she could tell him the things she had about Lawrence and be *certain* he wouldn't betray her?

"Poor old Tony! You get him into some queer messes," went on Lorenzo, disagreeably. Finishing, he got up and said: "I'll just walk over with you and see if Clarence can take us along before lunch. Here is this manuscript for you. You can look it over until we go."

It was *The Woman Who Rode Away,* Jeffers. All about the cave and the Indians. In it, you remember, Lorenzo had the woman offer herself voluntarily as a sacrifice to the Indian gods. And the Indian priests took "the mastery that man must hold, and that passes from race to race." Do you remember that ending, Jeffers?

When Clarence, standing in Tony's doorway, saw the Lawrences and me strolling up to the house, he was inflamed. Tony stood by with a deeply revolted look on his good face. He averted his eyes from Lorenzo. Frieda was as bland and smiling as ever until she saw Clarence begin to pace slowly towards Lorenzo with the most menacing expression on his face. Then a look of amazement flew into her eyes. I was so emotionally exhausted that I simply felt nothing at all except a kind of intelligent interest as Clarence, reaching Lorenzo, began shaking his long forefinger in the man's face.

"You devil! I *know* you now!" he cried.

"And I know *you*, now, to my chagrin," answered Lorenzo.

Clarence advanced upon him and he began to back in a way painful to behold. I turned and went into the house and sat down on the couch and began to read. The voices went on in their anger and I just sat and read with great interest that story where Lorenzo thought he finished me up. I looked up as Frieda came into the room. She was pale and put her hand to her heart.

"He said he would save you from being destroyed as Lawrence has destroyed me," she murmured. I never saw her falter before or since that moment.

"What *is* going on?" I asked, continuing to read so as to finish it before it was taken away from me.

"I am afraid they're going to fight," she said, going out again. I lost myself in the sheets of paper.

Lawrence was sitting by me, a little later.

"Do you like it?" he asked.

"Oh, it's splendid!" I told him.

"Well, we are leaving. Be careful of Clarence. He's not very nice. Don't trust him. Don't trust him right to the last," he counseled me.

It was Tony who drove them away.

Lobo, 7 July 1924

DEAR MABEL

I am asking Gerson's man to deliver this note to you, as you may not have had my letters. Will you please let the man put our trunks on his wagon: one of mine, two of Frieda's, and a leather trunk of Brett's: also a brown leather suitcase of F's. Frieda says she left some things in a drawer upstairs: would you be so good as to let Maggie put them in the trunks or the suitcase. Nothing of Frieda's is shut up. Mine and Brett's are locked. I find we shall be needing bits of winter clothing and other things we have left behind. And as I need things sent out on a wagon, this is a good opportunity to bring everything up. The rain has practically ruined the road: otherwise, I know, you would have been out to see us. I wish you would send word by the man, if there is anything we can put on the wagon and send down to you.

Best regards from us all.

D. H. LAWRENCE.

Yes, he must have wondered, after days of silence, whether a real break had come at last, and with a great aversion to being left in an equivocal position he had, on the chance, sent for all their belongings!

Clarence asked for the Two-story House now. Being quite the hero of the moment, he made the most of it. However, for the sufferer from persecution nothing is so bad as success. It seems to put him quite off his balance. Clarence moved into the Two-story House, and, buying yards and yards of white unbleached muslin, he hung long, full, white curtains all the way

across the two walls of the green living-room where the big
windows were, and these he kept drawn day and night to shut
out the world. Taos, the sunshine, and all of us were thus blotted
out of his sight.

I remember dear little Alice Sprague sitting on her porch in
the afternoon, sewing all the seams of these curtains. The white
stuff was billowing all around her. It seemed to be a sea rising to
engulf her. She was smiling with understanding enjoyment of
Clarence's idea. She thought it expressed a need to withdraw into
himself for contemplation.

When Frieda's much-labeled trunks had been taken out of the
small room adjoining her bedroom upstairs, Bobby Jones's chapel
emerged! This tiny, whitewashed room, with a small square
window deeply embrasured and high up near the ceiling, made
a perfect Jones stage-set. Bobby cut some tin candle-sconces out
of tomato-cans, with designs marked on them by a nail and a
stone hammer, just as the Mexicans do for their houses and
chapels, and he hung them on the walls. At the end facing the
door, he placed an altar table with a thin, old, white linen cloth
on it, a carved wooden Mexican crucifix on the wall over it, some
paper roses—and there it was! Clarence, of course, adored this!
He said he would pray there.

He had been filling our ears for a week with echoes of that
night he talked with Frieda. "He *wants* you *dead*," he told me,
over and over. "He wants to *know* that you are in the ground."
Tony didn't take this sensational news sensationally. I think he
felt I was able to withstand Lawrence's wish, he and I together.
But he said he was tired of Lorenzo. Clarence made him agree
that if Lorenzo ever came back there, they two would leave together! But he agreed laughing heartily as though it were a
great joke, for he was very sure of himself.

Clarence made me renew my promise every day until I was
tired of it. "Remember, Mabel, what you have promised." I
kept wondering whether Frieda had ever cleared up the con-

fusion by telling Lorenzo all she had said in the moonlight. Otherwise how would he understand what was happening? I knew *I* could never tell him. I couldn't give Frieda away if she didn't give herself away.

Yet—as ever before—nothing of all this mattered. I missed Lorenzo and the fun of his company, the thrill that got into everything when he was about. Comparing Clarence with him in my mind, the young savior lacked substance and appeared shadowy.

Tony said: "I think we done enough for those Lawrences. I'm going to send for my mare. Better my nephew use her." He sent Fernando up to get her from the ranch, but I sent no letter as I had always done before. When the boy came back, he brought one of my horses, too, one of those I had lent Lorenzo, though I had not told him to do so.

The days went peacefully by. Too peacefully, for me! When Tony and I went to Santa Fe for a night, I broke my promise and sent a card to each of them up at the ranch. Just saying: "Are you all right?" Lorenzo answered immediately:

Lobito, 3 July

DEAR MABEL

Had your cards. Yes, we're all right up here—been making a Porch over the kitchen door.

Come and see us up here—if you can get anyone to drive you to this lion's den. Don't mention our coming down—I mean don't speak of it, don't even suggest it: I have a vision of Tony and Clarence, with set faces, departing an hour before the arrival: C. said that he and T. had so decided: and I haven't the heart to disturb the nest to that extent.

But bring Mrs. Sprague if you come—give her our regards, anyhow.

And bring a bit of meat from Cummings, and a few vegetables.

I hope you got the piano. Perhaps it will have strains to soothe—etc.

D. H. L.

And Frieda added:

My sister wrote that she sent off on the *6th* 3 packets of manuscript as "insured" as she could make them! So look out for them, they are addressed to Taos to D. H. L. I hope they'll arrive safely and if it gives you a 100th part of the joy I get out of the ranch, you will get quite a lot. The pups are very gay; we don't know which is nicer. At first we had to take a lot of care of them, they were so little to be without a mother. Yes, we have flourished. Somebody, "The Drexel Institute" want to do a bibliography of L. We slept out one wonderful night with the stars entering into one and a most handsome squirrel very indignant in the morning. I suppose we have all calmed down again. I am still trying to find out *who* was Solomon's baby? We ride every day. The porch is such a success.

All good things to all of you!

F.

I liked my card.

Frieda's blithe reference to Solomon's baby shows her carefree nature, doesn't it?

"Oh, Tony, I want to see them again. Let's drive up!"

"You just want more trouble, don't you?" said Tony.

"Yes," I replied.

"But I do not," he answered.

After lunch one day I asked Tony to take me for a drive in the car. I said: "Let's go over to Valdez." I thought maybe from there I would get him to drive me forward to the ranch—only three or four miles farther. The sun was shining, but when we crossed the desert and came near to Arroyo Seco, the sky had grown black and the mountains were veiled in dark clouds that

were hurrying over from the north—from the direction of Lorenzo! I couldn't help thinking of the strange weather signs that
attended this man in critical moments. He seemed to be a part
of nature's storms and sunshine.

We drove down the mountain into Valdez, that village that
from the brow of the hill looks like a child's toy: a tiny plaza
with an old church in the center, and houses on either side. The
wind beat around us, and when we crossed the dry bed of the
creek, we went over to the post office to rest there a moment.
No sooner had we entered there than the postmaster, an anxious-
looking old Mexican, stuck his head out of the small window of
his pen and asked Tony in Spanish if I were Mabel Luhan.

"There's a package here for D. H. Lawrence," he said. "It
came today and it's addressed in care of Mabel Luhan, and as
that man never comes down here, she may as well take it."

This is a sample of our New Mexico laissez-faire! He shoved
the stocky, tattered bundle through the window and I took it.
It was the manuscript of *Sons and Lovers*. You will admit that
was a curious coincidence, Jeffers? It seemed as though we'd
gone specially to fetch it, for I hadn't been to Valdez for a year
or longer before that day.

Now, the moment I took it into my hands, there was a clap
of thunder and a rushing sound; then one of those sudden, incalculable cloud-bursts broke over our heads. The water came
down in sheets as though the skies had been rent. For five
minutes we watched it from the door, along with two or three
plaintive Mexicans who wondered about the young wheat and
corn, just pricking through the earth.

Then the sun came out as sweetly as though nothing had
happened—but something had: for the spot where we had
crossed the dry creek was a rushing angry-glad stream of yellow
water three or four feet deep, and we had to wait an hour before
we could cross it and leave that place. That cut us off sufficiently
from the ranch, for the roads would have been washed out. "How

strange!" I thought; "it is as though the gods brought me here to find Lorenzo's book and then threw the water between us as though to say: 'Pass no farther.' "

Well, I had the essence of him in my hands. Perhaps that should have been enough for me, you think? It wasn't.

We motored home in the late afternoon sunshine, with the wet sage smelling fresh and clean, and Clarence came striding to meet the car with a white, drawn face.

"*Where* have you been? Mabel, did you go to the ranch?" He spoke in a low, intense voice. "All the afternoon I've had a *feeling*," he went on, "that you were going there. Do you know what I've been doing?"

"*What!*" I snapped, feeling bored.

"*Praying,*" he told me, importantly. I could *see* him on his knees in Bobby's chapel.

But of course now I *had* to write Lorenzo and let him know the manuscript of his novel had come and the postmaster had given it to me. Writing that gave me a chance to tell him other things: how badly I'd felt when I saw his trunks all leaving the hill when he sent Gerson for them, and about Clarence's still being mad, and Tony's not being able to forget that night. I had written a parody for him called "Plum." I sent it him to read, for I wanted to give it to Spud for the *Laughing Horse*. It was quite good, I thought. Here it is:

PLUM

(Apologies to D. H. Lawrence)

Somewhere on the western slope of the mountain
Rides Lorenzo.
What of this Lorenzo? This never-never man?
Composite so delicate of all kinds of beings,
Yet forever not any one of them!
Not a fish.
Not a goat.

Not a snake.
Not a red wolf.
Not a lamb.
Not a blue-bird.
Not a bat.
Not a mosquito.
Not a mountain lion.
Not a humming-bird.
Not an eagle.
Not a kangaroo.
Not an elephant.
Not an ass.
Not a tortoise.
Not even a snapdragon!
Yet perpetually partaking of all of these,
Each in turn.
Momentarily coagulate.
Chameleon!
Yes! Maybe more essentially than any other, a chameleon!
Lorenzo.
And at all times ruddy, lustrous, bitter-sweet,
And sealed to a doom of continent, rich savor.
Enclosing in his form more starry space
Than ever he displaces in this dark universe.
This small vessel of radium! Lorenzo!
Why do women like Lorenzo?
They *do*.
Maybe because no one, so well as he, knows
How to stick in his thumb and pull out the plum
Of their available, invisible Being.
No one.
Yet why do men hate him? Hate him with a ready hate:
A quick, hot, ill-termed hatred?
Maybe because he is a fish,
And a goat,
And a snake,
And a red wolf,
And a lamb,
And a blue-bird,

And a bat,
And a mosquito,
And a mountain lion,
And an eagle,
And a kangaroo,
And an elephant,
And an ass,
And a tortoise,
And a snapdragon.
All of these, yet never to be caught!
Never to be snared,
Nor caged,
Not to be caught with a line,
Nor roped in a corral,
Not to be smashed under the heel,
Nor barred in the pen,
Never to be squashed
Nor bridled—
And not even to be picked!
How can man, the hunter, ever like Lorenzo?
Never will he!
But the women will.
Oh, yes!
For, willy-nilly, this Lorenzo, this intractable one,
This escaped atom,
This Jack Horner of the midlands—
Anakatergic—
Contingent upon Christmas pies—
Releases the fruit weighing so heavily in female bosoms,
Plucks the Plum, heavy like a stone
On the maiden's heart,
Hard like a stone in the matronly heart—
Plucks it, but devours it never.
No.
("What a good boy am I!")
For what would a fish do with such friuts?
Or a goat?
Or a snake?
Or a red wolf?

Or, indeed, even a snapdragon?
Or any of these?

Unassimilable!

Oh, bitter, sacred fruit of women!
Bitter, flaccid, perpetual harvest!
Lorenzo!
Thyself plucked only by thyself from women's hearts.
Thyself.
Eternal fruit uneaten of men—
And uneaten of all creatures.
Forever contiguous, but self-harvested only!
The mystic Plum.

I told him, too, how the rain came down and shut me away from the ranch just when I'd been hoping to get up there that day. "Oh, let's fix it, somehow," I finished up. I sent the note up with a few pounds of meat, just as in the past. He replied at once:

Tuesday Evening

DEAR MABEL

Do as you like about the poem. Tocca a lei.

Meat came this evening—many thanks. In that same storm, Saturday, I sat under the Hondo bridge, holding Poppy—en route to the Wayne's to get eggs. But got so wet, went back.

I was very much annoyed when that boy—I didn't recognize him—suddenly arrived yesterday and demanded *Tony's two horses*—as if we had stolen them. However—poco me importa.

Clarence's being mad or glad doesn't affect me. He is only a stranger. And what has Tony to remember? or to forget?

No, don't let's fix it—better not. Let them stay mad, and me go my own way—plum or poison-berry—non mi fa niente.

Basta! to all that nonsense.

We'll think of each other kindly, at a distance. The world is too full of mere people—like a forest of nettles and weeds.

I wrote and asked Gerson's to collect my trunks and send

me up things. I waited for you to come, to arrange it. We really need the trunks. Do hope you won't mind being bothered.

No sign of MSS as yet—expect they'll come tomorrow. Come up and fetch yours, if you wish: else I'll send it.

F. wrote you, but we forgot to bring the letter down. She, too, in a peace-making, let's-fix-it mood.

But to me all this stuff of being mad and doing mean little things is just a bore. I say basta! bastissima!

CORNELA MYSTICA.

Now, Jeffers, wasn't it queer that he too was drawn down that afternoon towards Valdez, where we would have met had not that storm come to prevent it? You will agree that the man was somehow dominated by the elemental influences.

I wrote to him asking what else Clarence had said to him that morning. I had heard through Sara Higgins bits of the strangest versions Lorenzo had been giving to his neighbors, the Hawks, about the crisis through which we'd all passed. I had heard enough to know that Lorenzo didn't know what he was talking about: that as usual he was blaming me for all that had occurred! There was no satisfaction in his answer, and I couldn't clear up the misunderstanding.

Thursday

DEAR MABEL

Thank you for sending the things.

Would you like to hear all Clarence said to me? Pfui: You have some admirable young men. And ask Sara in detail for the "queer talk" to the Hawks, do!—and see what she'll invent.

And you know quite well there is no need for either Clarence or Tony to be "mad." It's pure bunk. But you always bring these things about. Think I care about their madness? However, I refuse myself to get "mad." We'll remain friendly at a distance —or at least, I will.

I'd rather you didn't send out that poem, at least with my name on it.

There is still another *brown* trunk of Frieda's down at your house. I'll send for it next time I order a wagon. Am very sorry you had to send Tony's wagon. Did you get the MSS you wanted? The postoffice said you took them.—No, don't let's be "mad," anyhow.

D. H. L.

There is a reference to the manuscripts in this letter, which I had fully explained in my previous one and which he had understood. Yet he forgets. Well, I let it ride for a while. Then he sent me a little note:

DEAR MABEL

We'll all soothe down a bit, then we'll come to Taos and see if we can't really get into a harmony. If everybody does his or her bit, I'm sure we can. Instead of being all wild like the horses. We'll all chew the cud of contemplation in our little corrals, then trot out for a reunion.

Anyhow, the hard work is *really* done here—and as you say, it should be done with. Too great a strain when it lasts so long. Now we lift off the strain.

Believe me, I *do* want us to be at peace together, all of us.

D. H. L.

That wistfulness, when it appeared in him, was perfectly irresistible! He distrusted it, though, and always tried to keep it out of him, and it made him furious whenever he capitulated to it in me. After I cried so hard that morning up at the ranch, he said to Clarence, some days later, who of course repeated it to me:

"And then she cries and grows wistful, but it's just a trick!"

I didn't feel it was a trick when it came up in him. I just felt it to be appealing and attractive. I wrote and told him, promise or no promise, I would come myself and see him, and he wrote:

Thursday

DEAR MABEL

Yes, do come up. It's silly of us to be in a state of tension.—
Only Sunday afternoon we're going out."

D. H. L.

And a letter from Frieda at this time just upset all one's con-
jectures, don't you think so? She writes nonchalantly of what
she calls "the destroying stuff."

DEAR MABEL

A book arrived from you last night, it's a godsend, we have
no books, except your bible!—Do you like the pups? We have
had such struggles with the horses, there's one nice new pony;
but last night Lawrence put turpentine on the fleabites of the
horses and there *was* a circus! *Lots* of strawberries. The Ufers
came one day, said the MSS of Sons and Lovers, they had "heard"
I had given it you (they always hear so much) was worth at least
$50,000, at least! Swinburne Hale told them!! It gave me a shock
to think of it in terms of dollars—a bit of one's life! I have not
got one of my trunks and the things in Clarence's house, in the
bottom drawer of washstand, put them somewhere else in a box
if they are in his way! I will come and get them some day! As
to the destroying stuff, it's all unreal and unwholesome *bunk* to
me! Not true—as if I would let it happen! It's getting lovelier up
here, red with flowers higher up where the young aspens are and
a white lily! Come and have a cocktail sometime and don't let
your men bunk!

Yours ever

FRIEDA.

That's all of that, Jeffers. That queer night was as though
it never had happened. Though it never was cleared up and none

of us have ever understood just what it was all about—what of it? You see, quarreling just doesn't matter. When Fate wills certain conjunctions, they are inevitable and no one can do anything to prevent them until they have accomplished their ends.

Clarence gave up. He couldn't seem to stay mad, either! Tony didn't oppose me when I went up to the ranch; he didn't say much about it. Clarence made a beautiful box out of pine-wood. It was the size and shape of a small coffin. He lacquered it red and sandpapered it until it had a surface like silk. He sent it up to Lorenzo—and also he gave him one of his best treasures, a small crystal rabbit.

You see, Jeffers, that's how life is. People aren't logical. They're changeable. Sometimes one thing and sometimes another. Lorenzo liked Clarence's box. He called it the Ark of the Convenant! The crystal rabbit sat on the chimney shelf among the other little special things Frieda loved. At that time Lorenzo gave me a present, too. It was a small moss-agate dish.

"There," he said, not very graciously, to be true, "my sister gave me that. It's the only possession I have left in the world, and now I haven't even got that."

Summer was passing and we were thinking of the Snake Dance in Hopiland. I had never forgotten my urgent wish to have Lawrence write and tell all about that country before it should die and become American like Buffalo and all the other towns and states. Imagine Buffalo before the Indians were gone! Then it must have had the same sound health as Taos Valley, for Indians are disinfectant. Nothing foul or morbid taints their neighborhood. I was born in Buffalo at zero hour when it was a town from which the native people had been driven out and those families who possessed it were sinking down into a diseased and melancholy inanition, for lack of knowing what to do to rouse the flagging blood current.

They had enough and more than enough to live on, those families on Delaware Avenue and all the other avenues, yet they

were sick and often bordering on madness. So they hanged themselves from chandeliers, or shut themselves into their houses and
turned day into night; one and another they nearly all bred
curious tastes and aptitudes. Yes, that was the time I was born.
Twenty-five years after, Buffalo began to grow active—active
and more rich. Now, fifty years after, it is frightfully busy and
simply steaming with gold. There are actually, in Buffalo, people
who eat off of gold plates at parties! There is no more madness in
the houses there, for you know, Jeffers, gold, too, is disinfectant.
It sterilizes the very souls out of people, and it takes a soul to go
mad.

Well, I did want Lorenzo to record the life, the kind of life
that exists where people have the true gold for which Buffalo
gold is but a deceiving counterfeit. Taos was a little living oasis
in a desert world, Jeffers. Where else did people live deeply and
thrive because they loved the sun and the water and the earth?
A land begotten, and not made, like old Europe and These
States!

But it was not to be. Lawrence really couldn't get it. You
remember I told you he had to go to Mexico to write down what
he did absorb of Taos? In *The Plumed Serpent* he has put the
facts of his Taos experience of Indians and drums and dancing,
but of actual Indian life there is very little told. All together
there are only three direct writings about New Mexico: an essay
called "Indians and Entertainment," "The Corn Dance," which
is a great tour de force describing a ceremonial at Santo Domingo
in which he succeeds in depicting, by a sequential cataloguing of
appearance and behavior, a vast, complicated, palpitating simul-
taneity, and "The Snake Dance." You have read these in *Mornings in Mexico*.

Even *The Woman Who Rode Away*, about the sacrificial cave,
he gave to Mexico! Why? I believe it was because he belonged
to those centuries of civilization that come between the bright,
true golden age of pure delight and the brilliant age of gold;

between those two "soulless" periods when men wandered piti-
fully wondering what was the matter with the world and with
themselves that they should so unaccountably suffer.

Though Lawrence believed he was through with what he
called inessentials, they were not through with him, and "history," which is concerned with the behavior of men turning
somersaults in a vacuum, never really lost its importance for
him. That is why Mexico mattered more to him than New Mexico, though maybe he would not have acknowledged it. Mexico
has some written "history"; New Mexico has none.

Well, Jeffers, it seemed to me that if Lawrence could emanci-
pate himself from that limitation of the known, the grip of
the manifest fact and folly of mankind, he, of all men alive,
could perceive and record the peculiar vestiges of another mode
of life that have miraculously survived in the undisclosed valleys
of the Rio Grande River. But somehow he could not give himself
to it. He never freed himself from his past or the past of his race.
He recognized that life there was pristine, but he could not
breathe for long in the rarefied air. Too much oxygen will burn
out the lungs. He ran to save himself from purity and died in
the old country.

But in those essays he managed to write in Taos, about Indians
and their dances, he captured a few fragments of a cosmos that
he barely glimpsed and that could have regenerated his falter-
ing spirit, had he been strong enough to stay by it.

Monday

DEAR MABEL

This in a hurry.—If Hal and Spud are coming, would you
give this list to Gersons. If Sabino is home, would he bring the
things in his wagon—if not, Gersons can hire a man.

When they come, would you bring some meat as usual.

I'll let you see my story when it's done—it goes very slow.

We should like to go to the Snake Dance. But not on August

4th, because of the two journeys. And soon it will be time to go to Mexico.

Hope you get this tomorrow.

D. H. L.

Did I say everything was the same again between us all? It was not. There was not even the recurrent happiness we used to share. The flow was gone, and in its place there was a calamitous pause that made one feel dammed up and irritable. Alice Sprague departed for New York and I planned the journey to Hopiland.

Only the Lawrences and Tony and I were going, and this left Clarence and Brett behind. You can imagine how they felt and looked. But more than four on a camping trip in an automobile is too many to manage, and they had to be left. Besides, I suspected them both, now, of making trouble, and I wanted to be free of them. I heard at this time that Jaime with his wife and baby was thinking of coming back to Taos and we all hoped to get away before they came, so they would not join us in their car!

Kiowa. Lobo. Sat.

DEAR MABEL

Brett says she would rather stay up here in her little house while we are away (we had the soap and letter, many thanks)— so let someone suitable come up—if it's Indians, Geronimo and wife. Throat still sore, but not so bad. Hope Señor de Angulo y Mayo will *not* turn up. We'll be ready Wed. afternoon.

D. H. L.

(How everything had to be arranged in those days! It seems strange to find Lorenzo planning Brett's security at the ranch when one remembers how she has lived up there alone for weeks at a time during these last years.)

Manuel and Albidia are at the Pueblo—it would be very

good if they would stay up in the little house while we are away. Will you ask them? They are not due at Del Monte till Thursday, but they might be persuaded to come Wed. afternoon to us, so Brett won't be alone: otherwise she can sleep at Del Monte a night. There is everything in the little house that Manuel and Albidia would want—bedding and everything.

The flowers are lovely.

We'll be ready Wed. afternoon.

And here we are, almost on the eve of departure, with Lorenzo complaining of his sore throat. He was never well after that, really.

Thursday

DEAR MABEL

I was thinking, if the Younghunters would like to stay here while we go to the dance, they are very welcome.—Or if they perhaps are going with us, the Gaspards. They seemed to like the place so much, perhaps they would enjoy a week here on their own.—Will you, if you feel like it, ask them. I wish I'd asked you to bring me a good gargle for my throat: it hurts like billy-o! this evening. I should hate it if it kept me back.

The fishermen aren't home yet—nearly six. Afraid the dish of fish are still aswim. They have become a fable.

Thank you so much for the books and things and all the trouble we have given you: not to mention the terrible event of the broken Catellack: done en route here or hence, alas!

D. H. L.

There was a passage about Lorenzo in a letter Leo Stein had written me some years before: "I wonder which will give out first: his lungs or his wits." Was he destroying himself instead of me, I wonder. In his struggle to free himself, did he find *himself* in Frieda, in me, and in the world around him? Oh, little Atlas, what a burden was on you!

Across the high valley and over the brim, we dropped down the steep mountain road till we came to the river. Now that it was August, the greens along the shores were growing sombre, and all the weeds flowered in purple colors. The peach orchards in Rinconada were heavy with fruit and we bought handfuls of lovely ones as large as apples. No one who eats California or Florida fruit can even guess how New Mexico peaches and apples taste, for they are allowed to mature on the trees and not in packing-boxes.

We kept on and on, eating a lunch we brought with us, until we came to Albuquerque, and there we stopped at the Harvey House for dinner. When we went into the large and luxurious dining-room, Lawrence altered the ease and naturalness we had somehow maintained all day, by becoming all of a sudden extremely conscious of Tony. He went through a byplay of which he himself was not aware, nor was Tony, either, so far as I could see. But of course with Tony it is always impossible to tell what he notices and what he doesn't.

Lorenzo tightened up and flashed a quick, half-impatient, half-protective glance at him. He had seated himself with unperturbed majesty and was calmly unfolding a large napkin and tucking the end of it into his shirt-front. Lorenzo threw looks of hatred up at the head waiter, who was a large, efficient woman with a manner aloof, and at the pleasant waitress, standing with the menu in her hand. His glances were confined for the first moments to our own small circumference, though he imagined a roomful of hostile critics surrounded us. His malaise made him snappy with us all. He began to ridicule American food and to nod his head violently to emphasize the words. His foreign flavor became apparent, advertised as it was by his manner, so that by the time his timidity allowed him to gaze a little farther than our neighborhood, he found smiles on traveling men, half concealed behind large fin-shaped hands, heads leaning together, eyebrows rising and falling. As is frequently the case, he had provoked the real event which at first his imagination had summoned up to give an opportunity for his prejudices to exercise themselves. There was a hostile atmosphere in the room, directed, however, not at Tony, but at him.

That meal, our first one in public, was disagreeable. We decided to drive on a way farther instead of sleeping there, so we climbed into the car and went towards Gallup. We passed Las Lunas and we passed the bridge of Rio Puerco. The night was dark and still and warmer down there than in the high country. We were soon running along the highway beside the railroad that goes through the Navajo Reservation. It is laid for miles and miles between mountain ranges, with near-by buttes on the right-hand side that stand motionless like the rear ends of numberless great elephants. Lawrence was appeased by the night and the mild stars.

"The lonely stars," he said. "Would you like to be a star?"

"No," I answered him, "I would rather be just what I am: the space between the stars."

We slept at a small adobe inn at New Laguna, three miles from the Laguna Pueblo. It was kept by an Indian man and his wife. At breakfast we sat at a long table in the front room off the office and ate along with two commercial travelers, a priest, and several indefatigable, anxious American women. Lawrence was far more comfortable here than in the lofty Harvey House. He felt no need to protect anyone, and he even chatted with a freshly shaved, pop-eyed man next to him, who told him that his "line" was shoes.

You see, Jeffers, in this state so little populated, as yet so unexploited, where there are few industries and no large stores, the traveling men are the chief source of supply. They come in from the cities of other states bringing the newest fashions from quaint Western creators. They travel swiftly along in their Buick or Dodge roadsters, their samples in neat leather cases, and they bring brushes, stockings, shoes, dress goods, hair-nets, hats, or perfumes. They stock up the small wayside stores with all the "lines" of groceries and with all the other necessaries of life. They are a strange race of men. Their life, as for us all, conditions their fetishes and their taboos. They love a close shave with strong-smelling soap, clean shirts, and long cigars. They loathe the night from ten o'clock on, and often kill themselves in hotel bedrooms, so every hotel in our country places a Gideon Bible next the bed to soften the loneliness of the resourceless hours when there is no one to whom they can sell anything! I have heard that there is nothing in this world to equal the desolation of traveling men in hotel bedrooms. Who would think it, to see them stepping briskly from the dining-room, seizing a toothpick from the glass in front of the blonde cashier, flashing an electric smile, strutting in checks and stripes, newspaper under the arm? One can know them, though, from their emanations, for one must perforce come after them in beds and bathrooms. They leave an odor in the pillows and along the walls of rooms. Closets in New Mexico are sickening with the faint, sweet smell of departed commercial travelers, with the lingering odor of hair, soap, cigars, and the unaired suits of bachelors. This is a lonely smell and makes the heart faint and depressed.

Out from the low-keyed atmosphere of fried eggs and coffee into the clean morning! What a bath of sparkling life! We motored on through the valley. Mount Taylor, which had faced us in the evening, was behind us now. Past Grants, a group of wayside buildings and oil-stations, with the railroad water-tank for the trains; past other small clusters of houses and stores, a few miles apart from each other in the desert; past Gallup, called the toughest town in the United States, though it looks quiet enough. Here we turned another way and left the highway beside the railroad that leads to California.

The land is fierce in there, Jeffers, where the Navajos ride singing, and the Indian women herd sheep. Everything tries to keep one out. The roads are sandy and engulf the wheels. Frequently quicksands swallow entire cars unless their drivers are vigilant. One night I saw a car embedded in sand up to the hubs of the wheels. When we came along, it had already been given up by whoever had been in it. We camped there by the roadside, and in the morning that car, sucked under, had vanished.

There is a wilder look to this land than along the Rio Grande. Rivers make mild their borders with willows and sedges, and the people who live at the river brink do not burn as the desert Navajos do, with dry-eyed, molten, black glances from haughty, metal-hot eyes. It is said to be harder to know a Navajo than any other Indian. He does not need to know anyone else, not even the Indians from other tribes. When Tony goes into a trading post anywhere on the reservation, the silent Indians stand looking at him with no more interest or any other sign of affinity than at the rest of us. All other tribes of Indians act like brothers. They seem, when they come upon each other in unfamiliar places, to scent each other out so as to clasp hands and pass to each other the life from the eyes. But Navajos are different. They feel separate and they seem to like it.

We came to a little place called St. Michel's by noon-time. There is a monastery there and, I think, a school for Indian children, but I am not certain. All I remember there is Sam Day's place, for that's the house where we always stopped.

With rolling sandy hills covered with small, wind-beaten evergreens, and tough prickly bushes on every side, this green oasis bloomed with trees and flowers inside a picket fence. Sam Day came there fifty years ago and started a trading post. His wiry little old wife knew how to make a home in the wilderness, and her house is a repository of old furniture, piles of ancient magazines, and shelves of faded brown books and is noisy with canary-birds. Geraniums bloom in the windows, and the big kitchen has a great shiny black range, where the large coffee-pot has a perpetual brew in it, and the black iron pot is always full of brown beans.

When we first went there, the trading post had already been given up, for Sam Day grew old and tired. Outside the house there were barns and sheds and off at one side a single room where the Navajo wife of Sam Day the Second sat on the floor in her red velvet shirt, her full skirts spread out in a circle, weaving Navajo blankets all day long. Sam Day the Third, a little four-year-old boy, half Yankee and half Indian, ran back and forth between the two women, his unbending Yankee grandmother and his unbending Indian mother. These two women smiled and smiled, but they never made friends, even though love held them firmly together in that narrow circle.

Sam Day the Second, born in the Navajo country, grew up with the Indians all about him. Where his mother and father never penetrated, though they lived for half a century in daily contact with those people, he entered and was initiated into the secrets of the tribe. What Sam Day could tell if he would might open curious knowledge to ethnologists and scientists, for the Navajos hold power over fire, and apparently over the laws of gravitation, molecular change, and the instant variability of matter. But no member of this tribe—Indian or white—tells these things. It is possible that they cannot transmit what they know. Some secrets can be learned, but not told. You know this, Jeffers.

The Days were glad to see us. Two tall, lanky, blue-eyed men and a small, bustling home-maker! Their house was warm and musty, with a deep, rich life lived behind closed windows. The air was not stale, but it was close. The rocking-chair by the sunny window in the overcrowded sitting-room had worn cushions covered with Turkey-red calico, and a canary shrieked excitedly overhead. Mrs. Day was thrilled because Lorenzo was a writer. She had never heard of him, of course, but other writers had passed along there before him, and afterwards had sent their books back to her to remember them by. She hinted plainly! Lawrence made a comical face.

"Yes, yes, I'll send you one of my books," he assented. But afterwards he wondered what ever could he send her that would not upset her! "Perhaps *Sea and Sardinia*," he said, "is sufficiently blameless, or maybe *The Lost Girl*."

Tony and Sam Day the Second were repairing something in the car, for those roads always loosened everything in the machinery. We spoke of the Navajo woman outside in her house, for I wanted them to see her weaving.

"Oh, Kate?" said Mrs. Day, pursing up her thin lips and looking obstinate. "Yes, you go out and see her if you like. She will be going out soon with the sheep and then Grandma'll have Sammy all to herself, won't she, Sammy?" and she took his hand. But he pulled away from her to go with us.

There was absolutely nothing in that large room except the sunlight and the loom. Kate Day went on threading the shuttle rapidly back and forth and clapping down the woolen thread with the heavy batten. Her hands were fine-textured and brown, with elegant bones. She was very pretty, with proud, small features and a great lump of fine black hair bound with purple worsted at the back of her neck. We stood looking at her after making the usual polite gesture called a *bow*. She smiled very faintly, but that was all. She did not mind our being there. We made no difference to her at all, no more than a row of cows looking over a fence.

Inscrutable, small woman, vivid and willful and alive, what intelligence in your cells imposes upon you the need to remain in this alien enclosure, linked to Sam Day?

"What would Kate like for a present?" I asked the old lady, when we returned to the cluttered house. "I'd like to send her something." Perhaps I felt some sympathy for her, some untellable, secret knowledge that we both carried in our veins and that similarly ruled us.

"Oh, Kate? Velvet. That girl likes velvet better than anything else." She looked down at her black and white checked gingham and smoothed its folds with her ugly old hand, worn with the countless and never-ending duties of a house.

I took a picture of Lorenzo standing between Mr. and Mrs. Sam Day. The print came out pale and shadowy and their forms were lank phantoms. I felt myself closer to Kate than to those diluted and uncertified people.

" . . . They are all mongrels between the present and the past. . . ."

As we pushed along across miles and miles of Arizona sand and mud, we left all the familiar aspects of habitation behind us. The land was strangely accented by sudden peaks that reared themselves like explosions arrested in mid air, and occasional mammoth rocks that had boiled up and were left congealed on the surface of the earth. The sky was vast and blue, and the clouds formed themselves into colossal horses with warriors astride them, or took the shapes of mountain cities, in the peculiar calligraphy of Nature, who writes for those who can read her signs, in the sky or on the ground, somewhat of the life of the neighborhood. As eagles speed across Taos Mountain in cloud shadows, so in Buffalo one can observe great automobiles pursuing each other down the avenues of the pale sky on windy afternoons; for every place is reflected in the mirror of the ether.

There seems to exist in human beings a deepening reservoir that contains all these pictures of the movements that are taking place in both nature and man. One person, one small human creature, may be the repository for it all. But by some law regulating the currency of the soul, unless he gives back to life as much as he takes from it, his acute receptive faculty fails him. Man is the transforming animal; that is his function, and his fate depends upon its activity.

All my life I had been receiving impressions, for with unusual luck I had been allowed to go on taking in more and more and I had only occasionally felt any urgent need or wish to do anything about them. Once, away back as far as the days in Florence, a piercing shaft of desire thrust itself up from somewhere deep within me in the shape of a prophetic pronouncement, and I wrote, for myself, one night, a crude poem that had in its strong, emotional, sudden uprush from the depths the foreshadowing of the inevitable and prescribed human wish:

TO SOMEONE WHO WILL COME

All these years and all these paths that I have trod
Have led me here to you.

The beginning and the goal and the road, long, long to infinity
That I have broken wearily, are one, and strewn with thoughts of
you.

Here at the summit of the world whither we have pressed,
We are raised above it and can judge of it at last.

Far above the world and encircling it, Nature breathes
Like a vast flame,
And together in this high place we are part of her
And one with her at last.

In these great spaces far above the world
The flame of Nature rushes like a clean wind
Carrying from us fear and all blighting thoughts.

My love, how long and how long have I waited for you
And starved for the warmth of your flame?

All through the world go the sympathies seeking their counterparts
Waiting for union, yearning they go, and rarely finding completion.

Ten thousand sympathies have been offered to me,
But no one of these could lighten my darkness.
Ten thousand sympathies have I proffered in pity, but never with
love,

And no one of these could warm or fulfill the soul of another.

Long and long I have searched for the vision that you and I only
  may see fully together.
Thousands are the dreams and the hopes, but only one for you and
  for me.
Only one fair view that we two may see fully together.

Long have I gazed into the dreams of men, but never once have I
  seen them;
Long, long have I dreamed their dreams, but only yours have I
  ever known.

But your soul, my love, I have found at last. In your eyes only now
Do I read all the meaning. Understanding has come.

Naught remains for us now but to give back to life
Our interpretation of all we have found her.

Now go, my love, I have found you. Go back to the place whence
  you came.
Take with you my soul for your warmth and your light.

For I give you my soul. Your creation it is, and lives only through
  you.
It will always be with you now and you never can quite forget it.
What creature can ever ever forget his creation? Not God and not
  man.

Go where you will and live as you may, I will live in you the life
  of your life,
Never apart from the warmth of your deeds.

Look with my eyes through the eyes of your soul. Intensely see life,
And your soul will expand with the flame of your vision.

Then clarify life. Pour back upon earth all the stream
Of interpreting and magical definitions that flow from our union.

So may I help you. . . .

But it faded out like a dream, that yearning to render an account to God, for the someone in my poem had never come and never come, and I had gone on alone. Harvesting, gathering the nuts and pearls of experience, trying to understand and assimilate them, trying to docket them, placing them in their pigeon-holes, laying them away; for a woman cannot and never will be able to do anything without the man, who releases her into creative action. This is incontrovertible. Only a man can change a woman from the devourer into the creator.

How often Lawrence would seem to try to hurt me! Once, while we drove along through the desert, he suddenly exclaimed:

"Mabel, Frieda is the freest woman I have ever known . . ." and she, with healthy justice, interrupted him roughly, crying:

"And do you think I care for your compliments when you only say them to annoy Mabel?"

Perhaps I had dimly and intuitively expected Lorenzo to be the Transformer for me and had summoned him for that purpose from across the continents. Well, he had come. He had vivified my life and possibly I had done as much for his. But apparently nothing significant had come of it beyond the momentary illuminations that flashed between us and that always ended in the fretful and frustrated hours of bewilderment.

Now on this journey across the empty land of Arizona, devoid of distraction, I suddenly awoke to the fact that I was thrice alone for all the contiguity of three people near at hand, and I felt myself dead. Nothing was happening in me. I saw, beneath that lofty sky that carried its signs and omens in a joyful activity, that nothing meant anything to me. I had ceased registering. I sat like a smiling, embalmed mummy on the front seat of the car with Tony, and Frieda and Lawrence rode behind, sometimes joyfully exclaiming, sometimes, with digging irritability, knifing at each other while Tony sang. There we were, the quick and the dead! Right out there in that lost land that Washington has not yet recognized to be commercially interesting, I ran down like a clock and verily, I believe, almost stopped! So from that time on, Jeffers, I cannot tell you about our journey. It is not as though I had forgotten it; I did not notice it—it made no impression on me.

I know we came to Mishonghovi, and we camped below the great rock mesa that was capped, on its summit, with the Hopi village. Vague rumors come back to me of our night there, and of the Snake Dance the next day. But no *living* recollection remains in me, as other scenes have stayed, vivid and real, unconditioned by time, being now, as then, so that I can transfix them on this page by the curious faculty of transformation that enables one, by going into that space where life holds the past (as well as the present and the future, I suppose) in solution, to make manifest reality.

I could fake it, Jeffers. I could tell you all about the people and the place and the ceremonial, because I had been to that country before, and other times and experiences are there for me to enter and recount. But it would not be that particular day and hour that Lawrence saw it and I with him. How it was then I just don't know, and I will not lapse into just writing of it. There is too much mere writing in the world already. This thing I am making for you is another thing.

After the Snake Dance ceremonial we motored to the Canyon de Chelly, because I thought Lorenzo would like to see Montezuma's White House. In a swirling sand-storm we pushed through the broad, high-walled fissure, Frieda and I in a wagon, sitting on bales of alfalfa, our heads bent down to escape the clouds of hot sand; Tony and Lorenzo and another man pushing along beside us on horseback. Lawrence was good-tempered and quite full of fun, for any kind of physical struggle relieved his inner tension.

Later on, our two men climbed the steep wall of the cliff up to the compact, white stone palace of the Aztec Emperor, where it rests serene and seemingly forever on the ledge of the crevice. While men outside endured the Sturm und Drang of living, the heated winds of the world were blowing through those bleached chambers, making each year an imperceptible change.

When we stopped to relax at one of the lonely trading posts, we had all been silent for a long time. I turned towards Lawrence to find his eyes upon me, vivid and alight with an inscrutable elation. Only such glimpses come back to me from the long journey!

We were not happy. On the summit of the Continental Divide, where we slept one night among the pine trees, our camp was divided. Tony and I, and Lawrence and Frieda made two separate companies. Tony and Frieda were all right, but I was very cross, and Lawrence had an ear-ache. Lawrence wanted the coffee made weak, I wanted it made strong, and there was only one coffee-pot. So we made it twice, in a venomous silence, each conducting furiously an inner dialogue with the other. Everything seemed impossible to endure. I saw Lawrence and Tony and the whole of the sickening panorama of life from the under side—negatively—and it was unacceptable to me, a reversion of the promise and the hope. I felt I could stomach no more. My soul turned in me and I retched. . . .

When we reached Santa Fe, I flung myself on the bed in the De Vargas Hotel and lay in a dark mood of disgust until the hour came for sleep and I roused myself to go into the Lawrences' room to say good night. Lorenzo handed me a few sheets covered with his small, clear writing, and I read it standing beside the bureau; and then, without a word, laid it down and, saying good night, left them.

He had written a dreary terre à terre account of the long road to the Hopi village and of the dance, a mere realistic recital that might have been done by a tired, disgruntled business man.*

* This was published in *Laughing Horse*, No. 11, Sept. 1924.

It had no vision, no insight, no appreciation of any kind. I grew inwardly colder and more aloof towards Lorenzo. I had not taken him to the Snake Dance to have him describe it in this fashion. Disappointed and incensed, I decided to let them go on without me and I remained behind for a few days in Santa Fe at Alice's house.

Before I left them—as I stood frozenly, saying good-bye at the roadside—Lawrence pushed through the wall that had grown up between us and said:

"I know you didn't like that article of mine. I'll try and do another one."

He sent me the following note after they reached the house:

Taos, New Mexico

DEAR MABEL

Too late to telegraph. We met Eve leaving—met her in the stage at Velarde. Clarence is packed, and thinks to go Tuesday. Saw the Jaimes: Jaime is Jaime—the wife seems nice. For the rest, all quiet. Emilie complains of pains in her shoulders. I gave her the *baume*. I think we shall go up tomorrow morning—Sunday—if I can get my Gersons goods.

For the rest, everything quiet here.

I'm glad I made the trip—the only really bad thing was that ear of mine, and I felt real sick that part of the time. I liked the rest of it.

I'll write a sketch for the Theatre Arts, and draw one, too, if I can: not for the Horse to laugh at.

D. H. L.

We all liked the baby—John's—so much.

After he had been home for a few days, he wrote the wonderful, deeply understanding description of the dance that you have read in *Mornings in Mexico*.

(DARK OTHER-WORLD MAN

Dark other-world man!
For our unlikeness there is no cure.
It is slow, terrible, and sure.
The arrow, the swastika, and the star
Your symbols are.
The cross, the book, and the dollar-sign—
These are mine!
Shrive me—you other-world man!

THE BLACK KING

He walks aloof along the ranks
Of falling men whose lesser blood
Counsels them naught of coming days
That sleep before the loosening flood.

His eyelids fall below the scene
That carries naught of lively score
To quicken earthly tides in him
Whose vision guards the life before:

The life of other days and times
Lies dreaming on his darkened brow—
The time to come is his, he knows,
His fruit hangs ripening on the bough.)

The singular drought within me endured. I came upon these
words in Nietzsche and was reminded of my own plight: "These
young hearts have all become old—and not even old! only
weary, vulgar, indolent! Round light and freedom they once
fluttered, like midges and young poets. A little older, a little
colder—and quickly they have become—obscurantists and
mumblers. . . . If they *could* do otherwise, they would *will*
otherwise also. Half-and-half ones spoil every whole. That
leaves wither—why lament about that? Let them go and fall,

O Zarathustra, and lament not! Rather blow among them with rustling winds!"

What had Lorenzo done but push me to the wall, beyond which I could not pass? He would not let me live my life in the only way I knew, and actually the man had overcome me. Constantly remembrance came back to me of his expressed intention to destroy me—repeated so often—so often defied. It occurred to me that had Frieda let him write that book with me, he would have attempted by that means to annihilate the strong creature whose will was so evil in his eyes, for he held me to be the prototype of that greatest living abomination, the dominating American woman. And I found myself sorry now that she had thwarted him, for it would have been an easier and a quicker end of struggling had he done it with the magic pen rather than by the reiterated blows he gave me with the strange power of his presence. For his proximity had become deadly to me, to my way of being.

Had that frail failure of a man among men really attempted to cross continents and oceans to put an end to what he conceived to be the great enemy to life in the world—the overbearing feminine will that flourished, terribly vital and undaunted, in America?

I was shaken and stricken. Nothing mattered. The people on our hill became more and more phantasmic as the wavering nerve force declined in me. In a final panic I hastened to New York to consult Dr. Brill, good old Brill, sitting in his office like a kindly ghoul, laughing at mysteries, with a quick name for any subtle dilemma.

As he saw it, the matter was not obscure, nor was it even strange. He said he had been waiting for the time to come when I must face—what? Well, I had been lucky. Luckier than anyone he'd ever known, to have gone on as long as I had, to have been able to go on as long as I had without—oh Lord, Jeffers, the language they use!—sublimating! Here I'd lived all these years in the primary urges and perceptions of youth, had been able to continue *successfully* living far beyond the period when, apparently, primary living for its own sake makes a transition into some kind of formulation—or realization. There I was now, though, up against a need to—well, he called it *work*!

If you knew, Jeffers, how I'd always scoffed at *work*! It always seemed to me the most pitiful escape, unless one had to, for economic reasons.

"Well," said Brill, "you've *got* to work for your *living*!" I saw he meant I must work or die. Oh, the unclean compromise and capitulation!

I won't go into all that again. Enough that he told me to return later on and we would deal with the problem together, and that he made me realize it was necessary. Since I had already rented Finney Farm in Croton for the winter, I had only to go back to Taos to wait a month or two. I wrote Lawrence from New York somewhat of the talk I had had with Brill and he answered:

> *Del Monte Ranch,*
> *Questa, New Mexico,*
> *14 Sept., 1924*

DEAR MABEL

I had your letter about Brill last night. I knew it was very much as he said: that there was a fatal disconnection, and that it was passing beyond your control. I am glad you are going to put yourself into a doctor's hands. Because you have now to submit to authority, and to a certain measure of control from outside. And except to an authority like a recognized doctor's, you would never have submitted.

The thing to do is to try, try, try to discipline and control yourself. And to remember that, even if all the people in the world go negative and futile, and you yourself have stuck to something which is more than all people or any people, the real thing which is beyond anybody's malevolent reach, then you yourself will never feel negative nor empty. One should discipline oneself never to do things which one's own self disapproves of—and then one can't go to pieces. But it will be hard for you to get over your disintegrative reaction towards people and circumstances—everything. As you say, you went that way so long ago.

We shall be going down to Mexico in October. My chest and throat stay sore, I want to go south. I don't want to go east for the winter: no. For this winter you must fight this thing out more or less by yourself. It is your job.

I don't know if this will reach you—but send it to the club on chance.

D. H. L.

And this from Frieda, written on the back of Lorenzo's letter:

I wrote to a nephew to come and see you, but I daresay he won't be in time. At first you sounded quite gay and now this last letter! I have felt myself like a tiger with a steady suppressed growl, going on inside me! Just things in general! And yet it's so lovely up here now, let us know when you come back and tell us all your news! Get better. I won't bother you with vests!

F.

And again a second letter came to me from him while I was still there:

Kiowa, Friday Evening

DEAR MABEL

I found your letter this evening: and here's the answer:

1. Yes, one has to smash up one's old self and get a new one *with* a new skin (slow work).

2. One must kick bunk when one sees it: hence one must be a destructive force. You have hurt yourself, often, by letting

the bunk get by and *then* kicking at random, and getting the victims below the belt. You *must* discriminate sufficiently and say: That's *bunk*! Kick it!—not kick in the wrong place.

3. One does talk too much—and one shouldn't. I speak for myself as well.—Though I don't think it matters terribly, unless one deliberately makes bad mischief—which happened this summer, in *talk*.

4. About Tony—I'm afraid you and Clarence *caused* him to take a violent prejudice against me, that time. I really have nothing against him: except that it is foolish even at the worst to be swayed too much.—About his relation to you, yours to him, I would never venture *seriously* to judge. (You really shouldn't mind the things one says casually—only the things one says really, having considered.) I do think you have a terrible lot of the collective self in you. I do think this helps to split you rather badly in your *private* self. I do think there is a good deal of subtle feminine sort of *épatez le bourgeois* in you: sometimes crude. I think this encroaches into your better relations, with men especially—that is, with Tony. It's a very difficult and tiresome thing, the mass self: and perhaps far stronger than you allow. Always allow for it in yourself: then you can get your own feet of your *own* self, and make your *real* decision. Do, do be careful of your mass self: be very careful to preserve your real, private feelings from your mass feelings. In this instance, your mass feelings will ruin you if you let them.—And don't, through a sort of feminine egotism, want Tony to live too much through you. You know how bad that is.—It is a pity you ever made Tony jealous of me: it caused a bad confusion in his feelings, which he won't easily be able to straighten out. Because, as you know, he was not naturally jealous of me: his *instinct* knew better.

5. I wish there could be a change. I wish that old built-up self in you, and in the whole world, could give place to a new, alive self. But it's difficult, and *slow*. And perhaps the only thing

that will really help one through a great change is discipline, one's own deep, self-discovered discipline, the first "angel with a sword."

To your P.S.—You need have no split between Tony and me: never: if you stick to what is *real* in your feelings in each direction. Your real feelings in the two directions won't cause any disharmony.—But *don't* try to transfer to Tony feelings that don't belong to him: admit all the limitations, simply. And never again try to transfer to me: admit the limitations here too.

Try, above all things, to be still and to contain yourself. You aways want to rush into action. Realize that a certain kind of stillness is the most perfect form of action, like a seed can wait. One's action ought to come out of an achieved stillness: not be a mere rushing on.

D. H. L.

To these I replied when I returned to Taos:

Taos, New Mexico
Sunday

DEAR LORENZO

Please do not get impatient with me for asking so many questions, but what is so queer is that I seem to know quite clearly for other people and am absolutely blank for myself. For instance, you wrote me I must learn to discipline and control myself severely. I am ready to if I knew in what way. Do you mean I should begin to serve the concrete? Such as to get up deliberately in the morning and begin deliberately to *make* myself *do* things? Such as housework? You know my tendency is to lie in bed and muse or half-think, and try to reach my own centre—or try to meditate; then to get up and dress with a great economy of attention (a genius for short cuts well accomplished!), hurry downstairs and give everybody a few *orders of things to do*; then to muse around some more, talk some, maybe, offering bright ideas to anyone around of what *they* should *do*; write some letters, do an errand, eat, then muse until the churning energy in me is beating me wild—and I decide to go and *walk* somewhere to get rid of it. . . . You know the kind of days.

Doing things is a kind of agony for some reason. As you knew, just to decide to hang up those grapes with you whom I like to be *with* made a subtle peculiar pain run along my nerves. I suppose you don't know what this is like? So is that what you mean? I should force myself into it, hating it?

Now, I'm going to tell you. There is something that takes this away—this uneasiness in action. There are two things. One is being in love. Then everything is glorious and easy and a pleasure. I am efficient, doing things easily. But it's silly for me to think of being in that condition, though not impossible, ever! I mean I call it being in love, but it is merely a kind of flow that is accomplished by somehow getting my life-tube in alignment with someone else's and having *his* life-flow run into my tube and *run my machinery.* This is what many people call being in love. It is a kind of vampirism. I can live at top strength if I get someone else's life in alignment with mine. I know the answer to that, though. "The Kingdom of *Life* is *within.*"

The other thing that releases me from this gummed-up state is *writing.* If I can overcome the terrible resistance and inertia that seizes me before I begin—if I can once get started and know I want to say something—it comes. Then I am off —in a good running pace. And *after* having done some writing, everything is different. The room I sit in seems beneficent, and the light bathes one in a mild peaceful glow. All the misery and tug and pull are gone. Then I can *do* anything. Easily. Or I can walk out into the street and take an *objective* interest in *anything.* Feel pleasant. And the negative criticism is gone. Everything is in a mild glow. Living isn't a mess and a struggle, and the beating blood inside doesn't beat at one any more. It goes along like a river at the same tempo as the sun.

But the terrible inertia to overcome in order to *start* writing! Also I can only write *for* someone and you are positively the only audience I care to say anything to. Besides the inertia, I always remember your words: "I shall never consider you a writer or even a knower." And these words paralyze me except for occasional letters and poems or parodies that *are* letters.

But one thing I have found out this morning. Life in action, in *doing* things or experiencing activity outside one, is only possible as a *secondary* thing. There must be some *primary* thing to *use one* before one can even take a walk without agony of continence. Do you understand? If one lets oneself off in the vampire love—or, rather, starts the movement by someone else's presence—then one can *bear* to wash dishes without absolutely groaning and cursing. Or if one can do some writing for some-one, then after it the world appears mild, sober, lovely, or interesting. At least one isn't *pinioned*.

Now both you and Brill feel *I* have to do all the work this winter. With guidance I have to *do* the thing, whatever it is.

Can you tell me *what* this thing literally is? Finding my-self? I believe I've been a kind of werewolfess.

What kind of control and discipline did you mean? *Would writing do* as a cure and a help? Shall I try to start a life-history or something? Save this letter if you think it would help Brill. It's so hard for me to formulate things, maybe it would aid him.

Yrs,

M. L.

P.S. Now you see Tony *per se* gives me the sense of *zest* in life—in doing things—sometimes. But so much spoils it. I suppose we must admit our different cultures—our surface lives —have taken different directions. So that there is practically nothing for us unavoidably to *do* together. For he likes Mexican dances and I don't. He likes the simple movements of life, like the plaza life, and I don't. And there is little we can talk about of *current* life. About general essentials and the eternities we are in agreement and can speak together about them. If we sit in a room, it is in silence. We do not afford each other the surface outlet, yet we both feel reality in each other, and through each other.

I do not *try* to make him live through me as you say I do, but I *wish* he did—that we both could. I try to—for when he is at the table I know I enjoy my food better. When there are only the others there, they are only pale shadows of me. When he has come in at midnight from a dance, I sleep better. If I wake up and find he has not come in and is not sleeping next my room, I am in a panic of terror lest something has happened to him. He is my security for living. My whole personal life. Have I got to give up the wish for a personal life? Have we *all* got to give it up?

M. L.

I never was able to explain to Lawrence that Tony's coldness to him did not come from any jealousy, but from Tony's observation of the curious accumulative effect of Lorenzo's powerful effort to change the part of me he did not like, coupled with Clarence's insistent belief that Lorenzo wished most literally to destroy me. That pasticcio never was disentangled, for although Lorenzo and Frieda came down and passed a few days here before they left for Mexico and we for Croton-on-the-Hudson, and we passed all together, apparently, a few days of tired serenity, yet underneath the smooth surface there were currents of suspicion and misery. Lawrence never knew me as he so much wanted me to be, and Frieda and Tony and Brett all had their secret discomfiture.

Yet it was somehow peaceful, though perhaps more sadly so than happily. One day we all drove together almost in silence through the valley: through Arroyo Seco and back across Taos to Cordovas. Again the cottonwood trees were yellow against the dark-blue sky and there was no wind—not a breath or a breeze in the rich autumnal air. The mountains hung quietly purple around the crescent horizon, and the vast magnanimous mountain, above the pueblo, continued its unperturbed life as it has done for so long. Yes, we were peaceful and I felt it and said, as I had said once before:

"It seems like nothing, yet perhaps we shall look back on this afternoon and think how happy we were."

The next day, when they went away, Lorenzo leaned out for a last good-bye. There was a wistful look in his wide-apart blue eyes.

"We'll write," he said. "I know you're going to feel better soon." And then they left and I never saw him again.

After a day or two Tony drove me to Santa Fe to put me on the train for New York, for I was to go ahead and put the house in order and he would follow me when everything was ready. I had a little feeling of hope in me then that came from an acceptance of the realization that had finally arisen to my mind, that a real change was before me, no induced or emotionalized mood, but a hard, stiff change of attitude that I was ready to try to bring about in myself. I felt Lorenzo believed in me, and I believed, too, in myself. I believed I could do anything I set myself to undertake. But I was not to be bolstered up for long by the thought of Lorenzo's encouraging faith. No sooner did I reach Santa Fe than the friends with whom he had spent the evening before leaving for Mexico told me of his criticism and vituperation against me. I was "hopeless," I was "destructive," and, of course, I was "dangerous."

It seemed to me then that there was no single stable element in the universe, either outside or inside my own brain. That was possibly the instant that I recognized once for all the immutable truth that actually there is nothing except what one creates for oneself. If I wanted stability, I must create it—and anything else

I needed. This realization, truly experienced, is the liberating and lonely and last farewell to youth and the wish for supremacy.

I gave up Lawrence then. That is, I gave up expectation, so far as he was concerned, and I wrote him a letter on the train as the land and rivers widened between us. I told him it was no use, no use at all, to believe in him, in his friendship, his affection, or even his actuality. I told him he was incapable of friendship or loyalty—and that his core was treacherous.

Alas! That letter took too long to reach him and he sent a postcard to me on his own journey south:

DEAR MABEL

It was a lovely drive: very beautiful, and about 22 miles further. Bynner comes Saturday. Spud is hesitating—one of the "is lost" sort. I don't think he'll come with the car. We shall get away if possible today—if not, we shall have to stay till Sunday, as we'd get no Visas if we arrived El Paso Sunday. If you want to write your apologia pro vita sua, do it as honestly as you can—and if it's got the right thing in it, I can help you with it once it's done. You haven't enough restraint in you for creative writing, but you can make a document. Only don't go at it too slap-dash—makes it unreal.

D. H. L.

When he reached Mexico, he wrote a letter:

> *Hotel Monte Carlo*
> *Av. Uruguay, Mexico D.F.*
> *29 Oct. 1924*

DEAR MABEL

We've both had flu colds: everybody in this damned city coughing and sneezing: it's been very chilly: snow low down on Popocatepetl. And the town uneasy and depressed: as if the bottom had fallen out of the barrel. Don't like it.

We think to leave for Oaxaca on Monday. Gamio is reported to be in Yucatan: but I don't care where he is. Somerset Maugham sent me a telegram: he left for Cuernavaca the day we came. But apparently he too is no loss: a bit sour and full of nerves and fidgets lest he shouldn't produce a Maughnum opus with a Mexican background before Christmas. As if he could fail!!

Don't talk to me about plays—the very word makes me swear. At the minute there's not a play-word in me, and I'd rather be in New Mexico. If we don't like Oaxaca, we shall probably toddle back. If I'm going to waste my sweetness on the desert air, I'll damned well choose my desert. But pazienza!

Best write % The Brit. Consulate,

2 Av. Madero. (not 1) Mexico, D. F.

If I can sit still in Oaxaca, I shall probably pull off a play. But quien sabe!

Wonder what happened to the Azul. I'll write and ask Dassburg.

And how is Finney Farm?

D. H. L.

How he must have hated to remember he had written to me, as soon as my train letter reached him!

Well, Jeffers, that is all I have to tell you about Lawrence in Taos. I called him there, but he did not do what I called him to do. He did another thing. Perhaps you are the one who will, after all, do what I wanted him to do: give a voice to this speechless land. Something interfered with Lorenzo's chance to do that. Perhaps it was because there was too much willfulness and passion and egotism surrounding him here. The irony of it is that if there is a greater freedom and purity in my wish now, that the life here may become articulate, and that you will be the channel through which it shall speak, it is Lorenzo who released me from my insistent self-will and brought me to the happy immolation that has in it no false desire. You are a clear channel and I think I am become myself a clear one, now, too.

I will not give you any history of the months and years that passed, or of the changes that came about. You have read the volumes that lead up to this one, and that, in their slow and painful compilation, taught me, through the observation of the behavior of a lifetime, to disentangle the hereditary and environmental motivations that made me what I was at the time Lorenzo came to Taos and knew me here.

How many enmities dropped away during the "work" on those volumes! If the dark compulsions and the assertive jealousies I felt towards Brett and Frieda and many others can so completely fade out of me, isn't it a pity they had ever to find lodgment in my heart and obscure all the lovelier relationships? Ah, well! That is perhaps what life is mostly composed of; as Nietzsche said, "More wrestling than dancing," until living for its own sake gives place to understanding.

So this is where I cease to come into these pages, Jeffers. I have told you all I know of Lorenzo. What follows are portions of his letters during the last years he passed in Europe. I am placing in the following pages parts of some of his letters, the parts that will hurt no one, I hope, and that seem to have some revealing of his own changes.

Though we both came back to Taos the summer following, I did not see him. He, up on the ranch, avoided me, and I avoided him. What took place between him and Brett and Frieda and others is their story, not mine. I never communicated with him until I completed the first volume of the *Intimate Memories* and wrote him that I wanted to send it to him in Europe, where he went the following autumn and from where he never returned to America.

So there you are, Jeffers; have I done what I attempted to do? Have I made you know Lorenzo?

Envoi

Envoi

Rock, bear these impressions kindly.
They are pictographs of an earlier day than now,
Telling of a time when a new world was forming
Out of the same old elements.

Photo Edward Weston.

ROBINSON JEFFERS, 1929

Part Five

Part Five

%o Frau Baronin von Richthofen
Ludwig Wilhelmstift
Baden Baden, Germany
2 Nov. 1925

DEAR MABEL

I have just got your letter. We are moving on to Italy in about two weeks' time, expect to winter there. When we get a settled address, I will write to Havelock Ellis, if you wish, for your MS. Then I will write to you what I think of it, as far as I can; and if you really wish it.

Frieda's mother seems really older, than two years ago. But still she is brisk. This place is quiet as death.

I didn't care much for New York, the eight days we were there this time. Seemed stale.

This morning I was up at the Altes Schloss, looking over the Rhine Valley: where we'd motored across, from Strassburg. Queer thing, to have a past!

Grüsse

D. H. LAWRENCE.

Villa Bernarda
Spotorno. Prov di Genova
16 Jan. 1926

DEAR MABEL

We had your Christmas Day letter, with the little story, yesterday. The story gives one the feeling of the pueblo and the country very much. I liked it.

I'm sorry I've mislaid Havelock Ellis' address. If you could tell him to send the MSS. here, we could read them and tell you how they strike us.—Heaven knows what it is, to be honest in writing. One has to write from some point of view, and leave all other aspects, from all the remaining points of view, to be conjectured. One can't write without feeling—and feeling is bias. The only thing to put down on the paper is one's own honest-to-goodness feeling.

We actually had two days of snow here, and the cacciatori are banging away at the tiny birds, it's like a festa with all the crackers going off. The robins and finches fly about in perfect bewilderment—and occasionally in bits. La caccia!

It's a quiet winter, but pleasant. Thank heaven the sun shines warm again, the almond trees are budding. Europe is easy, when all's said and done.—Where, by the way, was your Florence villa? Sounds like *où sont les neiges d'antan*. If you'll send me the address, we'll go and look at it. I expect we shall make a trip round about when my sister comes out in February.

I don't quite know what we shall do later in the spring. There is some talk of my going to Russia for a bit. But I don't know how that will turn out. How long are you staying in Croton? I ordered you a copy of *The Plumed Serpent*. You may perhaps like it: not many people will: but I do, myself.

Brett is down in Capri. She seems to be enjoying it, too, from what she writes. Frieda expects her daughter Barby this afternoon—la vita e tutta altra. Quasi quasi non mi conosco piu. I wonder very much what it's like at the ranch. William Hawk has taken the horses down to his pasture at San Cristobal.

Remember me to Spud and everybody—tanti buoni auguri!

D. H. L.

My publisher Martin Secker is here—quiet little man. I think I'll give him this letter to post in England, he'll go back on Monday.

Ash Wednesday

Nice of you to write so warmly about the *Plumed*. I haven't got your MSS. yet, but expect they'll arrive. They'll be quite safe. I'm going to Monte Carlo for a bit, with my sister. It's lovely sunny weather, thank Heaven. Did Spud get the poems?

D. H. L.

2-3-26 Villa Bernarda

DEAR MABEL

Your manuscript arrived safely, but Lawrence is in Capri. I wanted to see your villa in Florence, it and your life in it had left a vivid impression. I have the children here and something in me came to life again in them too. I hope Lawrence is taking a new lease of life, that Plumed Serpent took it out of him, it went almost too far. Hope your novel is doing you good. I was amazed at the people in New York, they were such terribly squeezed lemons, painful really! You sound nice and peaceful at your Croton. Yes, we will meet again (it sounds like a hymn) if Lawrence is only well enough. I want to go back to the Ranch. If your house in Florence isn't let, I would love to stay in it a day or two! Lawrence will soon be back, so I keep the manuscript here.

A rivederci

FRIEDA.

Ravello, 18 March, 1926

DEAR MABEL

I have been moving around a bit, while Frieda stays in Spotorno with her two daughters. Your article came along yesterday. I suppose it is true, one is struggling against all these mechanised emotions and motions, and one gets oneself a bit Laocoon distorted in the process. But à la guerre comme à la guerre. At the moment I'm feeling as if I'd had a kick dans le ventre. There was a rather sniffy note from Edwin Dodge to say he is staying himself, con famiglia in the villa. You shouldn't have bothered him. I had no idea of staying there. The plans for the summer are vague. Frieda talks of leaving Spotorno for good on April 10th and going to Germany. She has your MS. I shall read it as soon as I go up there again—perhaps next week —and let you know. Brett may be coming to America quite soon. I gave her your address. I do think we are all changing pretty drastically, even she.

Best wishes.

D. H. L.

Finney Farm
Croton-on-Hudson
New York
April 3, 1926

DEAR LAWRENCE

Your note from Ravello came the other day. I wonder if we *are* changing! I hope so. A real change is needed, not a growth, not to grow "bigger," not an increase of oneself as is! That, I thought for ages, was what one had to work for, so I apparently went on getting more and more *so,* which of course was orful.

I believe Gurdjieff says something like this, put into *my* language: we devour the world . . . we eat up the whole *outside ourselves* and turn it into consciousness, but the more consciousness we get, the less place we have to use it (for we have swallowed our exterior in this and many other lives). So the less place we have to function in, and, finally, it is a torment like having to carry the whole weight of one's body on the tip of one's own little finger.

It is like having used up New York and all the music and the theatre and books and people and ideas and motors and the whole damn show—having eaten it up and got it all inside one so one *can't* go into town any more—there is no such place *for* one. Besides which, once onto oneself and one's own chief feature (which is one's own particular mode of egotism, and *mine* is self-importance—don't tell!), one *can't* go on serving *it* and performing stunts to turn it into a monument to oneself and calling it by grand names like ambition, service, an influence on one's time, and such like, so that there one is—suspended "between two worlds, one dead, the other powerless to be born"—hung there between *ambition* or *self*-serving purpose and *inertia*.

Then Gurdjieff comes along with his Method or Solution, and it is this: if one will continue to go *on* instead of to drop down one's scale, a special effort is needed for self-creation. Nature, with heredity and sociology, has done all she's going to—has baited the hook all she can—has led us by the ego to *here*; now one has to do the rest oneself.

Gurdjieff says quite calmly, here's a way. Sounds crazy, sounds awful. Try it. Observe this organism. Observe Mabel. Stand back a bit and see her. What she *does,* what she feels, what she thinks. It is enough to observe just her physical behavior: her tone of voice, her movements, her changes of temperature, etc. Just behavior, for that is a new language to learn . . . it is what her feelings and her thoughts are saying.

This Mabel has three modes or centres: instinctive, mental, and emotional. They have eaten up the universe. She *must* create a fourth one herself—the I. Behind the brain there are potential muscles for the new mode. To develop them, observe yourself—all the time. Become conscious now of your self, it is a new universe, a cosmos, the world of self-consciousness. And it is terribly hard to know it. All the old life is against it. One can never make a habit of becoming conscious of this mechanism, one is so identified with it. One doesn't *feel like* becoming aware of it and at the same time non-identified with it.

This is the only activity without wish—and it develops Will as opposed to Self-will. Gurdjieff says that little by little the by-products appear . . . in the old centres *new* emotions—

active knowing and active creation. "Seek ye first the Kingdom of Heaven and all other things shall be added unto you."

So that's his Method. Self-observation. First with *non-identification,* then *participation,* then *experiment. His* kind of alchemy.

At the Institute in Fontainebleau he makes them all *work,* use their bodies, which is to attack the instinctive centre absolutely paralyzed in most people—to break up old *habits* and crystallizations. As they move and work, etc., they are to observe themselves and what goes on in them. *Not* introspection. *Not* one part of the mechanism watching another part—but really aside: *non-identified.*

I suppose I've made you mad as hops writing all this. I remember you got furious at a letter from Cal. all full of diagrams! But I *do wish* you'd go and see Gurdjieff if you're in Paris, although I believe he may be near you now on the Riviera, and *see* if he says things like this—and see what you feel about him as a person.

I might go over for a week or two in May to have some talk with him; but I'd rather wait to hear from you first. I wish he'd come over here.

I am dying to hear your opinion of the manuscript. It is a real effort to *see Mabel.* Did I send you the remarks to the second volume? Here they are if I didn't. I am having a hard time with it. Not interested in *her then,* though the people and the place make interesting material. Amusing, that is.

I do not think Edwin meant to be "sniffy." He is always a little embarrassed. He wrote me, too, that he and his wife are there for some weeks and he didn't see how it would be "practicable." You will understand him when you read my second volume.

Tony and Spud and an old friend Neith Hapgood and her two girls have all gone to New York for a matinée. I've had flu since three weeks ago and am just getting over it, so I'm all alone out here. The ground looks drab and discouraged, the trees perfectly stubborn, and the river flat and gray. Tomorrow is Easter and they will sing: "Christ is risen." I believe it's up to one to see that he *does*! But oh my!

Affectionately,

MABEL.

Better come to Taos. Will look for Brett here.

Villa Bernarda
Spotorno (Genova)
12 April 1926

MY DEAR MABEL

I have been back here a week, and in another week we leave this house, for where, I don't quite know. I don't want to come back to America just now—it's so hard and tense. I am weary of that tension, even the tension of the practice of relaxation. My I, my fourth centre, will look after me better than I should ever look after it. Which is all I feel about Gourdjieff. You become perfect in the manipulation of your organism, and the I is in such perfect suspension that if a dog barks the universe is shattered. Perhaps I should say, the I is also so perfectly self-controlled that nothing more ever can happen. Which perhaps is a goal and an end devoutly to be wished.

I do believe in self-discipline. And I don't believe in self-control.

In the end, if you Gourdjieff yourself to the very end, a dog that barks at you will be a dynamo sufficient to explode your universe. When you are final master of yourself, you are nothing, you can't even wag your tail or bark.

But the fact that your I is not your own makes necessary a discipline more patient and flexible and long-lasting than any Gourdjieff's.

I wish you had not written to Edwin Dodge again about the Curonia. Myself, I don't want to go there to stay. An hour would be enough. Since your Duse story, basta! And Edwin Dodge's note to me was very sniffy, as if I were wanting something of him. Heaven forfend! But he was of course quite polite.

I have finished your Memoirs, sent the first part back to Havelock Ellis, will send him the rest tomorrow.

In the first place, why oh why didn't you change the names! My dear Mabel, call in all the copies, keep them under lock and key, and then carefully, scrupulously change the names: at least do that: before you let one page go out of your hands again. Remember, *other people* can be utterly remorseless, if they think you've given them away.

"Memoirs of a Born American"—they are frightfully depressing, leave me with my heart gone way down out of my shoes, so I haven't any heart at all, feel like a disembodied corpse, if you know what that means. At the same time, I should say it's the most serious "confession" that ever came out of America, and perhaps the most heart-destroying revelation of the American life-process that ever has or ever will be produced. It's worse than Œdipus and Medea, and Hamlet and Lear and Macbeth are spinach and eggs in comparison. My dear Mabel, one could shed skyfuls of tears except for the knowledge of the utter futility of shedding even one. The only thing to do is to close down for the time the fountains of emotion, and face life as far as possible emotionless. But you've said a sort of last word —*That's that!*—to Jesus' *Consummatum est!*—It's not the absolute truth—but then nothing ever is. It's not art, because art always gilds the pill, and this is hemlock in a cup. It seems to me so horribly near the truth, it makes me sick in my solar plexus, like death itself, which finally breaks the solar plexus. My dear Mabel, I do think it was pretty hard lines on all of you, to start with. Life gave America gold and a ghoulish destiny. Heaven help us all! One thing, though, I do think we might learn: if we break, or conquer anyone—like P., it's like breaking the floor-joists, you're sure to go through into the cellar, and cripple yourself. It's the broken snake that's the most dangerous. The unbroken slips away into the bushes of life.

Never win over anybody!—there's a motto.—I mean never conquer, nor seek to conquer. And never be conquered, except by heaven. And if you don't set your will in opposition to heaven, there's no occasion for conquest there.

But one can't do more than live one's destiny, good or bad, destructive or constructive. One can do much *less,* like B., and chew substitutes all one's life. Or like E. D., not have much of a destiny anyhow.

Lord, what a life! It's pouring with rain, and I'm feeling weary to death of struggling with Frieda. I feel like turning to Buddha and crying basta! and sitting under a bho tree.

D. H. L.

Spotorno,
19 April 1926

DEAR MABEL

We leave here tomorrow, shall stay in Florence a few days. Then Frieda will go with her daughter to Baden Baden, and I shall probably stay in Umbria, and collect notes for that book on the Etruscans.

I heard from Brett that she is landing in Boston about May 16th: she sails from Naples on May 2nd. She wants to go back to Del Monte. She'll be able to keep an eye on the ranch. But heaven knows how she's going to be, out there alone. She must get some decent person.—And she's coming in on the quota: hope there won't be a fuss when she lands.

I discovered your little foreword to the Memoirs, when I was packing up: so it didn't get sent to H. Ellis with the rest of the MS.—It's a very clear statement of the very very very central malady of our civilisation, seems to me. To be born without any centre, any centrifugal I!—only this strange contripetal vortex of an ego. I think everybody is born both: their souls go

both ways, centrifugal and centripetal. But according to statement, yours was only centripetal: you only existed when something was pouring into you—some sensation, some conscious
registering. Of course that's not quite true. There must be a
central you, or you couldn't *know*. Most people don't know. I
believe the majority of people are like it. It's only that they have
no definite I, and they exist in the group consciousness; they
are so tribal, so entirely group conscious, that they don't need
to have any individual consciousness. I think that's what the
man meant when he said you never quite belonged to the human race. The group consciousness *of course* never knows the
acute individual consciousness: and the acute individual consciousness is always half oblivious, half hostile, to the mass consciousness, the mass consciousness is hostile back again. You
happen to have been born an individual, even if you were only,
in your own terms, an individual vortex. Those other swine re-
volve slowly in the vast, obscene social or mass vortex, and so
of course they never realise their own null negation. Yours anyhow was a fierce, direct negation: as there are gods of pure
destruction, pure in its way, and necessary as creation.

And that's what I think about Gourdjieff and all those
things: they can only help you more competently *to make your
own feelings*. They can never let you *have* any real feelings.—
That only comes with an acute moment of self-knowledge:
and you've had that: and a sort of anguish of repentance (it
only means a turning back, or turning round, or the crucial pain
of turning or revolving in the other direction). As for that, I
don't know.

But the Foreword gives the book away, don't you see. All
those terrible feelings, none of them, ultimately, real.—But to
know it immediately *makes* something real: in a sense, sets the
whole thing in a rhythm of reality.

Heaven knows how it will all work out in actual living.
Change is the coming of that which we don't expect. But the

breaking of a lifelong habit is also *almost* impossible.

Collect your MSS and keep them all in a safe. Don't show them to anybody else, just now. Labour and wait. Don't be in a hurry. It's one of your habits you must break. Let some change come. Then, after a few years, take out your MSS again, and do what you wish with them. But not now. For the moment, let them lie still.

Write % Curtis Brown, 6 Henrietta St., London, W. C. 2. tante cose!

D. H. L.

Florence, 25 April

We are here for awhile—if you come to Europe in May, let me know—but % Curtis Brown, 6 Henrietta St., London W. C. 2 is the quickest.

Had your letter today. But I contend (although Gourdjieff's method is sound, for what it aims at) that when the *I* finally emerges, that way, it will be half demon and half imbecile. That's the tragedy of that way. There's another way, but the change *has to take place* before you can start on it. However, every man to his own stride.

Don't you see Gourdjieff's ultimate I is the ultimate self important?

D. H. L.

Villa Mirenda, Scandicci,
Florence, 8 May 1926

DEAR MABEL

I had your letter with "Constance"—and also your following letter, where you say you—to put it short—don't feel anything any more. I believe one has to go through that. It's the change of life. I feel all Italy is going through it: the strange change of life. It's the breaking down of the Gourdjieff "habits." But the habits that are hardest to break down are habits of feeling and consciousness, and above all, habits of relationship. Our habits of emotion go so deep, we almost die before they break: and our habits of relationship have so many cancer-like threads, any one of which will start the whole old thing again—it's a case of *poveri noi*! The process is organic and ultra-organic. I feel it's a painful deadening process. But I don't feel that one can "do" it, *make* it! There has to be something else pushing. And one has to be on the side of the new unknown.—Anyhow it's a weariness!

Constance is quite a good sketch, but has not much to do with you. It doesn't matter. You see in Europe you didn't *fight* —couldn't. And if you only live in and try the fight, you couldn't live. But perhaps that habit of the fight has to go, with all the rest. O poveri noi!

I think quite definitely you should publish those memoirs yourself, and do them in separate vols, with separate titles, so that the different vols may be quite different.

We think to stay here till about 16th July, then go to Baden for two weeks, then to England for August. So address me either % Curtis Brown, London, or else % Frau von Richthofen, Ludwig, Wilhelmstift, Baden-Baden.

Tell Spud I haven't had his horses yet, and shall write him the minute they come.

I heard from Brett, safe in New York, and thrilled by it. So probably you've seen her. I don't even want to be thrilled.

I suppose we shall be back here in September, and I shall go around to the Etruscan places. I'm afraid I shan't get anything much done before we leave.

One's got to leave off wanting to feel as one has felt, and enjoying what one has enjoyed—at least, in the old way.

The weather's always unsettled and unsatisfactory. They say there's an astronomical reason.

D. H. L.

There just came from Taos about 1000 sheets of the drawing of me by Bynner for Spud's Horse. Were they all really intended for me?

Villa Mirenda, San Polo Mosciano,
Scandicci, Florence, 17 May, 1926

DEAR MABEL

We've taken this old and bare sort of farm-villa: or at least, the top half of it, for a year. But it costs very little, so we can just keep it as a pied-à-terre. It's very nice country, about seven miles out of Florence.

About your MSS.—I don't see much point in having them done into German—nobody would take half so much notice of them, if they came first in German. If you very carefully disguised all names, and your own identity, and got Orage and Little—or Littell, whatever he is—to swear secrecy—and were really careful—you might get them out in America. Or you might do as James Joyce did with *Ulysses,* get them published in a fat paper volume at the Shakespeare Library in Paris. You would have to see Miss Beach about it. But that strikes me as the best way. I think Frank Harris is doing something of the same with *My Life.* Or you might come to Paris with Spud and *publish it yourself,* next winter. It's not at all impossible. I should think that *Miss Beach, Librairie Shakespeare, rue de l'Odeon, Paris* (I give the address from memory)—would tell you all about it. She did the whole business of *Ulysses* herself, and you know what a great fat book that is. And she is very nice.—You could publish, if you like, the first Vol. first, so that there would be nothing to startle the prudes: and when they were quite used to seeing *Intimate Memoirs* going through the mail, then send out the second and third volumes: ship them in bulk. You ought easily to get your money back. (But you must very carefully alter *all* names and disguise the locality.)

It may be, also, that you need a break in the continual writing. Nobody one earth can pour out three, four, five volumes without ever turning off the tap. Probably the Florence part would come better if you rested a bit—or if you were in Paris again. Europe is very unreal, in America. And in Europe, America becomes like a sort of tormented dream to one.

Brett is due to land in New York tomorrow. I do hope she has no difficulties, and that she'll be able to look after the ranch this year. It is rather a burden on my mind.

As for Gourdjieff and Orage and the awakening of various centres and the ultimate *I* and all that—to tell you the truth, plainly, I don't know. History may repeat itself, but the repetition comes with such a difference, that you never can tell, till afterwards. There is no way mapped out, and never will be. Only we know that the process is long, and painful, and dangerous, and you're more likely to die or to disintegrate than to come through, if you do *too* much about it.

I'm sorry Spud's *Horse* wants to be born with five legs and its tail at the end of its nose. Quel monstre!

I'll go and look at the outside of the Curonia, if I can find out where it is. Somewhere up the Viale dei Colli, isn't it—behind Piazza Michelangelo?

I met a man called Loeser—is that how you write him?—he spoke of you and "Edwin."—Why do Americans always talk about their friends by their Christian names, to strangers and in piazza? I didn't care for him. There's an unholy bunch of rich Americans here.—But I am weary of people who talk like that.

It rains a great deal, the country is much too green, and the proper spring and summer seem as if they'll never come. Which is very disappointing.

Tante cose di noi due!

                                                                D. H. L.

Villa Mirenda, San Polo Mosciano,
Scandicci—Florence, 21 May 1926

MY DEAR MABEL

Your bit about G. and the article on the Curonia came today. I'll go and look at the outside of the villa very soon. Probably your bit about G. contains the germ of your resistance to these vols. You resist anything which is not resistance. The only other touch of real love in your book was for Violette in Paris, and that was deathly. With your men, you only want to resist them, fight them, and overthrow them: that was what you wanted with P.: "let's see who's stronger!" With G. it was a touch of the real old physical love, not from the *will* like all the others. So you rejected it, as you must have rejected it all your life. And this makes one of the great losses of your life. Because in that kind of love, you'd have had moments at least of escape from your ego. But you never finally wanted even the *momentary* escape from your ego. You wanted your ego *all the time*. This makes you resist Italy, for Italy for the first time "tempted" you. America never once tempted you, not even in the shadowy U. C.— And it is this which makes the peculiar rancid sort of bitterness one finds in Italy today: the permanent rejection, by the foreigner, of the natural physical flow, and the permanent insistence on the ego, the putting-it-over business. You'd better say to yourself: "In rejecting the *best* of the Italian 'thing' " (as you always call it—and G. is an example, though personally he's not very important)—"I made one of my life mistakes."— You know I always uphold, it is the sheer physical flow which is the healing and sustaining flow to the height, it is sex, true sensual sex. But it has a thousand forms, and can even be only a mere flow in the air, to be enough. But one needs the physical flow. That's why I can't stay long in America.

Don't leave your MSS. to anybody. They'll all edit them to emasculation. Rouse up and publish them yourself. Do it in Paris, or even here. Norman Douglas publishes his works now himself, here in Florence. But Paris I believe is better.

And don't have introductions. Don't be introduced and discussed before you're there. Don't have anybody write an introduction. Don't ask for credentials and letters of recommendation.

Publish your things blank straight as they are, without a word, and so put them down. If you sell a thousand, it's quite enough to establish the book permanently. Print a thousand, or at most two, and have done with it. Have it reviewed in about three good newspapers, and no more. As little publicity as possible, and the thing makes its own way and won't be quashed. And preserve your incognito as completely as you can, really. For once put your ego aside. After all, there's enough of your ego in the book, without having to write your name large on the title page. And never say die.

I do think one ought, if one can, to remove the fight (the fight *is* essential) from the field of one's personal relationships, and put it in the impersonal field of the combat with this fixed and rotten society. Put your fight into the publishing of your book, and let *people* alone. Even let your own salvation alone.

But there, you'll do what you need to do.

It's been atrocious weather—rain, rain, rather cold all the time. This afternoon I sit on the terrace in the sun, but there are mutters of thunder. I do wish it would clear up. If you can, try and prevent Brett doing anything rash, like going up to live on the ranch all alone. I hope she'll find some substantial person to be up there with her.

If I were rich enough, I'd hire the Curonia for a bit just to show these English-American Florentines how completely one wants to ignore them.—But even from San Polo Mosciano one can do it enough.

D. H. L.

Villa Mirenda, Scandicci,
Florence, 3 July 1926

DEAR MABEL

I am sending back the MS. of the "Villa" now. It seems to me all right as it is: a wee bit absurd, but expressive of the phase you want to describe. As for its lacking the human quality, it's aboundingly full of Mabel—which is all that is intended, for this time. It is a perfectly coherent part of the Memoirs.

I can see you don't want to publish the thing in English: and I think, all things considered, you are right. I wrote to Frieda's sister about getting it done in German. She did the *Boy in the Bush* and did it splendidly. She replied that she would like to see the MS. very much, and would probably like to do the translation. The difficulty is, with a book which has not yet appeared in English, the publishers would be willing to pay only very small translation rights—equivalent at most to $200—probably only $100—and it really is not worth while. You see you would, I presume, make a royalty contract with the publisher, as if the book were an original German work. You would have to make some arrangement with Else: either pay her a sum down for the translation and keep all the rights and royalties for yourself: or else share the royalty rights with her; if she feels she can do it. You would have carefully to alter all the names before you sent the MS. to Germany, because of course many Americans read German: and you would have to take a nom de plume. Else knows the publishers and the publishing world pretty well, she no doubt would get the thing placed. Her husband used to edit a fat political-economy quarterly. But think it over, then write to her yourself: Frau Dr. Else Jaffé, Bismarckstrasse 17, Heidelberg, Germany. We leave here in ten days time, for Baden Baden. I shall see Else and talk the matter over with her.

I don't think I want to go and see Gourdjieff. You don't imagine how little interest I have in those modes of salvation— or modes of anything. But later on, you go yourself to Fontainebleau for a while: it would do you good, even if you went away again deciding it was not for you. It would give you something to accept or reject.

I'm glad you met Brett and you got on well together. It's quite true, one should by now be old enough to take no notice of things said—specially things repeated—and we surely surely needn't get into "states" any more.

The postman has this minute handed me the new batch of MS. I will read it at once.—Of course this vol. isn't so wildly interesting, but it's just as much an integral part of the memoirs, and just as necessary as the first two parts.—If you want to send it to Germany, don't send this Vol. II yet awhile. Send only as far as where you leave Buffalo. Better never offer too much at a time, to anybody.—You may take it as a fair test, that what didn't bore you to write, won't bore the reader to read.

Best address me % Curtis Brown, 6 Henrietta St., London, W. C. 2.—I expect we shall be in England for August.

Am glad you like Taos: it *is* very lovely there, with the fine pure air. I continue to like Tuscany: the cicalas are rattling away in the sun, the bells of all the little churches are ringing midday, the big white oxen are walking slowly home from under the olives. There is something eternal about it: apart, of course, from villas and furniture and antichita and æsthetics. But we see few people, and live rough, which is what I prefer.

Frieda calls me for dinner. Remember me to everybody.

D. H. L.

I have read the new MS. and return it also.

The part about Edwin is excellent, and gives one a sense of true experience. The part about Bindo isn't so good. You are never so good, apparently, when you are doing a relationship with one who is *not* an American. It was the same with Marcelle. The hammer doesn't ring on the iron, quite. I don't know why that is. Even the Eyres the same.—But it is just as well it is so, because that conveys the sense irrevocably that you *are* an American, and foreigners *don't* really come into immediate contact with you. It gives value to the Memoirs.

I wouldn't linger too much, I think, over occasional people in Florence.—But don't listen to me even there.—Do only that which *really interests you*, with a bit of a burning interest. And anything that does burn in you, do it without reflection.

The part about Edwin is very good indeed.—But what about his feeling to *you*, as time goes on, in the Curonia? Do you give that?

D. H. L.

Villa Mirenda

DEAR MABEL

Of course I was most interested in your novel. I think you ought to be satisfied, you have "done your bit" and been what you were meant to be: what more can any human being want! As for myself, I *learnt* from it, from your successes and from your failures. Alas for the failures, they are like the wounds in battles e cosi e la vita!

After the ranch, I appreciate Tuscany's otherness and delicacy very much! I almost feel immoral because I loved that ranch life, but now I love this, the subtle richness and floweriness! You must come in the autumn! I wanted to write before and I like to think of Tony and the Spud, but I don't like the Gurdieffs and the Orages and the other little thunderstorms.

The way you wrote the chauffeur story was splendid! Thank you for thinking of the embroidery for me; do bring it along when you come! And we will have some good times yet! Let's have done with our grands serieuses, tres grands serieuses, I want to have a "good time!" at last!

Yours ever,

FRIEDA.

25 Rossetti Mansions,
Flood Street, Chelsea,
London, 8.8.26

DEAR MABEL

Always now and then a batch of your past life appears and I devour it. Lawrence is in Scotland, I am glad; London lowers one's vitality. Monty and Lawrence met on the stairs and were all "loving kindness" to each other "all of a heap!" It came so suddenly, it made me gasp. The boy's struggle to get somewhere moves me and interests me and how little use one really is! When I said don't let's take ourselves too seriously, I said it to *myself*, but I laughed at your attack certainly deserved—had I not preached it at myself! Do say how Tony is, Lawrence was also quite distressed, surprisingly so. Of course Tony is a "possession of ours." I don't feel the coal strike here, but everything seems like only half emerged from the sea and drowsy. The flat is a studio and looks over the roofs. While Lawrence is away I have for each meal an egg, a tomato and a cup of Bovril, to get a little thinner, so if you find this letter "thin" you'll know why. We have seen Aldous Huxley—charming, cultured, thin, my word, you can get him in half an hour! Then a charming youth who wants to reform the world by dancing. He was thrilled about the Indian's dancing. Then we went to the Richard Aldingtons—Arabella comes in Aaron's Rod. She is so like a mixture of Trinidad and Rufina, so black-haired and Richard is so fair and blue eyed and Germanic! Arabella loved my Indian rings, one you gave me and one Swinburne Hale gave me. I feel superstitious about them, thinking they bring me luck and always wear them. Do send Arabella a *bracelet,* she *ought* to have one: and tell me what it costs. It would please her so.

Lawrence has had a crisis in health and is better. He does not want to write anything much just now. I am glad. He gave more than he could afford.

Yours,

F.

They are doing "David" and are *keen*—so am I!

14 August 1926

DEAR MABEL

I am glad you are back in Taos. Poor Tony, I was thinking of him, sick there in Albuquerque. I think you mustn't take him so far from the Pueblo, really. I don't think he can stand it, it saps his vitality. Seems to me he ought not to do more than take little trips in the West.

As for publishing the *Memories*, I don't think it's wise, while your mother lives. Keep them safely locked away, and wait. And then one day publish them yourself.

I am up here in the north of Scotland for a couple of weeks. It is nice, but rather rainy. The heather is out on the moors: the so-called mountains are dumpy hills, rather sad and northern and forlorn: it is still daylight till about half-past nine in the evening.—But I wouldn't care to live up here. No!

We shall be in England for a week or two. The stage society is giving a couple of performances of the play *David* in Oct. or Novem. I should like to see the first rehearsals, anyhow. But I don't want to stay long in England. I have said I will go back to Baden Baden and take an inhalation cure, in the Kurhaus, for my bronchials—for twenty days. Then towards the end of Sept. or in October, go back to Florence. That seems to be my programme for the moment.

The MSS. you sent are still in London. Frieda didn't forward them here. As soon as I get back, I shall read them and tell you my impression and return them to you. I hear Spud has gone to New York. What will you do for a secretary?

I do hope Tony will be all right now. Remember me to Ida!

D. H. L.

30 Willoughby Rd.
Hampstead, N.W. 3
23 Sept. 1926

DEAR MABEL

I am sending back all the MS. today. It is all very good—but towards the end gives a great feeling of weariness: the weariness you no doubt felt in Italy there. It depresses me, of course: the long, long indictment of our civilisation, the strange focussing of female power, upon object after object, in the process of decreation: or uncreation: as a sort of revenge for the compulsion of birth and procreation: becomes in the end like a sandhill slipping down on one. Ce ne finira jamais! It is as if the hourglass of time were reversed, and the sands of an eternity were streaming backwards down on us. The struggle with the sands of time is worse than useless. Let the soft dry deluge continue, out of the reversed heavens. C'est la femme.

Tony's mother was your enemy—so she too is gone!—and I shall never see her look up at me again, sharply, as I sit in the car: with so much sharp understanding—and with so pathetically little, since our psyche is equipped with a whole extra box of tools.

Bobby Jones' letter doesn't strike me as a pure bronze resonance of sincerity. To my feeling, it would be a bit cruel to bring Tony to Europe. But you will do what your doom makes you do, so why ragionare? Jung is very interesting, in his own sort of fat muddled mystical way. Although he may be an initiate and a thrice-sealed adept, he's soft somewhere, and I've no doubt you'd find it fairly easy to bring his heavy posterior with a bump down off his apple-cart. I think Gourdjieff would be a tougher nut.

We leave here on Tuesday, and stay a few days in Paris, on our way to Florence. It is warm and sunny and autumnal, as I remember it in 1915 when we lived for a few months here in Hampstead. I have seen a few of the old people: and yesterday the Louis Untermeyers: extraordinary, the ewige Jude, by virtue of not having a real core to him, he is eternal. Plus ça change, plus c'est la même chose: that is the whole history of the Jew, from Moses to Untermeyer: and all by virtue of having a little pebble at the middle of him, instead of an alive core.

The autumn sounds very lovely in Taos and at the ranch. Part of me wishes I was there—part doesn't. I heard from Rachel Hawk she had left. Hope Brett will manage all right alone.

I suppose we shall be at the Villa Mirenda, Scandicci, Florence, by the first week in October. The grape harvest won't all be over.

Remember me to everybody. You ought to number the pages of at least the sections of your MS.

D. H. L.

Villa Mirenda, Scandicci,
Florence, 9 Oct. 1926

MY DEAR MABEL

Your letter and the sketch came yesterday. I will offer the sketch to some magazine, but don't know if they'll take it. It's not really very good: not nearly so good as your Memoirs. As soon as you try writing from the imagination, not recording your own actual impressions, you become amateurish. Yet the most part of the Memoirs is not amateurish at all, very much to the point.

Richard Aldington says why not bequeath the "Intimate Memories" to the Académie Française. There they would be quite safe, and sure to be published some time.—But I myself know nothing about it.

By the way, did Frieda ask you to send an Indian bracelet to Arabella—Mrs. Aldington? I only heard of it yesterday. Don't you be bothered about it: I don't see why Frieda troubles you, for such a thing. And if you *did* happen to send one, let me know what it cost. It's not *your* present to Arabella, mon Dieu! But if you haven't done anything about it, *don't*!

I do feel it's rather rash of Brett to have a motor car, in that country, on those roads, and with her deafness. But I suppose there is a special kind of providence for such cases.

We got back here four days ago. They were just finishing the vendemmia. It is hot, rather sultry—I shouldn't mind a little rain. I suppose Taos is all blue and gold. It is very lovely out there: much lovelier than here. If it weren't for a certain queer exalted or demonish *tension* in the atmosphere, I would so much rather be there than here. Italy, humanly, isn't very interesting nowadays. Fascism, whatever it does, spreads the grand blight of boredom. But I suppose we shall stay here at least till spring.

Remember me to everybody!

D. H. L.

Many thanks for *Lolly Willowes*. I found it here. It was good, in a small way, and true. Only, like everybody else, she didn't know *how* to be a witch. Sabbaths and talks with satan are all beside the point. Being a witch is a much more serious and strenuous matter.

Do you remember, by the way, the owl Manby sent over? Is he just the same?

D. H. L.

Villa Mirenda,
Scandicci (Florence),
30 Oct. 1926

My dear Mabel

My agents sent back the little sketch, which I'd asked them to try round: said it wasn't good enough: and I agree with them. Why bother with those trifles! As I say, whenever you take a literary attitude, your stuff's no good. The novel, or rather, the *Memories*, is so good because you're not being literary: only occasionally a bit of a literary taint comes in. When you are only trying to put down your own truth, nothing else, the stuff becomes excellent. I do think the Memories extremely good. As for literature!—well, twenty years hence, W.'s books will be where most other books are, under dust. R.'s books don't exist even now. There's nothing in it all, this literairiness.

I was talking to Aldous Huxley about *Intimate Memories,* and he was pining to read them. But don't send that MS. round any more than you need.—And when there does come a chance of printing it, print it, even if you only distribute a hundred copies at present.

I'm glad everything sounds so nice at Taos. That must have

been a rare bean-feast, the rodeo. It all sounds very jolly, really, and a lot of me wants to be back. We'll see how we feel when the winter turns.

I can hardly believe Tony's mother is dead. I caught her eye once or twice, and she did not look like a dier.—But a man can't have his mother forever.

There are a few aspens on the hill here, and they drizzle slowly away in greeny-yellow. I think of the mountains at Taos and the ranch. No place can ever be more beautiful than that is out there. If only oneself were a bit tougher!

I've been painting pink roses on a dull yellow bureau: doesn't it sound Florentine?

It's a scirocco day, warm, moist, like a hot-house. Remember me to Ida, to everybody.

D. H. LAWRENCE.

If you send that bracelet, do let me know what it costs. The address is: Mrs. Richard Aldington, Malthouse Cottage, Padworth near Reading, Berks. England.

Villa Mirenda

DEAR MABEL

Yes, do send Arabella that bracelet. I will send you some of the lovely Florentine ribbons. Ever since in your novel I read about your Buffalo girl ribbon boxes, I wanted to send you some. Yes, your batches of novel are read with eagerness. You gave a good idea of the Duse, I am sure. One has passed *that* milestone and with your novel you have had a marvellous spring cleaning of the human emotions, so now one ought to be able to get on. Lawrence seems well. We are getting a sunny winter room ready, painting the furniture—it needs it! I wonder if we shall come! Of course we love the ranch, but Lawrence is interested in Europe and there are the children, too. Elsa is engaged to a Teddy Seaman, he is learning to farm and the new young element is good in our lives. Monty and Lawrence have also made friends, it's all come right—grazie a Dio! It's jolly here, too, our only neighbors 4 Wilkinsons, parents, a boy and a girl; had a well known puppet show. They have got them all: vegetarian, anti-vivisection, conscientious objector, socialism, etc. Of Florence we see little. I am bored with spite and that's all you get. . . . My love to Tony. You sound happy. The novel must have been a great thing for you. My best wishes to you.

F.

Why does A. think I am pining to get thin, or *ought* to be! My waistline is a great comfort to me and I wouldn't be cardboardy elegant, not I! Especially here in Italy. And why do you all think my life is a desperate struggle to hang on to Lawrence? It really does make me appear such a poor thing! I am jolly glad to be alone sometimes, so is he, but we are both glad to come together again, very glad! . . . Our lives, Lawrence's and mine, are so easy, if nobody makes any mischief! . . . No, I am not such a fool as you all seem to think me; so there is a bit of temper for you; but then I ask for something else! Good luck to you.

Villa Mirenda
Scandicci, (Florence),
23 Novem. 1926

MY DEAR MABEL

Your letter and the two Florentine sketches of Craig and Savage Landor. The last two are quite well enough, if you don't do any more like them. But you are losing the peculiar intimate flow that the *Memories* have had so far, and are getting a bit hard and journalistic. Perhaps people would like these two sketches very much: it's so smart and unhurt. But the genuine throb is going out of them.—Don't write if you're out of mood. Don't force yourself. And wait for grace.

I wrote at once to Richard Aldington, as you seemed keen on the Académic Française idea, to ask him to write to you direct, as soon as he had found out about the business of procedure. No doubt he will do so. The other idea is to alter all the names, carefully, and print the thing yourself, not more than two hundred copies, and sell them by subscription to people you can really trust. If you did it in Santa Fe—and did most of the work yourself—and didn't talk about it *at all* till it was finished, and then only very gradually—you could secure the distribution of two hundred copies—then print no more, at least for a time, but have the plates preserved.—This would be very little more than showing the MS. to people, as you have done: less dangerous, perhaps.—But a very good man to consult about this would be Harold T. Mason, The Centaur Bookshop, 1224 Chancellor St., Philadelphia. Make it plain that it is not money you are after—and be careful. You can do most things, if you obviously *do not want* to attract attention.

I wish we could come over for a bit. I wish I could come today. It is rainy and heavily dull here. I'd welcome even the snow at Taos. But how can one take that long journey so wearying and so expensive, all at once. We shall have to wait at least till March, and see then.

Many thanks for the Voltaire book: it interests me, but is sugared up horribly. I detest the masturbating kind of style it is written in. Afraid I've nothing serious to send you in return—only a story!

I shrink rather from trespassing on Edwin Dodge's preserves, at the Curonia. Last time I heard of it, he'd got some impecunious American professor and family living there.—How can I go and tread on their toes? It is known as Mr. Dodge's villa now. Imagine my butting in!—It's not merely your abandoned relic, remember.

We live very quietly here, see far less company than you do at Taos. Sometimes I wish things were a little more convivial. But one has to take life as one finds it, and the kind of conviviality one *does* get doesn't help much.

I wouldn't worry about Bynner—he's a belated sort of mosquito.

Don't write your Memoirs unless you're really in the swing. And if you've had enough of Florence, finish that part off now.

Yrs,

D. H. LAWRENCE.

Villa Mirenda, Scandicci,
Firenze, 6 December 1926

DEAR MABEL

It's nearly Christmas, and Frieda hasn't sent you your ribbons yet. But we've not been in to Florence for quite a time. We'll go in and get them, though. I sent you a little book.

I went out the other evening and looked at the Curonia, from outside. I didn't go in: it was getting late: a grey evening with the olives all washing up in silver, in a chill wind. You hadn't made me realise how splendidly the villa stands, looking out over everything. A beautiful place! I'll go again one day, now I know just where it is, and as for the gardener—Pietro, did you say.

It is tramontana here, and quite cold, but rather pleasant. We've got a good warm stove, and a nice room—and the olives and the pine-wood outside. And I've taken to painting for a change: now doing quite a biggish canvas of Boccaccio's story of the nuns who found the gardener asleep.

Secker wants to publish those Indian dance essays, that came in the Theatre Arts—also some Mexican esasys—*Mornings in Mexico*—in a smallish book in the spring. Knopf will do it in New York. And it is to have a few illustrations. You haven't one or two nice photographs of Indians dancing—or an Indian dancing—something a bit suave and beautiful—that we could reproduce, have you? If you have, I wish you'd send them to me. But be sure you have the right to reproduce them.—I'll dedicate the book to you, if you like: to Mabel Dodge Lujan, who called me to Taos.

I'm glad you get on with the Brett and that she has a comfortable corner to come to, in your house. The ranch weighs a bit on my mind. I think, when we come in the spring, we shall have to think if we should sell it. What do you think? Now there are oil kings about, it might be easier. And you would always let us a house of yours. I feel very uncertain about what the future will be.

The man Frayne sent me this letter: very funny. He has never paid my taxes—and I never wanted him to. Why does he suddenly butt in? Would you hate to hand him the cheque, with thanks? Or let Brett do it. I suppose he *has* paid the money!

Hope you'll have a good Christmas.

D. H. LAWRENCE.

I only did three Indian articles, didn't I? *Corn Dance, Snake Dance,* and *Indians and Entertainment.*

Had a letter from Christine Hughes in Rome! Suppose we shall see her soon.

DEAR MABEL

We got such a thrill out of your ribbons, just a shop full of boxes full of ribbons. I hope you like velvet ones, and the young man who sold them thrilled too! We are very cosy and quite "elegant" for us, rushmatting all over the floor in a big, good room with bright, light things in it, and a piano and cyclamens, Lawrence painting on an easel—a Boccaccio picture *not at all* proper, and when it's fine, my word, it's fine—the weather, I mean. Of course it grieves me too much to think the ranch might go, but then we have so little money and Lawrence is so English. He is writing another short novel. We have a gay little dog for a friend and go down with a very small horse and a board of a waggon, driving like blazes and the peasants round us are very friendly. I think in Florence we're a myth. We hardly see anybody. One knows them! Of course we must come back to Taos. Lawrence seems awfully well this winter. Not many forestieri this year. We read "Helen of Troy." They are doing Lawrence's play Mrs. Holyroyd on Sunday. Good luck to you in the new year. If you came to Florence you would want to buy—such braids and silks and paper and embroidery, they have such clever hands! Thank you very much for Arabella's bracelet. Lawrence of course grumbled at me for taking it from you. You still have a lot to do for your novel, so many years!

Greetings to Tony.

FRIEDA.

Christine Hughes wrote from Rome.
What about Spud?

Villa Mirenda,
Scandicci (Florence),
10 December, 1926

DEAR MABEL

We went in to Florence today—and here are your ribbons. I think there are sixteen bits—hope they're right colours. If you want any more, let me know and *say what colour*—send a bit of stuff to match. We told the man in the shop it was a present —and he said *proprio un bel regalo, un bel regalo darrero*— but to me it seems not much of a show.

I hope the Piero della Francesca is the one you like. Anyhow it's beautiful. If you had another in mind, tell me more in detail and I'll find it. Tell Brett we are sending her a scarf— thin wool—gaudyish.

Hope you have a jolly Christmas.

D. H. L.

I'll tell Huxley about the MS. if you really wish—but I'm scared of it going round with all names left. He is at Villa Ino Colli, Cortina d'Ampezzo, Italia. It's in the Trento region, north of Padua, in the mountains.

Where is Mary Foote and when is she due to appear?

Tante belle cose!—tempo bellissimo qui, le montagne tutte nevi-
cate, l'aria chiara e fresca—e un po' di allegria.

> *Villa Mirenda, Scandicci,*
> *Firenze, 16 Dec.*

DEAR MABEL

I enclose R. Aldington's letter. You'll see he says more or
less what I say. But you *must* alter names. No point in keeping
them, absolutely.

Awfully nice of you to keep Poppy for me—wonder when
I'll ride her.

Molta nebbia qui.

> D. H. L.

We sent off the ribbons—have you got them?

No sign of Mary Foote.

> *Malthouse Cottage*
> *Padworth near Reading*
> *Berks*
> *11/12/26*

DEAR LORENZO

I have been slow in answering your last letter for several
reasons. This is a busy season of the year with me because of the
numbers of books which come for review. In addition I had to
write a lecture and then go to Newcastle to "deliver" it before
the Literary and Philosophical Society. I got fifteen guineas
thereby, and incidentally an invitation to lecture at Cambridge
next year. I was a bit nervous for the first three minutes but
afterwards rather enjoyed making them listen.

Now, to Mme Lujan and her affair. I consulted Professor
Renwick about the project and he says that he thinks there is
not the slightest chance that the Académie Française would
undertake the job. They would only do so if it were both

historical and French. I was therefore wrong in what I said.

The only alternative plan that occurs to me is this. There is a printer at Dijon who produced Ulysses. Might not Mme L have her book privately printed by him, say 100 copies, and discreetly circulate them among her friends? This would ensure enough copies existing for the book not to perish. France has almost complete freedom in publication. I know the French representative at Geneva refused to give any but a formal ratification to Hugh Cecil's ridiculous resolution for the international suppression of "obscene" literature, on the grounds that such suppression was contrary to the law of France. Libel actions may be taken, but it would be practically impossible to bring a libel action against the author and printer of a book by an American privately printed in France. The one snag might be that she would not want this done in her life-time. Could she not have the book printed, wrap up and address the copies to various people, deposit them with the printer (who has to be well paid) with orders that they should be despatched directly she was dead?

All these posthumous arrangements sound rather ghoulish.

How are you getting on at Scandicci and what are you doing to conjure down that ennui which inevitably waits upon the Romantic Soul? All your "fixings" in the villa sound real dandy to me. Gee, you must be pining for a lil real home-life and a hundred per cent clean uplift.

Au revoir. We look forward to seeing you in March. Arabella sends love.

RICHARD.

Villa Mirenda
Scandicci, Florence
29 Dec. 1926

DEAR MABEL

If I were you, I'd *never* bother to have books sent all that way. Why $700 would print you the first two volumes of your

Memoirs—which surely is much more important to *you* than books to High Schools and such stuff. Why don't you have a small selection of the books, not more than 100 volumes, made for your *own* library, and sell the rest in job lots in Florence. Give $100 worth of miscellaneous books to the library—and save the rest of the money. Seems to me madness to cart old books to Taos—madness. And let somebody bring the three pictures when they come—have a regular agent just ship them to the boat—or let someone like Gondrands ship them to New York, to somebody you can trust, then pick them up some time. Don't waste all that money on transport, when you can print your memoirs with it. You got my letter with R. Aldington's suggestion: that you print 100 copies of your memoirs, wrap them up addressed to the people you want to have them—to be forwarded after your death—or at your order later on. But I would always advise you to change *all* names, and names of places, before you send the thing to print. And ask the Centaur Bookshop about the business. Bind just in paper wrappers, and keep it quiet.

If you really want me to look over those books in the Curonia, I shall have to wait for warmer weather. The villa will be icy as a church. But far better sell them here, and give the *proceeds* to the Taos library and the High School. Sheer waste of money sending the stuff 6000 miles.

Yrs,

D. H. LAWRENCE.

Villa Mirenda, Scandicci
(*Florence*), *17 Jan. 1927*

MY DEAR MABEL

We got the parcel of books and herbs yesterday: very nice of you to send them. The herbs smell *so* strong of Taos: when we went into the trattoria at Vingone, the padrona kept sniffing: ces'è? ma cos' è questo profumo?—and we had to open the parcel and give her a bit.

I went to the Curonia a week ago with Orioli. We thought we'd be able to get in, without that Romanelli, who must be a marvellous thief, asking you $700, when $70 must be nearer the mark. But we could find nobody—house shut up, cypress avenue empty and triste—the whole place of a tristezza da morire, though a lovely day. On the big terrace a fat marble baby lying flat, but its tootsies broken off: and your old stone dogs! After ages we found Pietro—he's very nice—remembers you affettuosamente. Acton had been up and told him you were *dead*—great blow to him. But he had corrected that. He and his wife are quite alone at the Curonia, and he says it is *molto triste*. I gave him money, as from you, and he sent you ringraziamenti e ricordi no?—e tante cose, alla Signora Mabli! I liked him. He told me how you made him do things, alla moda Americana, subito, subito Pietro! E poi, quando era fatto. When he'd done it—it was some sort of a rockery—you came and said: Pietro, ho sbagliato. Porta tutto via. I can see it all. We went in the down-stairs servants rooms, cold and sad, but all the fine copper pans! Pietro hadn't the keys of the living rooms—only that Romanelli. It is like Edwin Dodge to get into the hands of a swindler. I hear Edwin D. wants $100,000 for the villa—which is Liras two and a half million. He'll never get it. Lucky if he gets half. It's a lovely place, but sad, and oh, the cost of upkeep nowadays! You've no idea! I shall go again as soon as there's a fine day and get the Romanelli and really look at the books. According to Pietro, they are not so *very* many—a few quintali—and the heavi-est are great bound vols. of magazines. Do you want those?

How did you like Buffalo? You'll be back now. Tell Brett Brewster is here for a day or two, looking round for a villa: but Achsah wants to *buy* one, near Rome—but not more than $6,000. Aschsah and Harwood are in Capri.

Did you get the ribbons? How is Tony?

D. H. L.

DEAR MABEL

Well, the books are here, and the three pictures, at Orioli's. We have been over to Egidi, and it will probably cost about five or six hundred liras to send the lot as far as Galveston, Texas. I will pay that, and you must pay the remainder. We are sending you *all* the sets: and everything worth having: *two hundred and eighteen volumes.* The rest, hundreds of vols, we leave at the villa, just rubbish, as far as I can see: most disheartening.— Then I am taking ten paper-cover Balzacs and about a dozen other trifles, mostly Tauchnitz, for light reading. I'll pay for them. Orioli is keeping about six Henry James, one or two Lafcadio Hearn, Burton's *Anatomy* and one or two Stevensons to sell—in all about 42: of which one or two Henry James are first editions—the only things that are. He'll pay a proper price for them. We gave Pietro liras 25.00—and paid a cart. The Condamine was *not* there—I never saw it—but Orioli thinks he has a copy of his own which he will send you along with the *Portraits of Mabel Dodge,* by post.—The Curonia, and especially the books, are most depressing. They must have been picked over very thoroughly, *all* the good things gone, and such a heap of rubbish—hundreds of vols.—The big yellow carpet is still on the hall floor—they say the moths rise from it in clouds, in summer. There is a nice painted cupboard, and very nice copper pans in the kitchen.—As for the silver, that man Romanelli says it is nothing—*niente, niente*! But he's awful. If you send an order for Pietro to have it delivered here at Orioli's, Lungarno Corsini 6, like the books, we can either send it you or sell it, as you wish. I've no idea what it is.—I think Romanelli hopes ultimately to lay hands on everything, and one feels like frustrating him.

I want to send you back all your MSS. You've wound up your Florence part. It's all right—just a wind-up. But you've lost the flow. The sketches aren't very good either. You've gone out of gear with your writing. But perhaps, innerly, you don't *want* to do any more. Let it rest, for a while.

I think it's going to snow here—and was so lovely. The wild tulips are all springing up.

I have Brett's "Adolescence." Most people experience *something* the same. The worst is, the body, *the blood* forms its habits of hostility or sympathy, and these are practically unbreakable: they don't yield at all to the mind, but remain underneath like a rock substratum. The mind and spirit may play their own game, on top: but it never passes through the rock-bed.

But I'm glad you are friendly. Today is a day when I can imagine Taos.

D. H. LAWRENCE.

Villa Mirenda, 5. IV. 27

DEAR MABEL

Today came your letter. I have just come back from Germany into the most bursting Tuscan spring, it almost rattles with eagerness. Am sitting alone (which doesn't often happen) reading the Hopi snake dance proofs. It is good to have one's past so safe in these writings. Yes, I am sure we wouldn't quarrel any more. All this winter we lived so peacefully, Lawrence and I, and with one's usual forgetfulness, I can't believe that we ever quarrelled so dreadfully! I shall go over to the Wilkinsons, "The Wilks," who have a good camera, and have L's pictures taken if it's fine. I don't know what they are without colour, but they do make the house splendid. Maria Huxley said they are "grand!" And so they are. And the first conception of one is very thrilling when Lawrence gets his paints and his glass bits, puts his overalls on, takes a bit of charcoal from the kitchen, is quite still and suddenly darts at the canvas, goes on for a few hours. I sit and watch and then it's there and we both feel dead tired.

Lawrence comes tomorrow and my daughter Barbara next week, panting to come. With my usual immorality of loving so many places, I like it here, too, but sometimes I *long* for the ranch. I never thanked you for the bracelet. Arabella was thrilled with it. If you would like some braid one day from a lovely braid shop, say so. I am glad you have the Younghunter house —it will make you so complete. Bynner sent me a cutting from the Nation, somebody taking up my defense— Violet Hunt's "atrocious" treatment of me: I had never noticed it!! I only remember that Ford Madox Hueffer and she and Mrs. Wells came to see me and when I said to him, "We are both German, aren't we?" she said, unhappily, "No, no, Russian." Now he is Ford Madox *Ford*.

This is quite a long letter. I enjoy the Balzacs we got from the Curonia.

F.

Scandicci, (Florence),
Villa Mirenda
14 April 1927

MY DEAR MABEL

It seems long since I have written you—but you will hear through Brett all the news, or lack of it, from us. I have just got back from looking at Etruscan things—tombs—on the coast north of Rome—Tarquinia, Cerveteri, Vulci, Volterra. It was very interesting, very attractive. I should like to do a book of sketches of Etruscan places.

When I got back I corrected the proofs of the tiny book of essays, *Mornings in Mexico*. They are essays I like—and they have one basic theme. I liked particularly the Hopi Snake Dance. I inscribed the book to you, as I said, since to you we really owe Taos and all that ensues from Taos.—Reading the New Mexico essays gave me a desire to come back—made me feel that, as the wheel of destiny goes round, it will carry us back. I should love to see the dances at Santo Domingo, and the winter dances at Taos again—and go to Zuñi, where I've never been. One has gradually to let life carry one round.

As for a change of life—there's a very nice poem on it some-where at the ranch—if somebody hasn't torn it out from the end of one of my books of MS. When it comes to changes, there's nothing to be done but to accept 'em and go through with them and put up with the penalty of them, in the hopes of coming through into calmer water. Myself, I'm in just the same way—just simply suffering from a change of life, and a queer sort of recoil, as if one's whole soul were drawing back from connec-tion with everything. This is the day they put Jesus in the tomb —and really, those three days in the tomb begin to have a ter-rible significance and reality to me. And the Resurrection is an unsatisfactory business—just *noli me tangere* and no more. Poveri noi! But pazienza, pazienza! The wheel will go round.

I haven't seen Orioli since I'm back, to ask about the final settlement of your books. I'm sorry we didn't get the child pic-ture—but we were only authorized to take the three. As for the other things you mention in Curonia, I remember none of them. I didn't look at all carefully. But the place seemed to me almost stripped bare.—There was no sign of any Arabian Nights —nothing one wanted. I just got eight paper-back Balzacs and one or two Ouidas, the last for mere amusement. But it seems to me you should have that silver.

It is lovely spring here—the red tulips in the corn, and the last of the purple anemones. I have said we will keep this house another year—it doesn't cost much, so is no matter if one abandons it half-way. I feel for the time a sort of soreness, physi-cal, mental, and spiritual, which is no doubt change of life, and I wish it would pass off. I think it is passing off. Meanwhile pazienza! But till it heals up, I don't feel like making much effort in any direction. It is *easiest* here.

My word, how you do but extend your boundaries, out there on the hill! You'll have a real Mabeltown before you've done. I believe that's your ambition—to have an earthly king-dom, and rule it. But my dear, it's an illusion like any other.

But if houses are your passion, why, then have houses. We'll no doubt come and sit in one of them one day.

Frieda was back from Germany a week before I got home. I found her with a bad cold and feeling very low. The day after my arrival came her daughter Barbara—of course with an elderly woman, as duena, in tow. But the elderly woman is put down in the inn, and we make the best of things.

I hope you're feeling really better from the flu. In my opinion, flu is one of the diseases of a changing constitution. It changes the very chemical composition of the blood—hence the bad effect on the heart—and the long time one takes to get round. And when one does get round, one has lost for good one's old self—some of it—though where the new self comes in, I don't quite see.

When is Spud coming back to you? I stayed two nights in Christine Hughes' flat in Rome. She seemed rather calmer in herself, but Mary Christine would be *much* better home in Santa Fe.

Best wishes, then.

D. H. LAWRENCE.

Scandicci, Florence,
Villa Mirenda
16 May 1927

DEAR MABEL

I have again shirked going to London, to *David*—I had a cold, and then I simply can't face mixing up with a lot of town people.—But I shall never go to Fontainebleau to see Gourdjieff, don't ask me. He's not interesting to me, and a good deal of a charlatan. Make that little visit yourself—you'll never rest easy in your mind till you've done it.

I read the Jung things—many thanks—but I'm sort of tired of so many words. One changes—changes inside oneself—and then old interests die out. One has to change and accept it—and one's mentality becomes different along with the rest. I think men have perhaps a greater "change of life" in the psyche even than women. At least it seems happening so in myself. It's often unpleasant, but the only thing is to let it go on and accept the differences and let go the old.

That's really why it's no good coming to America at present. One is in a state of flux, and decided movements are no good. I wish I could have the space and openness of New Mexico, and a horse, and all that. But my real inside doesn't turn towards America, and so there it is.

I wonder if you have the books yet. We haven't yet got the bill for the shipping as far as New Orleans. That is to be paid in Florence, and you have only to pay the railroad charge. Orioli has Ten Pounds Sterling of your money, from sale of a few Henry James, 1st edition American. He'll pay you the freight-age with that, and if there's anything over, I'll send it you. And I burnt that little 5 dollar cheque of yours—the few books I had can stand over against that.

It's been a lovely spring—the tulips were beautiful—now the pale mauve iris are just past their best, the rose gladiolus is in the wheat, and it is summer; sitting out all day under the trees on the grass. It is quite lovely really. Only I do wish there was a moor or a desert, and a horse. I think we shall stay on till mid-July, then probably go to Bavaria, the Isarthal, near Munich. I love that country. And in the late autumn we *may* go to Egypt. —I wrote to Brett telling her there was no need to go to the ranch, but to stay with you. She will do as she pleases, however. She writes furiously about my "inertia" and the "danger" of living "in this hole." But I wish she'd leave me to arrange my own life. She surely has enough to occupy her, with her own affairs! Anyhow it's useless for her to bother with mine.

We are expecting Christine Hughes in Florence, more or less on her way back to Santa Fe. I think she'll be glad to be back. Is Spud with you yet? He'll be glad of New Mexico too. But if one is born American, it is different.

About starting a new vol. of your memoirs, God knows. Perhaps you are too near to your American experiences, after Florence, to wish to put them down on paper. Probably you don't yet wish yourself to tell the truth about them. But when you have Spud back, you'll know better how you feel about it. I believe he is a good "medium" for your work. Though Summer is a bad time to begin. Summer is for holidaying, in autumn one can begin to work. But don't try to do it if your inside holds back from it. It is far, far better to do nothing than to try to force an inspiration. That only messes up the whole impulse.

I'm glad you've got a snow-white palfrey, like the maid in the Faerie Queene—"yet she much whiter." Dio buono, what a premium on whiteness.

The new vegetables, peas, asparagus, beans, potatoes, are in full swing—how good they are. And the garden is full of red roses.

I hope you're having a good time. It'll be June by the time you get this.

Frieda sends "tante cose." Remember me to everybody.

D. H. LAWRENCE.

Orioli sent you the "Portraits of M. D." and the other books.

Scandicci, Florence,
Villa Mirenda
28 May 1927

DEAR MABEL

You are about right about that "change of life" business. It's what ails me, as I said in my other letter. And partly the reason why I lie low here, is to let it happen, and not interfere with it, so it gets through as soon as possible. It's hell while it lasts—but I think I sort of see a glimpse of daylight through the other side. One emerges with a body all right—but a different one, perhaps, not so mentalised.

Anyhow I begin to feel like bursting out again. I doubt if Europe will hold me many more months. And the obvious thing is to come back to New Mexico. But I'd better wait still, to see how many more set-backs I get. It's no good moving till I am sort of sure on my pins. But I'm getting to feel very stuffy and shut in, here in Italy.

I hear Secker is publishing his *Mornings in Mexico* on July 9th—don't know if Knopf comes out simultaneously. He ought to. But I ordered you both an English copy—and I'll order you another American.

They produced *David* last week. I heard the audience was really rather enthusiastic, but the press notices are very unfavorable. It's those mangy feeble reviewers; they haven't enough spunk to hear a cow bellow. The worst of the youngish Englishman is, he's such a *baby*; one can't imagine his backside isn't swaddled in a napkin: and such a prig, one imagines he must either be a lady in disguise, or a hermaphrodite. We had Osbert and Edith Sitwell here to tea the other day. They were very nice. He loathed America. But my God, it makes me want to come back there, to get away from these European pap-drivelling little boys. They see *nothing* in America at all: not even the *real* menace: and none of the grim Yankee dauntlessness, which has *not* got its bottom swathed in a napkin. Anything, anything, anything for a bit of dauntless courage.

Italy is rather down in the mouth and pippy—over the rise of the Lira, the flight of the tourist, the necessity to put down prices and wages. Altogether nobody shows any sign of real spunk, anywhere; it's tiring.

I haven't been able to get my pictures snapped yet. But I've finished the Resurrection, also a story on the same theme. I think I'll bring my pictures to New York, and show them. Shall I? Never show them in Europe at all. I've got six big ones and some small. Shall we show them in New York—in autumn or early spring? And then move out to Taos and paint some more?

It would be rather fun. I'm just getting into my own style.

You don't owe anything over the books—we'll probably owe you some few dollars, as I said. But the bill for freightage to New Orleans hasn't come yet.

I'm glad Spud is back. After all, what's the world worth!—One can only kick it, when one gets a chance. I'm afraid change of life doesn't change one's feelings much in that respect. One can never make success *in* the world—only against it.

I'm holding my novel back—not even having it typed. Much better if I print only periodical stuff.

Do ever hear anything of Nina? It will soon be two years since we stayed with her. Wonder what she's like by now. We expected Christine Hughes through from Rome, but no sign of her so far—dead silence.

We may go to Bavaria in July, for a bit—but I feel I'm coming unstuck from Europe.

Hope all goes well. Remember me to everybody.

D. H. L.

Scandicci, Florence,
Villa Mirenda
15 July 1927

MY DEAR MABEL

I'm glad you've got the books and pictures. Were they more or less what you wanted? Let me know how much you pay transport; we have tried two or three times to pay the shipping, but the Egidi people haven't got the returns yet. You remember there is ten pounds sterling of yours in Orioli's hands.

I've had another whack of bronchials—due to sea-bathing when I shouldn't. But the doctor says it should clear up all right.

We want to go away to the mountains near Villach in Austria, about 2,000 feet up, as soon as I'm up to the journey—in about ten days. I'm not sure of the address, but letters will come on safely from here.

I had a letter from Bessie Freeman today—in Paris—so queer! Her beloved brother died: and she seems to have gone off some edge or other: been in India: and spending months alone in the desert with eight Arabs. "Why am I the only woman in the world who could do it safely?"—She wanted to be remembered to you and says she always liked you so much.

I can't say definitely about the autumn. I must see how my damned bronchials react. The doctors all say Taos is too high: good for lungs, bad for bronchitis. I'd like to see the open spaces again, though—and the cottonwood trees in October.

The man is supposed to come and snap my pictures to-morrow—if he does!

Tell Brett Mrs. Ashly wrote from Rome for news of her.

I dreamed so plainly of Tony.

D. H. L.

I suppose you and Brett got your copies of Mornings in Mexico. Knopf isn't getting his American edition out till September. Remember me to Spud.

D. H. L.

Thursday, 21. VII. 27
Villa Mirenda.

DEAR MABEL

We had a shock. Lawrence got a congestion bathing at the Huxleys. Thank goodness he's better and the doctor says he is really so strong otherwise; so here we sit in the heat, but not too hot, perched on our little hill in the stone square old house till he is better, then the Dolomites.

I'll send the photographs of the pictures soon. We had a very nice American here with a wooden leg who knew you in your New York days and who said how kind you had been to people who wanted to do something. Christine Hughes and Mary Christine quite upset us, something from "over there." I like them both! The Huxleys are coming this afternoon.

All good things. I am reading "Ouida" from your things and Balzac.

F.

The sunflowers will be out on the road. Greet Tony for me.

Hotel Fischer. Villach. Austria
25 August 1927

DEAR MABEL

Heard from Brett today—she says you are learning to drive the Buick and stepping on the gas like ten heroines. Don't do it. Camminando si arriva. Stepping on the gas one goes over the edge, which is not an arrival.

We've been here three weeks—me convalescing, and not very pleased with myself. I had a miserable month at the Mirenda with my bronchials and hemorrhages—seems to get me in July—and I'm still only about a third there. I do hate it. We're going next week to a house of my sister-in-laws in Bavaria, to stay a month, as arranged: but send me a line % Frau Baronin von Richthofen, Ludwig-Wilhelmstift, Baden Baden.

I think still with hankering of the ranch in the early spring— If I can, we shall come. A change of continent would do me good. Except that the altitude, for bronchials, is what the doctor calls a bleeding altitude. But who knows—I was so well again there that last summer.

What about the Memoirs? are you waiting a while?

And were those books all right? I'll bet when you saw them you only cursed them. But we did our best.

Austria is queer—seems to have gone quite void. It's like being at the centre of a vital vacuum. The people are healthy, rather handsome, and don't seem to care about a thing—a void, where caring is concerned. Most queer! But the peasants look unpleasant and stink of greed.—This queer vacuum is the centre of Europe. I wonder what wind will whirl in to fill it up. Anyhow the world is far past my understanding. A German wrote a book called Schopferische Pause—Creative Pause. I don't know whether this is one. It seems to me more than pause, even more than a blank full stop. Yet with such healthy bodies bathing and lying by the lake, you never saw. California on a small scale. L'ideale del vuoto.

Taos sounds nothing but a mad Valkyrie of motor cars in Brett's last. Send in a line to say you are all soothed down to ten miles an hour.

D. H. L.

Scandicci, Firenze,
Villa Mirenda
18 Nov. 1927

DEAR MABEL

I enclose cheque for $48.00—which is the equivalent of the Liras Orioli gave me. I drew the last remaining dollars out of an old account that I want to close, so if there is any hitch, don't be alarmed, it will only mean there's only 47 instead of 48 dollars in that bank. I think there are 49.—But if it's not right, I'll send you another cheque.

I was in Florence for the first time yesterday. Curious, something has gone out of me—towns mean nothing to me, only noise and nuisance. I'm not interested in them. I saw L. C. for a moment, stuttering and faded—and young N. came up the other day. But the way they talk of Tony makes me so mad. "I hear he comes to dinner in his war-paint!"—So I said: "And why not? Doesn't your mother and all the rest of your female friends? Tony is just as well bred." Dead and damnatory Florentine silence—nipped their little joke! Poor lot!

I met Michael Arlen, too, by chance—you know, The Green Hat. He too has been sick, and was looking diminished, in spite of all the money he has made: quite a sad dog, trying to be rakish.

The weather has gone suddenly cold and grey—very sudden. Gets my chest a bit. I bet you've got snow at Taos. I am busy getting my poems in order, to go into one vol.—all the poems. My word, what ghosts come rising up! But I just tidy their clothes for them and refuse to be drawn.—I think I shall publish my last winter's novel "Lady Chatterley's Lover!" here in Florence, privately, myself—and take in the badly-needed shekels and avoid all publicity. I must avoid publicity with it—it is so tender and so daring. I should print 700 copies only—at $10 a copy—and that ought to make me about 3 or 4 thousand dollars. There's an idea for you and your Memories, later on. I'll let you know how it goes—and you'll have to get me a few subscriptions, if I start.

I haven't heard from the Brewsters, whether they'll come with us in March or April to New York and then New Mexico. I think *he* would come—but Achsah in her long white robes and floating veils—oh, I'd love to see her in a side-saddle on an ambling pad—not Poppy—wafting between the plum-bushes towards the pueblo! *How* I'd love it! We might have a joint, slam-bang exhibition of pictures in N. Y.—Achsah's acres of Jesus and the blue Virgin, Earl's charming landscapes and stiff white horse—my incorrigible nudes—and Brett's Trinidad. I think we'd baffle everybody—and certainly not sell a rag.

Don't build *many* more houses—they'll weigh on you at last, like Oscar Browning. Stop in time! It's your lesson.

I hope Ida's better. It will be fun to be back and see everybody and sort of take the lid off. One's got the lid on all the time here. And Spud's printing press may lay golden eggs yet.

Compton Mackenzie, after swallowing one story in which he appeared as a character, was mortally offended by another more recent one in which I used him, and Secker wants me not to print it in a book. I call that cheek—he should be so honoured! Oh small beer gone flat!

Look out for my story *The Escaped Cock*—in the Forum, don't know when—I want you to say what you think of it.

F. says she'll send more ribbons, Christmas coming.

A rivederci,

D. H. L.

Scandicci, (Florence)
Villa Mirenda
12 March 1928

DEAR MABEL

Here we are back from Switzerland—and I'm a good bit better. The altitude was good for me. Now I'm so busy with my novel. I want to call it *John Thomas and Lady Jane* (John Thomas is one of the names for the penis, as probably you know): but have to submit to put this as a sub-title, and continue with *Lady Chatterley's Lover*: for the publisher's sake. But my own unexpurgated edition is being printed here now—quite thrilling. I want to have it ready by May 15th: and I want to post it direct from here, to those that buy it. I am doing 1000 copies, of which 500 for America, at $10 each. I shall send you a few of the little order-forms, and do please send them out for me, to Buffalo and New York and places like that, to people who are likely to appreciate the book. It is frankly and faithfully a phallic novel, but tender and delicate, as I believe in it: and as I believe is necessary for us to become. It'll infuriate *mean* people: but it will surely soothe decent ones. Anyhow do help me all you can, as you promised. Then really I'll have some money to come to the ranch: for I mean to come. And I believe the Brewsters and the Huxleys will come along with us. Which would be fun. If we don't come in the summer, I wouldn't mind coming in autumn, as we did the first time. But I must get this novel off my chest first.—You might one day print your memoirs here in Florence, in the same way.

I expect you have some resistance inside yourself to the New York socialist phase of yours. What is it, I wonder? You can't really sympathise with the Mabel of those days. But why?—

Unless you can sympathise with that Mabel, you can't write that section.

I am sending some of the order-forms for Lady Chatterley to Bynner and Christine Hughes, for them to distribute—so don't overlap. But do give Spud as many as he really wants, for people in California and out of the way places, to whom the book would be really attractive. I'll send a few forms to Idella Purnell. I shan't send out any copy until it's paid for—otherwise I'm left. Well, I hope I'll get through all right.

Yrs.

D. H. LAWRENCE.

Kesselmatte
Gsteig b. Gstaad,
(Berne) Switzerland
9 August 1928

DEAR MABEL

I'm glad you got *Lady C*, and that you liked it. I'm anxious about the other copies sent—about 200 in all—to America, as several people sent cables saying "don't send." It went into England all right, though there was a great scare in London—police were reported to have a warrant to search for it. However nothing has happened so far: and perhaps it won't, if nobody raises a dust. But most people seem to hate the book: some dealers have returned their copies—and altogether there is a lot of fuss and nuisance. Makes one hate hypocrisy and prudery more than ever and people as a bulk.

We sit here in this little chalet near the top of the mountains—been here nearly five weeks—and until this week I felt no better. But this week I really begin to feel a difference and can begin taking short sun-baths—they only made me worse before. If only I can get a real start, to shake off this accursed cough, I ought to come along all right. But this last year I don't seem to have been able to get back to myself. Now let's hope I can. Anyhow it's useless thinking of coming to New Mexico or anywhere far till I get this cough down.

The Brewsters are in the hotel in the village at present with *four* American spinster friends—quite nice women, but oh God! the meaninglessness that simply stares at one out of these women of fifty. They seem to have outlived any meaning they might ever have had, and are just rattling, rattling insistent spectres. Awful! They give me the jim-jams. If only they wouldn't *insist* on being there! If only they'd fade into the nothingness they really are! Then they might emerge again somehow. As it is, they rattle with the insistence of skeletons.

We are due to stay here till end Sept.—and shall, I suppose, if it really does me good,—pray God it may! I'm supposed to go to London to see my pictures exhibited first two weeks in October—and I may, or may not. Here I just dibble at tiny pictures, and potter about among the trees.—A bad few years for everybody. But let's hope we'll all get steady on our legs and manage with a bit of real equilibrium, afterwards. Poveri noi! Anyhow the weather is superb.

Now I'll go and hunt my spectacles, which I lost this morning! Hope you're feeling well. Regards to everybody.

D. H. L.

Hotel Beau Rivage,
Bandol. Var
19 Dec. 1928

DEAR MABEL

Yours about the article for the *Survey Graphic* came today. I'll have a shot at the aticle when I can get a bit of time—people here now.

My pictures are being kept back a bit—I think they are going to be reproduced in a book, rather expensively, $50.00.

We are staying rather vaguely here—can't make up our minds what to do. We are expecting Frieda's daughters for

Christmas—so shall stay here over the New Year anyhow, I suppose.

Tell Brett I wrote her three letters—hope she got some of them.

How do you like New York? Do you feel you've come a bit unstuck from the world altogether?—That's how I feel.

We'll have to see what breeze the gods will blow into our sails, to start us on a new move.

D. H. L.

> Hotel Beau Rivage
> Bandol, Var,
> 25 Dec. 1928

DEAR MABEL

I wrote what I think is quite a beautiful article on New Mexico—perhaps a bit too deep for the *Survey-Graphic*, I don't know. I'm sending it to Curtis Brown, London, to be typed and they'll send it to Curtis Brown, New York to give to the Graphic. If the latter think it's not quite suitable for their paper, I don't mind—probably someone else will do it. But I should like you to see it.—Writing it gave me a real longing to be back—and I should like to come in spring even if only to stay the six months allowed by the passport. Brett suggests creeping in unnoticed, but if I feel I have to do that I shall be spitting in everybody's eye. I'm not given to creeping in, and USA isn't paradise anyhow.—My picture show is held off—I think I'm going to have them all reproduced and appear in a book with an essay on painting, to sell at 10 guineas a copy—which is fifty dollars. That's what the Mandrake press say they want to do—seems to me a fancy price, anyhow. And the exhibition and book appear simultaneously.—I've done such an amusing book of rag poems—pensées—which I call my *pansies*—make them all cross again. But I'm holding it awhile. How are you liking New York? Christmas Day today, and we thought of you at lunch time and wondered where and with whom you were eating turkey. Anyhow, many greetings.

D. H. L.

I told Curtis B.'s, if you ask to see the MS., they are to let you.

Bandol, Var, France
11 February 1929

DEAR MABEL

Today I have sent to Marianne Moore a copy of the *Pansies*. It hasn't got my name on, or anything, because the police started a fuss in London over *Lady C.* and even confiscated two MS copies of the *Pansies,*—said they were obscene—a *lie*—I am suing for the return of the MS. But don't mention it in New York please, not to anybody, it'll only start the smut-hounds bellowing again. But do let me know if the Pansies arrive safely at the Dial office—perhaps they might have a typescript copy made, and charge it to me. Then I want Marianne Moore to send the MS. over to Curtis Brown, they'll have to place it. The Viking Press talked of doing my *Collected Poems* in New York—if they really did so, I suppose I'd offer them the Pansies—otherwise Knopf.

I got the cheque for $100 from the Graphic—many thanks— it should have gone via Curtis Brown, they get 10%. Glad you liked the article.

About coming—we really want to come, if only for the summer. But are you sure it's quite safe for me—won't somebody or other begin doing one dirt? If I were quite sure we'd come in all right and peacefully, and have a decent summer, I'd say we would definitely sail towards end of March. But even if we come, don't wait in New York longer than you wish. It's New Mexico I want to go to, really.

My pictures are being reproduced in colour to be done in a book, at fifty—or sixty dollars a time. I'm going to send over proofs when they are ready.

I suppose Gurdjieff is as you say an imaginary incarnation of Lucifer—but I doubt he'll never strike much of a light. All so *would-be*—and oh, so much talk. I hope we'll come, really.

D. H. L.

Write to me % Signor C. Orioli, 6 Lungarno Corsini, Florence, Italy. I expect we shall soon go back to Italy.

Hotel Beau Rivage
Bandol, Var
2 March 1929

DEAR MABEL

It's no good, I really don't think I'm well enough, with this cough, to come to America and stand the racket of journeys and seeing people. It makes me very mad. I *am* better—I am really quite well and quite myself so long as I stay fairly quiet. But as soon as I begin taking journeys, even going to Toulon and doing a bit of shopping and running round, I feel rather rotten and cough more. So it's no good. I shall have to give up again for this year. It is maddening—nothing is so wearisome as prolonged ill-health. Not that I'm an invalid or anything like that. I've not been in bed a day all winter, and I eat just as well as I ever did—though that's only since I am here in Bandol. But the minute I start walking at all far, especially uphill, and running around, especially in a town, I go all queer. It's partly psychological, of course. Some connection with the *current* world broke in me two years ago, and now I have to be different. I feel my inside energy just about the same. It's my outside energy I can't manage. And so I'm afraid of the long journey and all the people—and possible unpleasantness with authorities or public.

And I'm thinking, really, we ought to sell that ranch, so that perhaps we could be more free when we do come. It is a bit remote and strenuous when one is not well. Yet I should be sorry to think we couldn't go there and have it for our own any

more—so would Frieda. While Brett stays, I suppose it's safe
enough. But if ever she left it, it would soon get smashed up by
Mexicans and roughs. Last year when the Taos bank asked me
to sell, Brett said she would buy it. What do you think? You see
there are many MSS. there—some that are, and will be, really
valuable. They may easily be all lost or stolen. What should one
do? Don't say anything to Brett to hurt her feelings. Would you
suggest putting the MSS. and things we value in some safe deposit place? I've lost so many MSS. already—Seltzer has some—
Mountsier—some have disappeared unaccountably—and it seems
a shame.—As soon as I feel well enough and *confident* I shall
come. But now I feel unsure and a bit shaky—and Frieda isn't
very well either—no longer so strong.—Tell Maria Cristina—
yes, I like her too, I like the feeling one has of her. But don't
say anything particular to Brett. I would hate to hurt her feelings.

Did you get the *Pansies*—or did Marianne Moore? Have
you heard the row in London about them—seized by Scotland
Yard and now questions being asked about them in Parliament?
It's just March lunacy—those poor bits of *Pansies*. Everybody is
of course quaking, at the same time they are getting the wind
up against that imbecile Jix, the Home Secretary.—And the
colour-printers are frightened too, and refusing to reproduce
some of the pictures—perfectly harmless pictures. But the people
are going ahead—and I suppose they'll get the book out about
May: 500 copies at ten guineas each: I'll get them to send you
prospectuses with the reproduction of *Finding of Moses* in
colour, and you may get a few subscribers. I don't think the
pictures will have any difficulty passing through customs—they
certainly wouldn't, but for my bad name.

We are leaving here on Wednesday, I think to go to Majorca
—Spain—where we *might* take a house for six months or a
year. It remains to be seen.

I wonder how Tony will stand New York. I find big cities
are just too much for me now: or at least, all wrong.

And do give Maria Cristina all my news, and tell her I will write.

And you write to me % G. Orioli, 6 Lungarno Corsini, Florence. I think that will be as quick as any other way.

Why can't one make oneself *tough*!

D. H. L.

Hotel Principe Alfonso
Palma de Mallorca, Spain, Ascencion

DEAR MABEL

I think John was right to squash the dude ranch—and you must have been a bit loco to go and do it—after all, you mustn't humiliate your place like that. But I'm glad you've got it back, and sent the woman away, and can wash off the Philistine paint. It was a very "small" feeling, somehow, to think of your hill as a dude ranch with Jews and Jew-gaws. Better the houses stand empty, than that.

I can understand your feeling about it, however.

We have been here on this island—Majorca—two weeks. It is quite pleasant and Mediterranean, but not at all exciting, and less beautiful than Italy. I don't think we shall stay long. I want to do a little tour in Spain towards the end of the month, then go to Italy to see to a few things. I feel somehow that it isn't quite time yet for me to come to America—my instinct is against it, for the time being—but slowly the fates are working round that way. I am relieved that the dude ranch is quashed. And I feel we've all grown more tolerant, perhaps more whole in ourselves, so things should be easier.

I shall write to Mrs. Chambers—but don't in the least know, as yet, where we shall spend the summer. After June, Spain is uncomfortably hot. We may go to Lago di Garda.

Lately I have dreamed of the Indians, and all Tony's songs come back into my head. I wake up with an unfamiliar melody running in my consciousness, and it takes me a long time to identify it as one of Tony's or Trinidad's songs—that

I had utterly forgotten. Somewhere underneath in myself I feel a very deep sympathy with the Indians—superficially I don't really like them.

I wonder who is going to stay with you this summer? Is Ida? I'm sorry she's not been well.

Tante cose!

D. H. L.

Principe Alfonso,
Palma di Mallorca, Spain.
5.IV.29

DEAR MABEL

The thought of selling the ranch makes us both *miserable*, but it will have to be done, I think. Why don't *you* get away for a while? Lawrence is scared of M. C. He is so frail and anything emotional is more than he can stand. I just leave him alone and give him as much as I can, but make no demands—not of any sort—but I am at peace, thank God, at last, only a faith in things beyond one's own self does it. Surely Tony is a great sanity for you—make the most of him, or is that sad too, that dying civilisation—but it will be the coming thing that, and you can save it a bit. Ultimately only physical things matter.

My daughter Elsa is married. The young are coming our way. Have you a photograph of that adorable grandchild of yours? It made an impression on me.

It will be a relief if we have sold the ranch. Perhaps you or the Younghunters would be nice and send a few personal things. Those rugs (a red one you gave L, a blue and white one, and a Gerson floor rug). There was some music, some old photographs and a cookery book, a little book my mother wrote me, a Chinese jade Bynner gave me, the duck you gave L., a white skin waistcoat you gave us, some black embroidery you gave me on white linen, a tablecloth or two, that my mother did,—nothing else is worth sending . . . a candlestick, a Buddha embroidery, a nativity copy of L's. I wish you would go through the things and have somebody to pack us what is worth sending. You will hate doing it, but I wish you would. I can't *bear* to think of parting with the ranch but I shall always be terribly grateful to you that we *had* it all—and now an end.—L must tell you of the things he can think of. I hope the pack rats haven't eaten it all. The columbines, red and yellow, will be out at the ranch, how deeply I loved it all! The spring where the horses played when they went to drink. It was like the first days of creation, but the serpent was there all right, too, and the serpent triumphed! as of old! But I'll try again! And make a little creation on the Mediterranean on this island, perhaps. The sea is wonderful, Mabel.

Love

F.

I will send you one or two of L's pictures reproductions.

Palma de Mallorca, Spain,
20 May 1929

DEAR MABEL

Yes, I think I had all your letters safely—and I have written several.

We heard from Jack Young-Hunter this morning that he would like to buy the ranch—would like anyhow to rent it for August to try it out. I have asked him to write to Brett about *her* intentions. I have written her also. She said I was to make *her* the first offer, if ever we thought of selling, and she would pay five thousand dollars. That is a good price, perhaps too much. But could she ever raise the money? It's no good selling her the place if she hasn't a sou. Of course one would only want a fair price from her. What do you consider would be fair? We'd sell right out, horses, saddles, furniture—only take away our personal things. If there is anything of yours, you could reclaim it.

Jack Young-Hunter said he would pay cash down, and that would be nice, because we shall have to get a house, and then

Frieda could fix it up as she liked, with the ranch money.

It is bitter to sell the ranch, it is like parting with one's youth. Life is cruel, gives one things, then snatches one away and there is that awful bereft feeling. I don't want to talk about it.

We think to leave here in about a fortnight—perhaps make a little tour in Spain—then go to Italy to find a house. We must live in a house. We are tired of hotels. My health is about the same—certainly no worse—but nothing to crack about.

If you come to Europe in the winter, we might manage a little cruise in the Mediterranean. I should love that—go to Greece, and the isles of Greece, and Crete and Cyprus and perhaps Jerusalem—just move on in short flights.

You see, even if I was really well again, I don't think I should want to come to America to *live*—though I'd dearly love to come to New Mexico for a year or so. But the authorities are so hateful.

Are my MSS. rescued from the ranch, I wonder, and the deeds?

As one gets older, one's choice in life gets limited—one is not free to choose any more.

D. H. L.

Ludwig Wilhelmstift, Baden-Baden.
29. VII. 29

DEAR MABEL

I am so glad you are better and face life once more. It seemed a short affair, I wondered much how you were. Will you really be fit to go back in two days in the heat? I have had a jolly time in London, Lawrence's exhibition on, revelled in the children, people making a fuss of me, just because one doesn't care—but then, the pictures were confiscated. They are now in the police station cellars to be burned. Quite medieval, but it makes Lawrence absolutely sick with his native land. What cowards, natu-

rally so, people are of bogeys, public opinion! The trial is on the
8th! I only wish L were as strong as a horse! He isn't, alas! C. N.
came and saw Lawrence. I don't think it was a success. I didn't
see her—it would have been better had I been there. Lawrence's
fame seems to have grown over one's head, he has more irons
in the fire than he can cope with. *I don't really want to sell the
ranch.* I just don't.

What an end to Manby! Did his money and land go back to
the Indians and the Mexicans? It must be a joy to you, feeling
better again! I saw "Condamine" in London at a party they gave
me. He looked *28*, no older. We talked of you. My son Monty
came up to the scratch, enjoyed the fight with the police—said:
de l'audace et encore de l'audace! There aren't many English
like that! We want another house: sea and heat seems to suit
L. best, though we would both love a house in Tuscany. The
French Riviera is healthy but so ugly. I fear we must take a
house there. I still love and adore Florence especially when there
are no forestieri!

I hope you will soon be very strong again and pay us a
visit as the prophet can't come to the mountain. . . . L's health
is frail as a blue bird's egg!

All good wishes.

F.

Ludwig Wilhelmstift, Baden-Baden
18. VIII. 29

DEAR MABEL

Yes, it would be fun to come over in September, as we did
that unforgettable first time we came. *I don't want to sell the
ranch.* I like to feel we have a place in America, not to lose the
connection. L. feels the same.

Well, the pictures are free, the whole thing a terrific advertisement, Dorothy Warren can sell the pictures at a terrific price.
Thousands of people come—600 a day, often. It was all great

fun. I had such a jolly three weeks in London, the people treat-
ing me like the Queen of Sheba. The Agha Khan giving me a
dinner, and the children *entirely* with me at last—all three quite
independent and on their own and went out with me. And then
the antagonism those pictures aroused! I enjoyed it all! Lawrence
seems better, so we really will come back one day, I hope—but
this winter we must be by the sea. It suits L. best.

You must so enjoy feeling better. All good luck to you.

F.

Villa Beau Soleil, Bandol
Var, France,
29 Oct. 1929

DEAR MABEL

It's true it's a long time since I wrote you. But my health
went down with such a slump in Germany, and I got depressed
too. The doctors seem to think the lung is not troubling—it is
never very much—but the bronchials and asthma are awful, and
affecting my heart a bit, so I sympathise with you. However, I'm
so glad to know you are better, and at last feeling your real self.
There seemed to come a bit of the real you out of your last letter.
It's quite true, as you say, this being "mad" with people isn't one's
own real self functioning, it is something mysteriously superimposed. I say, as the ancients said, there is an evil world-soul which
sometimes overpowers one, and with which one has to struggle
most of the time, to keep oneself clear. I feel so strongly as if my
illness weren't really me—I feel perfectly well and all right, *in
myself.* Yet there is this beastly torturing chest superimposed
on me, and it's as if there was a demon lived there, triumphing,
and extraneous to me. I do feel it extraneous to me. I feel perfectly
well, even perfectly healthy—till the devil starts scratching and
squeezing, and I feel perfectly awful. So what's to be done!
Doctors frankly say they don't know.

We've taken this little house till end of March, right on

the edge of the sea. This place suited me so well last winter, I thought we'd better come back. Frieda seems happier and more peaceful, but of course not so strong, and sometimes unstrung—but on the whole, more restful. She likes the little house, and all the bits of curtains and so on.—The Brewsters are here, and are looking for a house for the winter. Harwood, the girl, is in school in England. I heard from Ida Rauh from Geneva yesterday. I suppose she will come and see us here. I liked Maria Cristina, but only saw her one week. She is "working" for me now in New York. Did you get a copy of my *Collected Poems* from me? It was sent you by Curtis Brown, London. And a copy of *Pansies* from New York. I hope you have them both. Let me know. Because the mail in America is so insolent.

I think these violent antipathies between people are in themselves a sign of nervous unbalance. Nobody matters all that; unless it's somebody very very near. So I'm glad you and Brett are friendly—so long as you keep cool about it, it is the best way, I think. Some things are inevitable, even some people. One can accept the bit then that is inevitable, and keep clear of all the tiresome accidental part of the relationship: as far as possible.

The Manby story was horrible. It somehow spoils Taos for me. I should always have to think of it. . . .

As I grow older, money bores me, and one smells it in people like a bad smell. Which is not because I'm hard up at all, because I'm not. I put myself on my feet by publishing Lady C. for myself.

Well, when shall I come to New Mexico again? God knows. At present it seems further off than Babylon or Nineveh, which are dreams in the sand. But the cycle of the greater year still goes round, and as it turns, it will probably bring us back. One has to wait for the auspicious day. I find one has to lean a great deal on destiny, when one's own will has been so thoroughly curbed by illness and things, and one finds one can't do anything, hardly, as one likes.

Regards from us both, and I do hope now you'll keep well and happy.

D. H. L.

Of course I want you to do just what you think best with your MSS.—publish if you can.

Villa Beau Soleil, Bandol
Var, France, 6 Jan. 1930

DEAR MABEL

Ida says she has written you about our coming to Taos in the spring. I think, if I felt safe about it, I have the energy to get up and start, and I feel that once I got there, I should begin to be well again. Europe is slowly killing me, I feel.

Ida seems pretty well. She goes around here with various friends of ours, and seems to enjoy herself all right. In fact I think she's really in a healthier state of mind than when I saw her last in New Mexico. We talk and make plans: plans of coming back to the ranch and having places near one another— and perhaps having a sort of old school, like the Greek philosophers, talks in a garden—that is, under the pine-trees. I feel I might perhaps get going with a few young people, building up a new unit of life out there, making a new concept of life. Who knows! We have always talked of it. My being ill so long has made me realise perhaps I had better talk to the young and try to make a bit of a new thing with them, and not bother much more about my own personal life. Perhaps now I should submit, and be a teacher. I have fought so against it.

For my own part, though I am perhaps *more* irascible, being more easily irritable, not being well, still, I think I am more inwardly tolerant and companionable. Who knows! Anyhow, people's little oddities don't frighten me any more: even their badnesses. I think we might get on easily together. Frieda is suspicious, but I think even she is weary of the old watchful and hostile attitude, and doesn't care very much when people affront her a bit. So many of our feelings are illusion. We don't *really* have them. I think we might all be a great soothing and support to one another.—I do really. I think we might even trust one another, sufficiently. It would be very good to have a real togetherness.

I wish we could start afresh with this year. You have never really trusted *anybody,* and you have never felt any real togetherness with anybody. Perhaps we might begin, and then do our best. We are too much cut off: I am too much cut off.

I hope you are feeling well, and fairly serene. I had your story. Of course it was *all* about yourself: just yourself. But I suppose, while you remain alone, you cannot escape yourself.

Well, here's to the Spring, and a little new hope.

D. H. L.

Villa Beau Soleil, Bandol
France, 21 Jan. 1930

DEAR MABEL

Your letter came yesterday—rather sad—and finds us rather sad. The doctor from England came on Monday—says the bronchitis is acute, and aggravated by the lung. I must lie still for two months.—Talks of my going into a sanatorium near Nice, but I don't know if it's suitable. And I don't know if I shall go. He says with absolute care for two months, absolute rest from everything, I ought to be well enough to come to New Mexico and there get quite strong.—I believe I *should* get strong if I could get back: but I'm not well enough to travel yet. I must see. As soon as I *can* come I want to come. The thing to do is to take one's hands entirely off the body, and let it live of itself, have its own will. It is by the body we live and we have forced it too much. Now it refuses to live. Yours does the same. Now I have got to be still till my body moves of itself, and takes its own life. It is very hard to yield entirely. You must do the same—

try to give up yourself, try to yield yourself entirely to your body, and let it take its own life at last. You have bullied it so much—even to having your womb removed. Now try to love it, to think tenderly of it, to feel tenderly towards it, and let it come to its own life at last. It is a bit late—but better late than never.—And that is the true way. And it is a thing you can only do by being alone, people will only prevent you. Lie still and gradually let your body come to its own life, free at last of your will.—It is what I have got to do, too.—If we can manage it, and I can come to New Mexico, then we can begin a new life, with real tenderness in it. Every form of bullying is bad. But you must help me about coming over, when the time comes.

Love from us both.

D. H. L.

Finis

A
NOTE
ON THE
TYPE IN
WHICH THIS
BOOK IS SET

*This book is set
on the Linotype in
Granjon, a type which is
neither a copy of a classic
face nor an original creation.
George W. Jones drew the basic
design for this type from classic
sources, but deviated from his model
wherever four centuries of type-cutting experience indicated an improvement or where
modern methods of punch-cutting made possible a
refinement that was beyond the skill of the sixteenth-
century originator. This new creation is based primarily
upon the type used by Claude Garamont (1510–1561)
in his beautiful French books and more closely
resembles the work of the founder of the
Old Style letter than do any of the various
modern-day types that bear his name.*

SET UP, KNICK-O-TYPED, PRINTED AND
BOUND BY VAIL-BALLOU PRESS,
INC., BINGHAMTON, N. Y.
PAPER MANUFACTURED
BY S. D. WARREN CO.,
BOSTON, MASS.